FOOD LOVERS'
GUIDE TO
KANSAS CITY

Help Us Keep This Guide Up to Date

We would love to hear from you concerning your experiences with this guide and how you feel it could be improved and kept up to date. Please send your comments and suggestions to:

editorial@GlobePequot.com

Thanks for your input, and happy travels!

FOOD LOVERS' SERIES

FOOD LOVERS'
GUIDE TO
KANSAS CITY

The Best Restaurants, Markets & Local Culinary Offerings

1st Edition

Sylvie Hogg Murphy

gpp

Guilford, Connecticut

Copyright © 2011 Morris Book Publishing, LLC

Editor: Amy Lyons
Project Editor: Lynn Zelem
Layout Artist: Mary Ballachino
Text Design: Sheryl Kober
Illustrations © Jill Butler with additional art by Carleen Moira Powell
Maps: Design Maps Inc. © Morris Book Publishing, LLC

ISBN 978-0-7627-7028-1

Printed in the United States of America
10 9 8 7 6 5 4 3 2 1

All the information in this guidebook is subject to change. We recommend that you call ahead to obtain current information before traveling.

Food Lovers' Guide to Kansas City is dedicated to my little boy, Quint, connoisseur of steak and rum cakes.

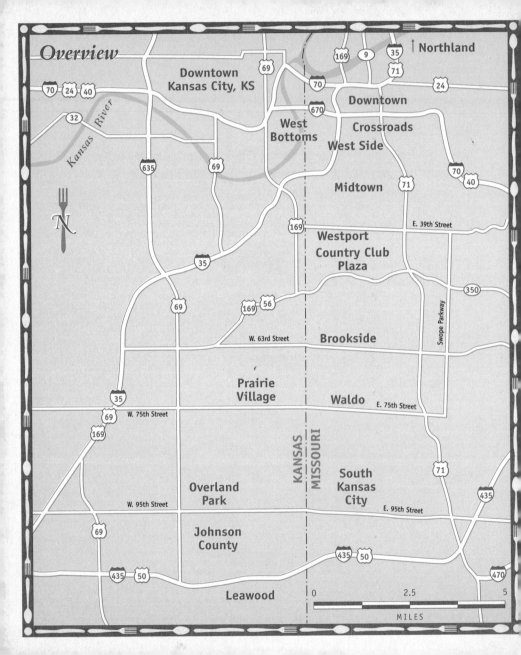

Overview

↑ Northland

Downtown
Kansas City, KS

West
Bottoms

Downtown

Crossroads

West Side

Midtown

Kansas River

Westport

Country Club
Plaza

E. 39th Street

Swope Parkway

Brookside

W. 63rd Street

Prairie
Village

Waldo

E. 75th Street

W. 75th Street

KANSAS
MISSOURI

Overland
Park

South
Kansas
City

W. 95th Street

E. 95th Street

Johnson
County

Leawood

MILES

0   2.5   5

Contents

About the Author

An expert on restaurants, hotels, sights, and culture, Sylvie Hogg Murphy has been writing travel guides for more than a decade. She is the author of *Frommer's Rome Day by Day* and *Frommer's Italian Islands,* coauthor of *Frommer's Italy Day by Day* and *Frommer's 500 Islands,* and she received a Lowell Thomas award from the Society of American Travel Writers for her work on *MTV Italy.* She has also written online guides and audioguides for several destinations in Europe and the United States. After living in California, Rome, and New York City, Sylvie now resides in Kansas City, where she is a freelance writer, Italian teacher, home chef, journeyman gardener, and head-over-heels-in-love mom to her little boy, Quint.

Acknowledgments

My heartfelt gratitude goes out to the innumerable talented, warm, and generous chefs, owners, servers, growers, producers, and fellow food lovers I met during the course of researching this book. Many of them have become my extended foodie family—you know who you are—and I would like to thank them all for the spirited conversations we shared, the insider tips and foodie leads they were kind enough to pass along, and of course for the quality and passion they put into their edibles and potables.

On a personal level, I am grateful to my in-laws, Susy and Tim Murphy, indefatigable and loving grandparents to my son, and without whose generous dedication to childcare almost none of my researching and writing would have been possible. And to my husband, Timmy, for accompanying me on so many epicurean errands around town, and for being such a wise and witty sounding board as I narrowed down my selections for this book.

(I do not wish to thank the burglars who, halfway through this project, broke into my house and stole my computer and with it an earlier version of this manuscript.)

Finally, huge thanks to my editor for all her patience and cooperation. You're a gem, Amy Lyons.

Foreword

I was living in the West Village of Manhattan when, out of the blue, I met the love of my life and future husband—a born-and-raised Kansas Citian—at a wedding in Puerto Rico. After a year of long-distance dating, I took the plunge and moved from the Big Apple to Cowtown. How does this love story relate to a book for food lovers?

In New York, I had had the extremely good fortune to be a frequent dining companion of the restaurant critic for the *New York Times*. At some of the most sought-after tables in the world, I ate food prepared by some of the country's most ambitious and acclaimed chefs. Hardly a week passed when I wasn't gulping down *foie gras*, truffles, or shiatsu-massaged sashimi on the *Times*'s dime. Manhattan, of course, is also the hungry urbanite's paradise where you can get any kind of food, at any hour of the day, delivered to your apartment. Before I lived in New York, I spent five years in Italy, where I still travel frequently as a guidebook writer. The Italian art of making masterpieces out of a few select, fresh, local  ingredients is well-known, whether it's a cheap pizza napoletana or a Tuscan bean soup or an expensive seafood entree. But eating out in Italy was only part of it for me: Zipping around Rome on my scooter, stopping at street markets and specialty stores for the best tomatoes, artichokes, arugula, clams, fresh mozzarella, pancetta, or focaccia was part of my daily rhythm—and I certainly didn't consider myself a gourmet cook. Properly made cappuccino, perfect espresso, and good-quality, affordable wine, too, were a given. In between all that, I came home to visit my family in the San Francisco Bay Area and the Napa Valley—the very cradle of foodie civilization in the United States. What I mean to say with all of the above is that for the best part of a decade, and without really meaning to, I'd been living a decadent epicurean lifestyle—a freewheeling food lover's version of Studio 54. Lo and behold, my privileged eating habits and exposure to the finest ingredients and suavest preparations had made me an accidental food snob.

So when I moved to Kansas City and looked around and saw—apart from BBQ places that I immediately fell in love with—a lot of boring but busy national chains, sad-looking Chinese buffets that apparently offered the only "exotic" cuisine available, and about 8,000 identical sports bars serving the same Sysco-supplied chicken fingers to Jayhawks and Chiefs fans, I was underwhelmed. Don't get me wrong, I have a lot of love for the canonical cooking of K.C.— BBQ, steak, and just about any form of meat—but I brought with me some major bias about the food scene here, and on the surface of things, that bias appeared to be grounded in reality.

But as I got to know the city better, and especially during the structured task of conducting research for this book, I found my eyes widening and my mouth watering more and more every day.

New York and Napa, eat your heart out: There are some amazing food finds here.

It has been an immense pleasure seeking out, or stumbling upon accidentally, all the foodie treasures strewn about Kansas City. It has also been an immense pleasure, now that I have a house, kitchen, and lifestyle that can accommodate much more of my own cooking than I ever did in Italy or New York, to ransack K.C.'s best local markets, delis, wine stores, butchers, and bakeries—almost as I did on my scooter in Rome, but with a lot more trunk space—and plan menus for my family at home.

As unlikely as it may be, I have become a major flag-waver for many aspects of my new hometown, and the food scene is a big factor. I am both delighted and proud to show off in this book the surprisingly varied epicurean highlights of Kansas City.

Food lover, yes. Harsh critic? No. I'm not too hard to please: I like quality ingredients, and I like stuff that tastes good. On occasion, even the right chicken fingers and spinach-queso dip can make me happy.

Yours in epicurean indulgence,
Sylvie

Introduction

From its roots as a cattle crossroads, Kansas City has always been a food town. A big-belted all-American city full of hearty appetites, enormous portions, and, most famously, barbecue. Only recently, however, has Kansas City come into its own as a bona fide foodie town, with sophisticated and diverse options, well beyond the realm of smoked meats, to please discerning palates. Culinarily speaking, Cowtown is a heck of a lot more sophisticated than outsiders might think. Even people who live here 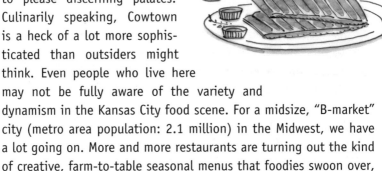 may not be fully aware of the variety and dynamism in the Kansas City food scene. For a midsize, "B-market" city (metro area population: 2.1 million) in the Midwest, we have a lot going on. More and more restaurants are turning out the kind of creative, farm-to-table seasonal menus that foodies swoon over, and more importantly, there seems to be a groundswell of Kansas Citians who are demanding—and thus, supporting—interesting, high-quality restaurants and markets.

I'm not sure this book could have been written five years ago, and certainly not without the breadth of food businesses I've seen crop up just in the three years since I moved here. Guess I had good timing. Farm-to-table, seasonal, and sustainable have become sacraments. Independent and sophisticated restaurants with internationally trained chefs are in every part of the metro area. But even as die-hard foodies here pledge allegiance to the craft of cooking and superior ingredients, most of us are still Midwesterners. We like comfort food, and our core value of thrift makes us very leery of spending a lot of money on style over substance. Whether out at a restaurant or entertaining at home, we generally like our plates to be full of reasonably priced, soul-warming fare. But as ambitious chefs all over town are proving, "comfort" doesn't have to come in the form of Crock-Pots and Velveeta, and even high-end restaurants are giving you a lot of food with that $30 entree (not to mention spectacular happy hour deals throughout the week).

Chalk it up to the Food Network or the globalizing effect of food websites and blogs, but the fine cooking movement is surging throughout America, and Kansas City is no exception. The food scene here is on the up and up in a major way. That's not to say that we've moved on from the simpler things; Midwestern  staples like biscuits and gravy, Reuben sandwiches, and Kansas City strip steaks remain beloved. But Kansas Citians are becoming as passionate about heirloom tomatoes and artisanal sheep's milk cheese as we have historically been about ribs and brisket.

Don't think for a moment, however, that all this hoity-toity stuff has, or will ever, dethrone the king of Kansas City foods. Barbecue (barbeque, BBQ, bar-b-q, no one cares how you spell it) has long been Kansas City's defining food characteristic, and I hope it stays that way. There are few aromas more comforting than wood smoke and slow-cooking meat; you are never far from that scent in Kansas City, and it greets you like an old friend—the olfactory version of Midwestern hospitality. BBQ will probably forever be the emblematic foodstuff of Kansas City, but if the past few years are any indication of future trends, progressive American, locavore bistros with internationally trained chefs are on pace to outnumber rib joints in the not-too-distant future.

Farmers' markets, the number of which has tripled over the past few years, are packed to the gills on weekends in season. Mainstream supermarkets have caught on, too, adding produce once considered "fringe" (oooh, arugula!) and expanding their ethnic food and gourmet cheese departments. Food trends and offerings are also reflecting the increasingly diverse ethnicities represented in the Kansas City population. International specialty food stores, with names like Hung Vuong and Namaste, are thriving. Elite food markets like Whole Foods and Dean & Deluca are doing brisk business, which just goes to show that even in a troubled economy, we still make room in the budget for great food.

We've got multiple James Beard–recognized chef-owners, one of whom, Celina Tio, has been on *The Next Iron Chef* and *Top Chef*

All Stars. We're also especially fortunate to have stellar local farms delivering their goods—dairy, meat, and produce—daily to our restaurants and markets from less than an hour away. Lots of K.C. chefs really do know their farmers, calling them personally every day, and in many instances, the morning's delivery determines the evening's menu. Just a bit farther north from our own metro area is Iowa's La Quercia, an artisanal pork curer that supplies prosciutto to the hottest restaurants and gourmet shops from coast to coast; but when that prosciutto comes to K.C. tables, the pigs don't have to fly.

Sophisticated coastal or big-city types reading this might be asking themselves, as they snicker and trade amused glances, "a vibrant food scene in Kansas City?" Cue the jokes about spit-roasted squirrels. Go ahead, I was once one of you. I am not a native Kansas Citian or even a Midwesterner: I come from the New York, Italy, and California schools of food expectations, but there's plenty in Kansas City that's impressed me. K.C. might be a few years behind the curve if you're talking about the latest culinary trends in the most cosmopolitan global cities. However, in the unlikely location of Smithville, Missouri, 20 miles north of downtown Kansas City, Justus Drugstore is a laboratory of the foodie avant-garde; Jonathan Justus is using animals tip-to-tail and doing an insanely committed version of the locavore ethic.

What Kansas City excels at overall, beyond barbecue, is uncontroversial yumminess. Restaurants all over town are serving contemporary

American and European food that's as comfy and luxurious as your favorite cashmere sweater. Even the more celebrated chefs here are doing burgers, because they know that a simple burger, done right, with great ground beef and a good bun, is still a terrific meal. Because it's not a New York or a London or a San Francisco, with a huge foodie market that's restless for innovation, or a constantly replenished supply of tourists, Kansas City food businesses have to be more timeless and less trendy to survive. The top tier of Kansas City restaurants are not about sourcing the most exotic or even the most expensive ingredients—it's about finding the best quality, locally whenever possible, and turning it into something better than what you'd come up with at home, yet not in an off-putting, ostentatious, or outré way. Kansas City is also less expensive than just about any food-loving town in America. If an entree at a nice restaurant costs $38 in New York or San Francisco, it might cost $25 at the same caliber restaurant here. Kansas City is also exceptionally friendly, and whether you're dining at a down-and-dirty burger joint or a white-tablecloth establishment with an award-winning chef, you'll be made to feel at home. In my book, warm and welcoming count for a lot.

Are there holes in the food scene here? Absolutely. K.C. is not, and never will be, as encyclopedic and deep in its offerings as such multicultural cities as New York, Chicago, or San Francisco. Sushi may not be hard to find, but it is hard to find it really fresh and tasty and in the kind of low-key atmosphere common to sushi places in bigger US cities. There's no Thai food that floors you with exquisite tang. Nor will you find any fully satisfying Greek or Vietnamese here, or a robust fleet of food trucks. (Not yet, anyway—this may be changing with new entries like Port Fonda, a converted Airstream with stylish Mexican street food, hitting the scene.) Visitors or recent transplants will also have to accept, as I have, that curb appeal isn't many K.C. restaurants' strong suit. Accept that there are some really great food finds in some really depressing-looking strip malls, and know that most locally owned food establishments don't have a ton of money to spend on fancy signs or even interior decor. But in America's current comfort-driven love affair with local, fresh, high-quality, artisanal, soul-satisfying food, Kansas City is hitting the nail on the head.

In terms of food consumption and appreciation, however, K.C. is still a city divided. There are those who geek out on farmers' market finds and will happily save up to splurge on a special meal at bluestem or Justus Drugstore. And then there are those who are happy as clams with the 2 for $20 special at Applebee's (love their grilled shrimp and spinach salad, by the way). Fortunately for the city and its food scene, the former group is on the rise.

As I researched and compiled this guide, some people asked me, "so who is this book for?" Well, ideally, it's for anyone who has anything to do with Kansas City, whether on a three-day business trip or as a lifetime resident, who has a genuine interest in food. This

Great Moments in
Kansas City Gastronomy

December 2008: **The Bacon Explosion** is invented by Kansas Citians Jason Day and Aaron Chronister, who blog about it and garner national media attention from CNN, the *New York Times,* and *Good Morning America.* A log of sausage with an inner core of crumbled bacon and barbecue sauce, the Bacon Explosion's suavest feature is the lattice weave of raw bacon strips that wraps around the log and holds it all together. The entire thing is then smoked for several hours. Slice and serve. It's a fairly simple recipe to recreate at home if you have a smoker. (The original blog post, with recipe, is here: www.bbqaddicts.com/blog/recipes/bacon-explosion/.) Otherwise, the Bacon Explosion can be purchased online ($17.99 for a half, $29.99 for a whole) at the BBQ Addicts website (www.bbqaddicts.com), at the **Kansas City BBQ Store** in Olathe, Kansas (www.thekansascitybbqstore.com; 913-782-5171), or at **Three Little Pigs BBQ** in Crown Center (www.three-little-pigs-bbq.com; 816-421-PIGS). It's a good idea to call ahead and reserve your Explosion to guarantee availability.

guide is meant as an introduction to Kansas City gastronomy for the particularly food-inclined who may be traveling here; a primer for the recently relocated who need some help navigating the food scene beyond the barbecue, steak, and chain fare whose high visibility often eclipses the real gems hiding a few blocks off the beaten path; and a go-to reference for longtime Kansas Citians who might like to branch out beyond their regular turf and discover the foodie finds across town, or who've been looking for a particular ingredient, like taleggio or tahini, and need some shopping resources. I've conceived this guide as a gently nudging reference for those who, like me, need reminding about certain restaurants or food markets because, in a town like Kansas City that is so spread out with so many isolated pockets where cool foodie stuff is happening, some areas just drop off your mental radar. So in the most practical sense, I hope it will be inspiration when you're faced with the perennial question, "Where should we go for dinner tonight?"

A Note on What's Included Here and Why

In narrowing down my selection of what restaurants, markets, specialty shops, and producers to list in the *Food Lovers' Guide to Kansas City*, I always posed the same questions: Does it enrich the food scene here? Does it perpetuate Kansas City culinary traditions that are worth perpetuating? Is it good?

I am all for palate broadening, but I haven't included a food business just because it fills a niche—there has been no "affirmative action" here, no inclusion of exotic but mediocre eateries just because they're exotic. The critical reader may also notice a dearth of locally owned steakhouses in this book. In a city known as Cowtown for much of its history, this is probably sacrilege, but while many classic K.C. steakhouses deliver on nostalgic atmosphere, there are precious few that consistently deliver juicy and delicious steaks to justify the high price tag of a steakhouse meal. Steak entrees, even at a casual place like Jess & Jim's out south, cost as much as a main dish at one of Kansas City's hottest foodieworthy tables, at places like Michael Smith or bluestem. For my money, I'd much rather buy a great cut of meat at a quality butcher like McGonigle's or Bichelmeyer and grill it at home.

Our Policy on Chains

Chain restaurants are a big part of the dining scene in K.C., no question about it. In fact, they are so glaringly dominant at high-traffic entertainment districts like the Country Club Plaza and the Power & Light district that visitors understandably think that your only options for a meal out in Kansas City, beyond a handful of well-known BBQ places, are Applebee's or the Cheesecake Factory. This isn't just a tourist thing; plenty of Kansas Citians are perfectly happy to frequent glossy, predictable chain restaurants for every anniversary and birthday. I'm not saying you can't have a tasty and good-value meal at a chain restaurant, but I've elected to devote space in this book to independent, local establishments, whether they're elegant gourmet/locavore restaurants or ethnic dives or greasy spoons. Most of the listings in this book have little to no advertising budget and lie a little off the beaten path. A few exceptions to this rule do crop up from time to time, in the instance of noteworthy local mini-chains (e.g., BBQ institutions like Jack Stack and Gates) that have multiple locations in the greater K.C. area only.

How to Use This Book

This guide is organized by neighborhoods or districts within the Kansas City metro area (see the Overview map on p. vi):

Downtown
The West Side
West Bottoms & Kansas City, Kansas
The Crossroads
Midtown: From 39th Street to Crown Center
Westport
The Plaza & Around
Brookside & Waldo
South Kansas City
The Northland
The Kansas Side: Johnson County

Price Code

$	Cheap eats: quick bites and entrees under $10 (even at dinner)
$$	A pretty good deal: entrees $10 to $16
$$$	Getting up there: entrees $17 to $28
$$$$	Splurgeville: entrees above $28 or prix-fixe menus at $40 or higher

Note: At lunchtime, $$ and $$$ places usually become $ and $$ places, respectively, with only slightly smaller portion sizes.

Within the chapters you'll find these categories:

Foodie Faves
These are restaurants where you'd go for tasty, interesting food, without breaking the bank, a few times per week. Foodie Faves can be farm-to-table bistros, Indian buffets, haute burger joints, tapas bars, Italian trattorias, even your neighborhood sandwich shop, if it's doing something outstanding.

HELPFUL TIP

In the back of the book there are appendices organizing establishments by Cuisine, Specialty Stores & Producers, and Special Feature & Atmosphere.

Old-Guard K.C.

Look here for the classics—BBQ joints, old-school steakhouses, and other historic pillars of the K.C. culinary landscape that have not, due to price point or level of formality, landed in the Occasions category. Visitors with time for only one or two meals should seek out listings under the "Old-Guard K.C." heading for the most representative food and ambience of this quintessential Midwestern town. Think lots of meat and zero pretense.

Occasions

Restaurants listed here are the splurge restaurants; the birthdays-and-anniversaries, $30-entree, amazing-service, fantastic-wine-list, special-atmosphere restaurants. We may not eat out at these places all that often, but when we do, we want to feel like we're their best customers, and we want to feel that both the food and the atmosphere warranted the splurge. In my experience, every restaurant listed under "Occasions" in this book fulfills those criteria. Keep in mind, too, that many an "Occasion" restaurant can double as a "Foodie Fave"—see above—and that eating at an "Occasion" restaurant for lunch instead of dinner usually keeps the expense way down.

Specialty Stores, Markets & Producers

This is our "et cetera" category, not only for things like farmers' markets, delis, wine shops, Asian grocers, sausage makers, and breweries, but for the one-trick-ponies of the food service business—ice-cream parlors, bread bakeries, and so on—that sell a particular kind of food, which may be consumed on-site, but aren't real restaurants. Also lumped in here are some fabulous stores whose focus isn't food itself but the tools and accessories that restaurant professionals and avid home chefs use when preparing and serving it—see **Pryde's** (p. 126) and Ambrosi Bros. Cutlery (p. 103).

Navigating the Area

In Kansas City, Missouri, and in Johnson County, Kansas (Overland Park, Leawood, Prairie Village), addresses along north–south streets correspond with the numbered cross street. As an example, 1727 Brooklyn (**Arthur Bryant's Barbeque**) is at the corner of 17th and Brooklyn; 1617 Genessee St. (**R Bar**) is at the corner of 16th and Genessee; and 10563 Metcalf (**Namaste India**) is at the corner of Metcalf and 105th Street. Whenever you see a listing in this book without a cross street given in the address line, just look at the street number—the first two or three numbers of the address will be your cross street.

Keeping Up with K.C. Food News

Many resources exist, across all forms of media, for staying on top of what's happening in the world of food and drink here in Kansas City.

Newspapers & Magazines

The *Kansas City Star* (www.kansascity.com) publishes its food section every Wednesday, in print and online, with reviews of newly opened restaurants, articles on local growers, seasonal recipes, etc. They also post a handy food events calendar every week. The monthly newsprint magazine *Tastebud* describes itself as "Kansas City's guide to food, drink, places, and people." Each monthly issue features seasonal topics and content on food happenings. *Tastebud* is free and available at many food markets and restaurants around

> "The restaurant scene in Kansas City is far more diverse than outsiders can imagine and has been, for the most part, far more vinously adventurous than people know. For decades, it's been a given that any K.C. restaurant offer not just a handful of wines by the glass, but a very robust and varied selection; in frankness, Kansas City came to that game a lot sooner than some other cities I know, like New York City."
>
> —Doug Frost, Master Sommelier, Master of Wine, and host of the TV show *Check, Please! Kansas City.*

town; find out where to pick one up on their website, www.taste budmagazine.com.

Both of Kansas City's alternative weeklies, *The Pitch* (www.pitch .com) and *Ink K.C.* (www.inkkc.com), have sections devoted to food and drink, both in the print version of their publications and online. Pitch restaurant critic Charles Ferruzza is a particularly noteworthy writer whose reviews are always entertaining but fair. Once or twice a year each of these alt weeklies publishes special food- and drink- focused issues.

TV & Radio

I am always learning something new about food (and food lovers) in Kansas City when I tune into the TV show *Check, Please!* (Thursday evenings on local public television affiliate, KCPT; check local list- ings for broadcast times). The highly entertaining *Check, Please!* is a restaurant-review show where three normal citizens choose their favorite restaurant in town; all of them dine incognito at each person's selection, and then they all meet back in the studio to discuss. The show is hosted by local wine guru Doug Frost, a Master Sommelier and Master of Wine who also shares great wine tips and factoids in the form of "Frost Bites" each episode.

On Saturdays from 11 a.m. to 12 p.m. on KCMO 710 AM, the entertaining and well-paced *Live from Jasper's Kitchen* features affable local "celebrity chef" Jasper J. Mirabile Jr. (of Jasper's res- taurant), and topics ranging from cooking tutorials to the local food scene to national dining trends and more.

TEST KITCHEN KANSAS CITY

Die-hard foodie, blogger, and columnist Jenny Vergara runs an underground supper club in Kansas City called the **Test Kitchen.** At each Test Kitchen dinner, a notable local chef "auditions" new recipes, cooking techniques, or anything else he or she might not be prepared to launch back in the restaurant just yet. Experimental or not, these are high-caliber meals where extremely talented chefs let their creative juices flow. To be part of it is to be part of a very special one-night-only food love-in. With space limited to only 20 people per dinner, the experience is "insider" and intimate, and comes with first-class service. Venues change from month to month but have included everything from downtown rooftops to luxurious suburban garden homes. To get on the list for Test Kitchen dinners, go to http://testkitchenkc .com and follow instructions to join. Dinner reservations each month are awarded on a lottery basis, and the set price of $100 per person covers the food (which is a set menu—picky eaters need not apply) and drink.

Blogs

No one is more clued in about the K.C. food scene than Jenny Vergara. She is a wealth of information about current foodie happenings all over town and especially loves to blog, on *The Making of a Foodie* (http://jv-foodie.typepad.com), about local, independent, and lively places to eat and drink. Check out her monthly "Table Hopping" feature (excerpted from *Tastebud Magazine,* where she is a columnist), which reviews a handful of metro area eateries large and small around a theme. Jenny's write-ups are always very finger on the pulse and rarely negative.

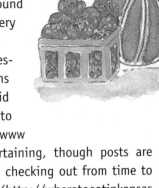

Another great blog for food and restaurants is *KC Napkins* (http://kcnapkins .blogspot.com). Humorous and candid reviews run the gamut from scathing to effusively laudatory. *K.C. Lunch Spots* (www .kclunchspots.com) is also quite entertaining, though posts are infrequent. A bit less useful, but worth checking out from time to time, are *Where to Eat in Kansas City* (http://wheretoeatinkansas city.com) and *What You're Missing KC* (http://whatyouremissingkc .blogspot.com).

User-Generated Content Sites

"Yelpers," the member-reviewers of the restaurant-rating site www .yelp.com, are a pretty wise and literate bunch in Kansas City. Collectively they provide a lot of excellent and entertaining wrap-ups about restaurants in town. Just keep in mind as you peruse reviews that the Yelp.com demographic tends to be younger, more clued-in about food, and more budget conscious than the population as a whole.

A similar restaurant-rating site, http://urbanspoon.com, has not been as widely adopted in K.C., and reviews there are a little less reliable than those on Yelp.

As the foodie trend continues to grow in Kansas City, more and more food-themed events are being added to the calendar every year. Keep track of the latest food and drink happenings through local media outlets like the food section of the *Kansas City Star* (www.kansascity.com), *Tastebud Magazine* (www.tastebudmagazine .com), *The Pitch* (www.pitch.com), and *Ink* (www.inkkc.com).

But if you're ever in town the first weekend of October, you won't want to miss the biggest BBQ shindig in the world, the American Royal.

Kansas City Restaurant Week (www.kansascityrestaurantweek .com), in late Jan, is a chance to try out some of KC's best restaurants on a budget. More than 100 restaurants participate in the event, which is actually 10 days long and features wallet-friendly

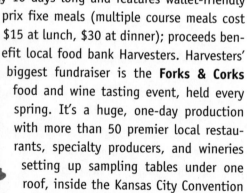

prix fixe meals (multiple course meals cost $15 at lunch, $30 at dinner); proceeds benefit local food bank Harvesters. Harvesters' biggest fundraiser is the **Forks & Corks** food and wine tasting event, held every spring. It's a huge, one-day production with more than 50 premier local restaurants, specialty producers, and wineries setting up sampling tables under one roof, inside the Kansas City Convention

Center. The event is normally held in late April; tickets are about $90 at the door or online. www.harvesters.org.

American Royal BBQ, American Royal Complex, West Bottoms; www.arbbq.com. First weekend in Oct; public gates open Fri 3 to 10 p.m., Sat 8:30 a.m. to 11 p.m. General admission: $13, does not include any food or drink. Covering more than 20 acres of blacktop in the former stockyards of Cowtown, USA, the American Royal BBQ is the largest barbecue competition in the world. It's Kansas City's version of the state fair, if all the state fair had were hundreds upon hundreds of professional and amateur BBQ booths. Held every year for one weekend only in early October, the American Royal rightly calls itself the "World Series of Barbecue," but as many of the 10,000-plus who attend every year are here as much for the opportunity to taste all different kinds of  BBQ as for the Indian-summer party atmosphere. In addition to a haze of hickory smoke hanging over the West Bottoms, there's a lot of loud live music and a lot of beer. The physical extent of the American Royal BBQ is massive; even on an ambitious day of walking around you may only cover half of it. Most attendees stick to the booths where they know someone, or a friend of a friend, who's entered in the competition—because that means free food and beer. If you don't know anyone with a booth, you can still get into most team areas by paying a small entrance fee (on top

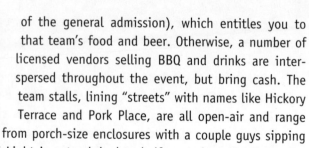

of the general admission), which entitles you to that team's food and beer. Otherwise, a number of licensed vendors selling BBQ and drinks are interspersed throughout the event, but bring cash. The team stalls, lining "streets" with names like Hickory Terrace and Pork Place, are all open-air and range from porch-size enclosures with a couple guys sipping Bud Light in a truck bed to half-acre plots complete with stages, live bands, full bars, and festive lighting strung overhead. The bigger setups are usually corporate sponsored but by no means less decadent. With all the music blaring and kegs flowing full throttle, it's easy to forget that this is a real food competition for which teams have prepared intensely. Ribs, pork, brisket, sausage, sauces, and side dishes are judged on Saturday and Sunday, with an awards ceremony on Sunday at 4 p.m. capping off the weekend. (Sign up to be a judge on the AR website a few months in advance; the $15 fee includes free admission to the event, free parking, a commemorative pin, and—wait for it—four pounds of meat!) Note that the weather this time of year is usually mild to warm during the day but can be quite chilly when the sun goes down—bring layers if you're planning on an evening down here. The American Royal is the only event—or situation, period—in Kansas City where parking is a problem. The lots immediately adjacent, near Kemper Arena, all charge a $20 flat rate, but you can park for free at one of several lots a bit farther afield (like at Union Station), and free shuttle buses will transport you to the American Royal west entrance gate and back at the end of the night. Beat the crowds by buying your AR tickets in advance, as the line at the box office on the day of the event is long and slow, and not all windows take credit or debit cards.

Wine & Brew Ha-Ha, Hale Arena, American Royal Complex; www.americanroyal.com. One Sat in July. $25 in advance; $30 at the door. This event, held on one Saturday in July at the American Royal's Hale Arena, is a must for anyone with a curiosity about locally made beers and wines. Or for anyone who likes a "structured" excuse to drink in an air-conditioned room on a hot summer's day. The Wine & Brew Ha-Ha was inaugurated in 2008 and has been such a success in its first few years that virtually every winemaker and brewery, big and small, in Missouri and Kansas now has a table here. In addition to hometown favorites **Boulevard Brewery** and **Amigoni Urban Winery,** and greater-Midwest beers like Colorado's New Belgium (of Fat Tire fame) and St. Louis's Schlafly, participants include breweries from Vermont, Ireland, and even the Czech Republic. The atmosphere is loud and convivial—what I imagine a political convention to be like, if booze instead of politics was the main focus. The entrance fee gets you a commemorative glass and unlimited tasting pours, from nearly 50 booths, of all the beer and wine you like; and yes, you can go back for multiple rounds. For an extra dollar, you can make yourself a pretzel necklace and eat from it, soaking up some of the alcohol, as you make your way around the exhibition. Each table, whether it's Les Bourgeois (a winery in Rocheport, Missouri) or Free State Brewery of Lawrence, Kansas, pouring or drawing about four of its products, so you really can get a solid idea of what they make and if you like it. The education in Missouri wine grapes—Vidal, Vignoles, Seyval, Chambourcin, Norton—alone is worth the price of admission.

Downtown

Kansas City's downtown loop, with its Art Deco skyscrapers, corporate towers, and government buildings, used to be a 9-to-5 business district with little of interest for the food lover. Uninspired sandwich chains represented hungry office workers' only lunch option; there were few full-service restaurants—and none to compel a real foodie—to make it a real nighttime destination. K.C.'s respectable downtown skyline might have looked the part of a bona fide urban core, but that round-the-clock vitality was missing.

It wasn't until a few years ago that Kansas City (and a megadeveloper called the Cordish Company) realized some of the potential of downtown and flooded the area with investments like the Power & Light district, with its corporate-chain bars and restaurants and spacious covered party piazza, and the Sprint Center, which is now K.C.'s premier concert and events space. The initial blitz of requalification began in 2008 and has been so successful that a steady stream of dining and entertainment businesses has been setting up shop downtown ever since. The concert season is back in full swing at the historic Midland Theater (reopened in 2009 after an extensive renovation of the 1927 building), and the K.C.–based AMC movie theater chain has opened its gorgeous, state-of-the-art Mainstreet cinemas in the 1921 Beaux-Arts Empire Theater.

All this development has breathed much-needed life into Kansas City's downtown: The area is enjoying a rebirth and beginning to resemble a real urban core again. People actually live down here now in significant numbers, in lofts and other contemporary housing developments that didn't exist 10 years ago, and residents from farther out in the metro area now flock to downtown's new restaurants and boîtes. While much of the dining in the glitzy Power & Light district itself is forgettable chain fare, there are some treasures (like the **Bristol Seafood Grill**) turning out great food. And the sheer amount of hungry and thirsty traffic these new entertainment venues have brought to the downtown loop has trickled into neighboring areas, like the River Market and Columbus Park. (The latter, originally K.C.'s Little Italy, is now beginning to resemble Little Saigon, with Vietnamese markets on many corners.) The foodie renaissance taking place downtown seems poised to flourish even more in the coming years.

Downtown is also home to a few K.C. bastions of Italian-American food, **Garozzo's** (526 Harrison St.; 816-221-2455) and **Anthony's** (701 Grand Blvd.; 816-221-4088), beloved by many for huge portions of red-sauce-and-garlic fare, midcentury nostalgia, and comfy family surroundings.

Foodie Faves

Bo Lings, 20 E. 5th St.; (816) 423-8036; www.bolings.com. Mon through Thurs 11 a.m. to 9:30 p.m., Fri through Sat 11 a.m. to 10:30 p.m., Sun 11 a.m. to 9:30 p.m.; $$. The best full-service dining bet within the City Market complex proper is this downtown outpost of K.C.'s own Chinese mini-chain. (There are six locations in the metro area; the flagship restaurant near the Country Club Plaza is reviewed in that chapter, p. 133.) Bo Lings is consistently tasty, and the portions, unless you're an Olympic athlete, are huge enough for several meals' worth of leftovers. Although the menu at first blush may look similar to that at your questionable local Chinese takeout—you know, the standard lineup of General Tso's chicken, spicy Mongolian beef, pork fried rice, and crab rangoon—the food at Bo Lings is in a completely different league, which explains why it's a buck or two per dish pricier than other Chinese restaurants in town. The ingredients are always fresh and flavorful and clearly prepared on the spot. Never mushy, never overly salty or greasy, Bo Lings delivers Asian flair with just the right amount of piquancy. You can't go wrong with their noodles ($8.50 to $14), like Singapore-style rice noodles with curry, Cantonese pan-fried egg noodles with stir-fry veggies and choice of meat, or pad thai. Vegetarian options are some of the best items on the menu, whether it's spicy curry vegetables with herbs and coconut milk ($9.50) or green beans Sichuan-style, with garlic, ginger, and chile in a light soy sauce ($9). And their dipping sauces, should you order dim sum or anything else dippable, are incredible. Selected dim sum is offered daily from 11 a.m. to 4 p.m., but for the full Bo Lings dim sum experience, which is the only full dim sum in town, go to the location at 4800 Main St. But whereas Bo Lings at the Plaza has a sort of old-fashioned Oriental dining room feel, Bo Lings downtown is much more contemporary and stylish, equally suitable for a casual first date, a group of friends, or families with small children. In mild weather, snag one of the patio tables facing the inner square of the market complex. Lunch combos (try the cashew chicken, with vegetables and a heavenly brown sauce, $8.50) include egg drop soup, crab rangoon, and your choice of rice. Happy hour (Sun through Mon 4 to 9:30 p.m., Tues through Fri 4 to 6 p.m.) draws a lively after-work crowd for deals like $4 crispy eggplant and $2 domestic bottles.

The Farmhouse, 300 Delaware St.; (816) 569-6032; www.eatatthe farmhouse.com. Mon through Tues 11 a.m. to 2 p.m., Wed through Thurs 11 a.m. to 2 p.m. and 5 to 10 p.m., Fri 11 a.m. to 2 p.m. and 5 to 11 p.m., Sat 9 a.m. to 2 p.m. and 5 to 11 p.m.; $$. Before settling back in his native town of K.C. to open this locavore restaurant in mid-2009, Chef Michael Foust worked with high profile chefs from coast to coast, and even in Hawaii and Europe, and did a particularly formative stint at New York's Union Square Cafe, under Michael Romano. But all that highfalutin training did not diminish his belief in good old Midwestern comfort food. What Foust does at the Farmhouse is a winning mix of refined technique and down-home cookin'—a cross between the classical French culinary style and "what my grandma taught me." The Farmhouse is located just a few blocks from the farmers' stalls at the City Market, where Foust grew up going every Saturday—he recalls when they still sold live rabbits there—and even though he has direct purveyors for produce and meat (80–90 percent of the food comes from local sources), he still shops at the City Market a few times per week. While the menu at this restaurant changes throughout the year (and sometimes day to day), there are a few core items that are always available, give or take a seasonal side dish or two. Some have become legendary, like the chickpea fritters ($9/$8 at lunch, and more famous for their accompaniment of apple, pecan, and smoked pepper salad, garlic aioli, and herb oil), the house-made corned beef sandwich ($8.75, lunch only), the 360-day aged hanger steak with salsa verde and blue cheese ($17, or $11.25 at lunch), the seared polenta cake with smoked mushrooms, braised greens, and red onion *gastrique* ($15, or $8.50 at lunch), or the panko-crusted fried green tomato sandwich ($8.50, summer only). Order any of the above dishes, and I can practically guarantee you will be singing the praises of the Farmhouse. The restaurant is spacious and handsome, with dark wood contrasting with pale green in a rather large (164 seats) and lofty space that can sometimes feel a bit too big. Opt for a table in the front part of the dining room, near the bar, where it's livelier. Once a month, Foust organizes a farm-to-table dinner where customers can meet and dine with a local producer, whether it be a chicken farmer or cheesemaker. Names of the Farmhouse's local suppliers are listed on a prominent chalkboard, but individual menu items do not name-check specific producers, curiously.

Happy Gillis Cafe & Hangout, 549 Gillis St.; (816) 471-3663; www.happygillis.com. Tues through Sat 8 a.m. to 4 p.m., Sun 9 a.m. to 2 p.m.; $. A vintage COCA-COLA AND SUNDRIES sign hangs out front of what used to be a mom-and-pop grocer serving the insular Columbus Park neighborhood; reclaimed sofas in citrus shades of brocade from 1940-something and midcentury cafe tables and chairs furnish the interior. But that dreamy music on the stereo isn't Dion and the Belmonts, it's the Smiths. Happy Gillis is hipster eating minus the hipster attitude. If cafes were high school students, Happy Gillis would be that cute, alternative guy who sits behind you in English class; that soft-spoken skateboarder-type who, when the teacher calls on him for his observations about *Hamlet,* always has the most amazing insights. I have a major crush on Happy Gillis, and I am not alone. So what is Happy Gillis exactly? It's a sandwich shop, and in an era where the word *"artisanal"* has become an overused catchphrase, Happy Gillis honestly deserves to be called artisanal. In developing the concept for Happy Gillis (which has evolved from a soup delivery business to what it is today), owners Todd and Tracy Schulte and their close-knit staff thought, why not apply the concept of a seasonal, farm-to-table menu—typically the realm of once-a-year, splurge places like Michael Smith and bluestem—to a simple sandwich shop? Its approach to food pays homage to American

VIETNAMAVORES

Downtown Kansas City, from the River Market area through Columbus Park and along Independence Avenue to the east, has a thriving Vietnamese population and quite a few Vietnamese food businesses that serve them. In Columbus Park, **Vietnam Cafe** (522 Campbell St.; 816-472-4888; Mon through Sat 9 a.m. to 8 p.m., Sun 9 a.m. to 6 p.m.) is generally regarded as the best all-around Vietnamese restaurant in Kansas City. The menu is vast, with tons of noodle, rice, seafood, chicken, beef, pork, and rice dishes, and many of the choices cross over into familiar Chinese-fare territory. It's a casual and energetic place with lightning-fast service and ridiculously affordable tabs (entrees are about $6 to $7). Although I have never been completely blown away by the food there, it has legions of fans and is certainly always packed with Vietnamese customers. On the border between Columbus Park and the River Market, **Kim Long** (511 Cherry St.; 816-221-8892; daily 8:30 a.m. to 8 p.m.) is a Vietnamese grocery that does a brisk lunch business with its yummy hot foods, like pho (the beef is the best), bun (rice noodles with BBQ pork), and banh mi, all priced at $5 or less. Also reliable in Columbus Park is the hard-to-find hole-in-the-wall—is it a sketchy massage parlor or a cafe?—**Pho K.C.** (315 Cherry St.; 816-471-2224. Daily 8:30 a.m. to 7 p.m.). If you can brave the somewhat menacing environs of Independence Avenue, to the east, try **Pho 97** (2605 Independence Ave; 816-241-0222; Fri through Wed 9 a.m. to 7 p.m., Thurs 9 a.m. to 3 p.m.).

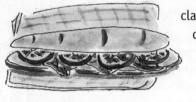

classics while simultaneously embracing the culinary aesthetic of the present day, incorporating cross-cultural influences and local, seasonal ingredients. You'll always find a classic egg salad sandwich ($7) and a BLT ($8) on the menu, but farther down, look for more intriguing options like the sweet soy and star anise–braised flank steak with pickled vegetables sandwich ($10), the eternally popular *banh mi* (marinated chicken with tangy Vietnamese-inspired accoutrements and peanutty sauce on warm ciabatta), or my recent obsession, the curried chicken salad with cashews, cilantro, and sweet chili sauce ($9). "Special" sandwiches also appear from time to time, the inventive creations of Happy Gillis staffers. But as innovative and foodie-fabulous as some of the listings on the chalkboard behind the counter may be, taste and quality are always paramount. These are $9 sandwiches, so they can't just be an aggregate of pretty-sounding ingredients. To pay New York prices in Kansas City, they'd better be pretty special on the palate, too. And they are, so rest assured that your $9, no matter what you select, will be worth it. Happy Gillis uses local bread from **Farm to Market Bread Co.,** and the stellar quality of that K.C. bakery sings in every sandwich here. True to the second part of its full name, Happy Gillis really is a warm and friendly place where you are welcome to while away the morning, utilizing the free Wi-Fi, refilling your coffee mug or ice water glass ad nauseam.

Arthur Bryant's Barbeque, 1727 Brooklyn Ave.; (816) 231-1123; www.arthurbryantsbbq.com. Mon through Thurs 10 a.m. to 9:30 p.m., Fri through Sat 10 a.m. to 10 p.m., Sun 11 a.m. to 8 p.m.; $–$$. We might think of BBQ as a country thing now, but Kansas City barbecue was born in the inner city. Arthur Bryant's continues a tradition that the godfather of K.C. BBQ, Henry Perry, began in 1908 when he started serving smoked meats from a trolley barn just a few blocks away from here. Although the market in this town is now flooded with BBQ joints, Arthur Bryant's is as original as it gets. "It has long been acknowledged that the best restaurant in the world is Arthur Bryant's Barbeque at 18th and Brooklyn in Kansas City," once wrote acclaimed columnist, author, and K.C. native Calvin Trillin. Bryant's is the quintessential Midwestern BBQ package: Unpretentious and brightly lit, its Formica tables always packed, Bryant's serves meat that is out of this world—whether brisket, pulled pork, or ribs, it's always perfectly tender and juicy. Although there are now outlets in the Ameristar Casino and at the Legends shopping center near the Kansas Speedway, this is the original and best Bryant's, a stand-alone temple of smoked meat in the middle of vacant lots and industrial plants in a particularly bleak part of downtown. Beef sandwiches are the grand pooh-bah here—and what you should get if you have never been to Bryant's before—but there's also ham, sliced or pulled pork, turkey, chicken, sausage, or burnt ends, another house specialty. Sandwiches are around $8.50, which may seem high for BBQ at such a spit-and-sawdust establishment as this, until you see that approximately 5 pounds of meat (OK, I am exaggerating, but this is the most generous half pound you've ever seen) has been piled on your hapless white bread, whose fluffiness is immediately flattened by the heaps of juicy goodness. There is no eating an Arthur Bryant's sandwich like an actual sandwich, so get a fork and knife. A full slab of ribs is $18.95, and meat by the pound is $11.40. Do note that Bryant's signature sauce is polarizing: It's not the tart and piquant flavor that's controversial, but the grainy, almost sandy texture isn't everyone's idea of BBQ heaven. If in doubt, order your food without sauce or with sauce on the side. Arthur Bryant's has become a sort of culinary ambassador for the city itself, and presidents campaigning in Missouri always include a stop for ribs and brisket here on their K.C.

What's a Burnt End?

If you're a Kansas City native, you learn the term "burnt end" around the same time you acquire the words "mama" and "dada." For transplants and visitors from other locales, a definition may be necessary. Burnt ends are the edges of smoked beef brisket; as the brisket cooks, the burnt ends take on a tough, charred consistency (here, the definition starts to seem rather obvious) and a rich, smoky flavor that is considered a major delicacy in the pantheon of K.C. barbecue meat cuts. Before being served, burnt ends are usually sliced into smaller bite-size pieces.

junket—it's a down and dirty place that helps the candidates look like "one of the people."

Gates & Sons Bar-B-Q, 1221 Brooklyn Ave.; (816) 483-3880; www.gatesbbq.com. Mon through Thurs and Sun 10 a.m. to midnight, Fri through Sat 10 a.m. to 1 a.m.; $–$$. If you don't hear an aggressive bark of "Hi, may I help you?" when you walk in the door of Gates, you've come to the wrong place. The signature greeting at Gates BBQ might have been conceived to express genuine hospitality, but it has morphed into a sort of automated, urgent scream that contains zero expression of actual eagerness to assist you— and if you don't collect yourself and spit out your order within the next breath, well, clearly you are an idiot who doesn't really want BBQ today, and they'll move on to the next, hopefully more-experienced Gates customer. This "Hi May I Help You!" shtick is totally part of what makes Gates such a fun outing. Gates is among the elite of historic K.C. BBQ establishments, so beloved that local rap artist Tech N9ne named his 2010 album The Gates Mixed Plate. It traces its pedigree to the founding fathers of 'Q in this city—it was cofounded in 1946 by George Gates and Arthur Pinkard, a cook who had worked for Henry Perry in his seminal trolley-barn BBQ joint downtown. More than six decades later, Gates is going strong with six locations around the metro area, each of them with their

trademark red roofs. The intersection of 12th and Brooklyn is Gates Plaza, a red-roofed Gates mini-empire (with Gates-owned shopping centers on each corner, and the actual Gates BBQ restaurant on the northeast corner) and part of current patriarch Ollie Gates's community development efforts downtown. Gates is a no-frills, cafeteria-style BBQ joint, in the same vein as Arthur Bryant's 5 blocks away, with bright-red brick interiors and well-worn trays emblazoned with the top-hatted "struttin' with Gates" logo figure. What sets it apart from the other pillars of BBQ in town is its sauce. K.C. is, unequivocally, a sauce town: The meat-smoking process doesn't vary a whole lot from place to place, but the condiment does, and while the typical K.C.–style sauce is tangy-sweet with molasses, Gates's original sauce has no molasses. Instead, it's a tomato-based, smoky sauce with subtle heat, and it's addictive. (They also make an extra-hot sauce and a sweet-and-mild variety for those who like more sugar.) Go to Gates for the sandwiches (beef, ham, pork, or turkey "on bun") and douse 'em with the sauce; we're talking a simple and heavenly taste of K.C. Some Gates devotees swear by their home-cookin' dessert, a sweet potato tart called the Yammer Pie. Gates also has all the standard array of meats by the pound, ribs, chicken, even mutton, and sides like coleslaw, fries (cooked in lard!), and baked beans, but for me, Gates is all about the sandwiches.

Bristol Seafood Grill, 51 E. 14th St.; (816) 448-6007; www
.bristolseafoodgrill.com. Mon through Thurs 11 a.m. to 10 p.m.,
Fri through Sat 11 a.m. to 11 p.m., Sun 10 a.m. to 9 p.m; $$$. For
all you doubting Thomases out there: Yes, you can get really good
fish in the Midwest. And if you are looking for one place that has it
all, from raw oysters to crab cakes to ahi to scallops to lobster tail,
Bristol is the only name you need to know. Serious seafood is what
it's all about here, with prices to match (most entrees hover close
to the $30 mark, higher for lobster and crab), but it's well worth
the occasional splurge. The Bristol started out as a K.C. independent
but has expanded (under Houlihan's Restaurant Group ownership)
to several locations in Kansas and Missouri; corporate or not, this
is hands-down the sexiest dining you'll find downtown (maybe even
citywide) and a nice contrast to all the mayhem and mediocre food
at so many other Power & Light district eateries. The room is sleek
and semi-nautical, like the inside of a Swedish yacht, with lots of
black, warm wood, and clean lines. All the seafood is airfreighted in
daily, whether it's striped marlin from Hawaii, king crab legs from
Alaska, or Wellfleet oysters from Cape Cod. The default preparation
for all fish is a delicate mesquite grilling that complements the
flavor and texture of the seafood beautifully. Among the starters,
soups, and salads, the Maine lobster bisque ($7.50) is legendary,
and the chipotle-grilled shrimp ($10) are a delightful detour into
Latin flavor with corn–black bean relish, chipotle butter sauce, pico

de gallo, and cilantro-lime sour cream. Favorite main dishes are seared Georges Bank scallops ($27.50, with wild mushroom risotto, shaved fennel salad, basil olive oil, and balsamic glaze), lobster cobb salad ($20, with arugula, white cheddar, sweet potato shoestrings, and tarragon ranch dressing). Plenty of couples come here for anniversaries and birthdays and order the seafood mixed grill ($31, shrimp, scallop, salmon, jumbo lump crab cakes, Yukon Gold potatoes, and grilled asparagus) to share. The chef's tasting menu ($29 for 3 courses, $35 for 4 courses; additional $15/$18 for wine pairings) is an excellent way to sample Executive Chef Travis Napier's inspired creations from both surf and turf. Come on Wednesday, and come early, for 1-pound lobsters at cost. (That's like $10 vs. $30—but call for availability.) Brunch at the Bristol ($21 adults, $13 children, Sun only) is adored citywide for its elegant buffet of seafood, fresh vegetables and fruit, made-to-order waffles, hot breakfast selections, and decadent desserts like the restaurant's signature carrot cake or the lemon meringue tart. Happy hour (Sun through Fri 4 to 7 p.m., Fri through Sat 9 p.m. to midnight, in the bar only) here is an amazing bargain—think $4 smoked salmon flatbread, $5 lobster rolls, $6 tuna tartare, and 75-cent oysters on the halfshell. The bar also does fancy, fun specialty martinis like the Margarita Float ($9.50) and the Hendricks gin-based Cucumber Dill ($10).

Le Fou Frog, 400 E. 5th St.; (816) 474-6060; www.lefoufrog.com. Tues through Wed 5:30 to 10 p.m., Thurs 11 a.m. to 2 p.m. and 5:30 to 10 p.m., Fri through Sat 5:30 to 11 p.m., Sun 5 to 9 p.m.; $$$$. It looks pretty godforsaken from the outside, like a derelict bar or dodgy Mexican place, and its name means "Crazy Frog." Unless you'd heard the rave reviews from Le Fou's many die-hard fans, you might think to give this one a pass. However, hiding out on a mostly dead block east of the City Market is what many regard as Kansas City's best French restaurant, and some of the best dining in town, period. Le Fou Frog trades not only on authenticity—Chef-Owner, Mano Rafael and most waitstaff are actually French—but also on atmosphere. Inside that rather baleful shop front on 5th Street is a cozy dining room that evokes a bohemian bistro in Paris, or at least New York's Greenwich Village. It'll be an expensive meal, but the luxurious preparations, intimate surroundings, service that's both familial and refined, and European pacing make for a memorable outing. It's an all-encompassing, special experience that really makes you feel like you've left Kansas City for a few hours. (Note that while Le Fou has white tablecloths, it's not at all stuffy; feel free to dress up or just wear jeans.) Settle in with some wine (Le Fou's *carte des vins* has a lot of excellent affordable choices by the glass or bottle, and almost all are French) and whatever *amuse-bouche* chef is preparing that day. For an appetizer, their salad with chevre, fig-honey compote, mixed greens, and citrus vinaigrette ($12) is a classic, or choose from the many hot hors d'oeuvres like *moules marinières* (Prince Edward Island mussels steamed in a broth of white wine, shallots, Dijon mustard, and cream, $10.25), *brandade* (salt cod whipped with garlic, mashed potatoes, and olive oil, $9), or escargot ($9 for 6, baked in a compound butter of tomatoes, garlic, and herbs), or cold plates like *assiettes* of charcuterie ($14) or *fruits de mer* ($35). If all of that doesn't fill you up, Le Fou's lobster tail entree ($29), with a Champagne–vanilla bean sauce, has become a signature dish that customers swoon over. *Viande* (meat) entrees include the Filet Le Fou (filet mignon with lobster meat in beef demi-glace and Boursin, over grilled asparagus and dauphinoise potatoes, $43) and the super-indulgent Wagyu filet (from local Majinola Farms, topped with *foie gras* and sauce périgourdine, $54). A distinguishing feature of Le Fou's menu is its game offerings: Ostrich and kangaroo (both $29) in sumptuous sauces are always offered. At some point during the meal, the pastry chef will come out and do a little cabaret-style entertainment, most often a campy rendition of Lady Gaga's latest chart topper. The performance might seem incongruous, but if you're on your second or third glass of wine, it's just plain fun. When the last tables have left for the evening, it's fun to hang around the bar at Le Fou for after-dinner drinks or late-night eats—the convivial spirit between patrons and staff completes that whole old-world European vibe. Lunch is served on Thurs only. Happy hour is a fantastic deal here: From Tues through Fri 4:30 to 6:30 p.m. you can get a handful of hors d'oeuvres and frites for about half the regular price (around $6.50 each) and a rotating plat du jour (fish or meat entree with vegetable side) for $6 to $15.

Specialty Stores, Markets & Producers

Baby Cakes, 108 Missouri Ave.; (816) 841-1048; www.babycakeskc
.com. Tues through Fri 10 a.m. to 6 p.m., Sat 10 a.m. to 4 p.m. The
whole cupcake trend may have jumped the shark nationwide, but
Baby Cakes was one of the first in Kansas City to specialize in these
single-serving desserts. It's a local, independent bakery and sells its
goods from a counter just a few feet away—the formula is perfect
for this adorable and up-and-coming River Market area. All cupcakes are made with real buttercream icing, and
year-round flavors include chocolate, vanilla,
red velvet, and lemon. Throughout the year,
a handful of specialty seasonal cupcakes—
pumpkin in the fall, pineapple in summer, egg
nog around Christmas—make an appearance
for a few months at a time. Even the icing has
different flavors, like cream cheese, peanut
butter, dulce de leche, and chocolate mint,
in addition to classic vanilla and chocolate.

Standard-size cupcakes are $2.75 each, and you can also special
order (at least 48 hours in advance) mini cupcakes ($10 for a dozen)
or jumbo cupcakes ($3.95 each). Baby Cakes can also deliver cup-
cakes to parties and events, or even to the patio of a neighboring
wine store—the rear of the shop abuts the rear of **Cellar & Loft**
(p. 19), and quaffers on their back patio there have been known to

order cupcakes, which are delivered via bucket and pulley from the Baby Cakes kitchen window above.

Bloom Baking Co., 15 E. 3rd St. (in the City Market); (816) 283-8437. Tues through Fri, Sun 7 a.m. to 4 p.m., Sat 6 a.m. to 4 p.m. Here's a challenge: Try to name a baked good—*any* baked good—that Bloom Baking Co. in the City Market doesn't make. You will likely fail, because this place bakes everything from rosemary focaccia to whoopee pies. In a relatively small space, this relatively new bakery has quickly gained scores of adoring fans with its encyclopedic range of scratch-made breads, pastries, and desserts. There are classic and creative breads (about $4), from jalapeño-cheese focaccia, challah (especially to die for), and brioche to potato and whole grain slicing loaves, *pain au chocolat,* and raisin bread; sweet and savory Danishes and croissants (ham and cheese, and even a spinach and feta "spanakopita empanada"), cookies and bars (try the perfectly tart-sweet lemon bars or the interesting selection of *macarons*), cupcakes (lots of flavors to choose from, topped with a gluttonous amount of either buttercream or cream cheese and mascarpone frosting), and cakes (their angel food is truly heavenly). They can also do special orders of any of their baked goods. The customer service could not be any more warm and welcoming, and often owner Steve will stand outside with generous samples of different products to lure in, ever so sneakily, City Market passersby. Once you're inside and rendered totally defenseless by the array of carby temptation in front of you, staff are eager to explain all the ingredients and processes that go into their lovingly made breads, pastries, and sweet treats. Everything is made on-site, and you can spy the baking in action through glass garage doors on the east side of the storefront.

Cellar & Loft, 525 Walnut St; (816) 283-0593; www.cellarandloft .com. Mon through Sat 11 a.m. to 7 p.m. With a stellar brick cellar that's enchantingly reminiscent of old Europe, this club-cum-shop is a fabulous addition to the wine scene in Kansas City. Opened in late 2010 on the Sesame Street–esque block of Walnut south of the City Market, it's the brick-and-mortar (more about that brick and mortar below) incarnation of a wine club that was operated for years by owner Bill Dane and previously known as Maggie's Attic. Cellar & Loft today is a joint venture between Dane and partner Eddie Kennison, the former Chiefs wide receiver (whose business card now reads "Professional Wine Receiver"), and the space they've created is utterly captivating. The "loft" is the narrow, street-level part of the shop, where there's a small counter area and a nitrogen bar dispensing top-notch wines by the glass. (Luckily for us, Cellar & Loft was able to obtain K.C.'s somewhat elusive by-the-glass serving license.) Not much wine is displayed on this level of the shop, except for the "20-under-20" shelf, featuring staff picks of great bottles under $20 that you might stop by and pick up for a weeknight or a dinner party. While the feel in the "loft" is airy and modern, the atmosphere changes once you walk downstairs to the "cellar," which is like something out of underground Rome.

Evocative exposed brick walls dating to the late 19th century, their former doorways and arches filled in with masonry over the years, frame the space, which is easily five times the size of the street-level room. A maze of beautiful wood fixtures displays the store's inventory of connoisseur-level wine (organized geographically; there's also a "90/90" shelf, with wines that have been rated at 90 points or higher by *Wine Spectator* and Robert Parker), specialty beer (sold by the individual bottle for $2.50 to $3.50), rum, and scotch; in one corner, the building's ancient elevator—a simple wood and rope contraption—sits like an archaeological find. Also down here are comfortable chairs for lounging and sipping, and a wonderful tasting table crafted from what are purported to be mast sections from a Spanish galleon. It's a captivating environment that is perfectly suited to perusing and appreci-ating wine, and the totally non-snobby, affable partners, and personnel make it all the more irresistible. You'll want to become a member after the first walk around. Cellar & Loft already counts more than 1,000 members in its various wine, scotch, rum, and beer clubs, and that number is only expected to grow. (All of the 96 lockers downstairs, which members can rent for $150 to $250 annually, have already been snapped up, and no more will be built, so get on the waiting list.) From $32.99 per month for the basic wine club (2 bottles of your category choice—red, white, or sweet), membership is a pretty good deal, and there are lots of perks. Dane and Kennison organize free tastings for their members every Saturday (nonmembers may attend once to see what it's all about) as well as other events throughout the month. While much of what Cellar & Loft does is members oriented, it's also a public wine shop (admittedly with a focus on pricier, special-occasion bottles), so at any time during store hours, anyone can walk in off the street, chat with the knowledgeable staff, or shoot the breeze with the owners over a glass of really nice Zinfandel.

The City Market, between 5th and 3rd Streets, and between Main St. and Grand Blvd.; (816) 842-1271; www.thecitymarket.org. Mar through Oct Sat 6 a.m. to 3 p.m., Sun 8 a.m. to 3 p.m.; Nov through Feb Sat 7 a.m. to 3 p.m., Sun 8 a.m. to 3 p.m.; also first Wed of the month May through Oct 10 a.m. to 2 p.m. That unmistakable perfume of farm-fresh produce—a little dirt, a little wood crate, under top notes of ripening fruit flesh and aromatic herbs and greens—permeates the City Market and several blocks surrounding it. This is Kansas City's biggest, best, and most popular farmers' market, with about 140 vendors selling plants, fruits, vegetables, herbs, cut flowers, and artisanal baked goods and other speciality foods. May to October are the ripest months for local produce, which in the fruit category means all berries, melons, apples, grapes, and plums, and on the vegetable side, beans, beets, broccoli, cabbage, eggplant, onions, rhubarb, sweet corn, tomatoes, and turnips, just to name a few. In summer, the market stalls are especially redolent with the aroma of luscious peaches and heirloom tomatoes, and visiting the City Market on a Saturday from June to September means negotiating a slowly shuffling crowd and heat that can be stifling. For a more manageable experience, just show up early (before 9 a.m.) on Saturday, or try coming on Sunday (when there are fewer vendors but a more peaceful atmosphere, even at high noon). The City Market is a year-round operation, so even when it's 2 degrees and snowing, you can still shop for fresh, locally grown winter squash, spinach, or asparagus. The permanent buildings around the four sides of the City Market house various restaurants (most good or at least interesting; **Habashi House** and **Bo Lings** are reviewed in this chapter) and shops (mostly oddball places with a vintage/antique bent), and on the east side of the market pavilion is the Steamboat *Arabia* exhibition (www.1856.com), displaying fascinating artifacts from the 19th-century cargo steamship that sank in the Missouri River in 1856 near Parkville and was rediscovered in 1988.

Cosentino's Downtown Market, 10 E. 13th St., at Main; (816) 595-0050; www.cosentinos.com. Daily 6 a.m. to 10 p.m. The gleaming, bilevel Cosentino's at the corner 13th and Main opened in 2009 to serve the growing number of people who actually live downtown or who spend extended time here because of one of the nearby entertainment venues (the Midland Theatre, AMC Mainstreet cinema, or the Power & Light complex of bars and restaurants). Hooray for this very tangible demonstration of belief in downtown's revitalization! The market here is a smaller, more urban version of Cosentino's beloved **Brookside Market** (p. 179), with half of its floor space dedicated to salad and hot food bars, prepackaged take-out foods, a deli, and a coffee bar. (There's also an upstairs lounge where you can eat your food and enjoy the free Wi-Fi.) The remainder of the market has well-chosen grocery items both basic and gourmet, as well as fully stocked beer, wine, and spirits departments. Park for free in the attached garage (enter on Main between 12th and 13th Streets), but be sure to have your ticket validated at Cosentino's checkout or guest services. In summer, bring your bathing suit and Miami sensibility and take the elevator to **The Jones** (www .thejoneskc.com), the building's roof-level swimming pool and bar.

Habashi House & Al-Habashi Mart, 309 Main St.; (816) 421-0414; www.habashihouse.com. Lunch served Sun through Fri 10 a.m. to 2 p.m., Sat 10 a.m. to 3 p.m. Market open daily 9 a.m. to 5 p.m. With a charming location along the portico of the City Market, the Habashi family's market and cafe are the best introduction to Middle Eastern cuisine in Kansas City. What began in 1992 as a tiny niche grocer serving the Middle Eastern community of K.C. has expanded into a well-stocked international food store that recalls the market stalls of such cities as Damascus and Jerusalem, and a cafe where you can get mouth-watering hot sandwiches at lunch. The market side of the business, Al-Habashi Mart, excels at spices, which are sold by the bulk scoop (a *huge* scoop) for $1 each. We're talking the freshest and most fragrant smoked paprika, chili powder, fenugreek, turmeric, and cardamom around, for mere pennies. Bulk dried fruits and nuts are also sold from bins in the center of the store, and shelves are filled with Middle Eastern staples like grape leaves, olives, tahini, pita bread and specialty grains, coffees and teas, and packaged treats like locally made baklava. Best of all, you can leave the cooking to them—the informal sit-down cafe next door, Habashi House, serves lunch 7 days a week. They claim to have the best falafel sandwich in K.C., and for $4.99, how can you afford not to test this assertion? However, you might also want to try the House Combo ($6.99), which is a sampler plate (that also happens to be vegetarian) of hummus, baba ghanoush, *dawali* (dolmas, or stuffed grape leaves), falafel patties, pita bread, and a side salad. Carnivores can devour the outstanding *shawerma* (gyro sandwiches, $5.99) and kebabs ($5.99).

Hung Vuong Market, 303 Grand Blvd.; (816) 221-7754. Sun through Fri 9:30 a.m. to 8:30 p.m., Sat 8:30 a.m. to 7:30 p.m. Asian markets abound in the River Market area, around Columbus Park, and along Independence Avenue, to the east of the downtown core. A great big store called China Town Food Market, on Grand between 2nd and 3rd Streets, is the most visible, and so draws a lot of traffic wandering in after a morning outing among the food stalls of the City Market. Less conspicuous, although it's actually bigger than China Town, is Hung Vuong, directly east of the Steamboat *Arabia* exhibition. Hung Vuong is the best Asian market not only downtown but in Kansas City, period. The aisles are wide and bright, making it a bit easier to navigate the expansive selection of exotic merchandise, and the goods displayed in the meat and produce sections always seem fresher than the competition.

Pieroguys, 307 Main St.; (816) 252-1575; www.pieroguys.com. Mon through Sat 8 a.m. to 4 p.m. The creation of two young KU alums, Frank Gazella and Andrew Misak, Pieroguys brings the pierogi—a Polish-style dumpling that is such a snack-food staple on the East Coast—to Kansas City. Although the word *"pierogi"* may be unfamiliar to some Midwestern ears, it's a pretty simple concept. Think of a cross between a Chinese pot sticker and Italian ravioli, but filled with potatoes and cheddar and other hearty, eastern Europe–inspired accoutrements like local sausage from **Krizman's** and **Cosentino's** spinach-artichoke dip. There are currently about a dozen different flavors available, including premium varieties (touted by Gazella and Misak as great hangover cures) such as the pizza-like potato, mozzarella, Italian sausage, and pepperoni. Whether you buy the pierogies here from the factory or you pick them up at one of several metro-area retailers who carry Pieroguys (check the website for names and addresses, but you can usually get them at Cosentino's markets and **McGonigle's**), they're generally sold frozen by the dozen (from $7.49). You can then choose to boil, bake, or pan-fry your pierogies. Or come down to 307 Main on Thursday or Friday from 10 a.m. to 3 p.m. or Saturday and Sunday from 10 a.m. to 10 p.m., when Pieroguys becomes a cafe serving hot pierogies prepared to order.

The West Side, West Bottoms, & Kansas City, Kansas

In Kansas City's heyday as a continental crossroads and livestock capital, the West Bottoms—the low-lying floodplain on the west side of the city, at the confluence of the Missouri and Kansas Rivers—was ground zero of commerce and comings and goings and the heart of its economy. In the late 19th and early 20th centuries, the West Bottoms heaved with activity: 55 acres of stockyards saw up to 2.6 million cattle received and sold in a year, and as many as 16 railroads converged here. Until Union Station opened in 1914, Kansas City's main train station was in the West Bottoms. The live-stock trade boomed until 1951, when a catastrophic flood wiped out the West Bottoms and its once formidable place in the economic life of the city. The stockyards never rose after the flood of 1951, and the West Bottoms became a ghost town.

The Cowtown, USA, heritage of the Bottoms lived on—and still does—in the American Royal livestock exhibition, horse show, and rodeo, whose grounds overlie the old stockyards. The American Royal is best known to locals for its annual barbecue competition (p. xxxv). For one weekend in October, more than 500 professional and amateur BBQ teams from around the nation set up their tents, trailers, and kegs, and all of Kansas City converges on the West Bottoms for one huge, hickory-tinged party. Until quite recently, the **American Royal BBQ** and an old-school steakhouse were the only notable food stories in the Bottoms; in the past several years, however, a couple of stylish little eateries with fantastic food have crept in (**R Bar, Genessee Royale**), and a neighborhood redevelopment association (www.westbottoms.com) is hoping to requalify the historic West Bottoms as K.C.'s latest frontier for the hip, artsy, and just plain curious.

While the north end of the Bottoms (now dubbed "the Stockyards District") has been the focus of the modest renaissance down here, the south end of the West Bottoms, where an industrial city had grown up in the early 20th century, retains that ghost town feel: Towering brick warehouses lie mostly vacant, although a few have been repurposed as cutting-edge galleries, architectural rehab shops, and at Halloween, terrifying haunted houses (www.fullmoonprod.com). For anyone with a weakness for American history and nostalgia for bygone eras of American history, the West Bottoms is a treasure. For now, there's still a bit of a forlorn air about the West Bottoms, but in plenty of other cities, similarly fringey districts have been transformed into sought-after progressive neighborhoods. So, keep an eye on the Bottoms and stay tuned for future foodie presences down here.

To the east, the bluffs above the old stockyards have always made for a sharp geographical demarcation between the West Bottoms and the "civilized" part of the city. In the Cowtown era, residents who lived atop those bluffs, in the Victorian houses of the district now known as the West Side, overlooked the swarming activity in the Bottoms and lived with the stench of manure that was a daily reminder of the literal "cash cow" that the stockyards were for so many Kansas Citians. Today, stink-free, those highlands are a burgeoning foodie district, supported mostly by the eclectic, art-and-design crowd that has made the West Side neighborhood their home. An urban gastropub and beer garden (**Westside Local**) and an all-vegan cafe (**Füd**) have opened here in just the past two years, and a restaurant that has been doing the farm-to-table thing (**Blue Bird Bistro**) since long before it became fashionable anchors the neighborhood at the corner of Summit and 17th Streets.

Down the hill to the east is Southwest Boulevard, an industrial thoroughfare best known, from a food-biz perspective, for its myriad Latin American restaurants. Southwest Boulevard is also home to the production plants of **Boulevard Brewery** and the **Roasterie** coffee company, and on the southern end of the street, where it crosses into Kansas, Rosedale BBQ is one of the oldest smokehouses in the city and still many an old-timers' favorite. (Note that Southwest Boulevard area businesses on the east side of I-35 are reviewed in the Crossroads chapter, p. 58.)

Also included in this admittedly gerrymandered "neighborhood" chapter are a few noteworthy Kansas City, Kansas, foodie entities (all, coincidentally, with a meat focus). The central business district and historic Strawberry Hill neighborhood of Kansas City, Kansas, are separated from the West Bottoms by the Kansas River.

Foodie Faves

Blue Bird Bistro, 1700 Summit St.; (816) 221-7559; www.blue birdbistro.com. Mon through Sat 7 a.m. to 10 p.m., Sun 10 a.m. to 2 p.m.; $$–$$$. When you want to feel really good about your carbon footprint and support of local producers, make a reservation at the Blue Bird Bistro. Blue Bird is the high church of farm-to-table in Kansas City, and as the anchor establishment of the growing foodie-mecca West Side neighborhood, it deserves a lot of credit for elevating the seasonal and sustainable concept to near-religious heights. Directly or indirectly, Blue Bird has influenced just about everyone else now doing farm-to-table in the metro area. Food lovers go gaga over the menu, which includes lunch entrees like pork and polenta Benedict ($14), with Rain's Farm all-natural pork sausage, mozzarella, and **Campo Lindo Farms** poached eggs on organic baked polenta with hollandaise made from Menno Brennerman Farm and local herb pesto. Or on the dinner menu, ravioli ($18) stuffed with Heartland Long Horn Ranch grass-fed beef and Nature's Choice Farm chestnuts in a chestnut cream sauce served on a bed of organic spinach. Each dish gets this same sort of exhaustive description, name-checking each local farm or producer that it employs. (Bring your reading glasses.) The larder at Blue Bird is certainly luxurious (and changing daily according to what farmers deliver), and the menu expansive (over a dozen main dishes, from trout to Moroccan stew are on the dinner list), but slow service and sometimes bland preparations keep Blue Bird from really soaring to foodie nirvana heights. However, the ciabatta French toast ($10, dipped in rich vanilla-egg batter and topped with pure maple syrup and local butter flavored with Missouri Northern pecans), on both the breakfast and Sunday brunch menu, earns unanimous rave reviews no matter how long it takes to reach the table. The restaurant is situated in an old house, and the seating on the ground floor is far more atmospheric than the upstairs area, which has the feel of your spinster great-aunt's spare bedroom. So, request a table downstairs. (Also, the stairs are hard to negotiate after a few glasses of wine.) Once a month, Blue Bird organizes a "Farmer's Table" dinner, a 5-course, prix-fixe event when diners can mingle with the very people who have grown the spaghetti squash or raised the chickens they'll be eating.

Chez Elle, 1713 Summit St.; (816) 471-2616; http://chezelle .homestead.com. Mon 11 a.m. to 2 p.m., Tues through Sun 8 a.m. to 3 p.m.; also first Fri of the month 6 to 9 p.m.; $. Kansas City's only dedicated creperie is a jaunty addition to the foodie enclave of the West Side. Chez Elle occupies the most historic building in the area, the old Summit Theater, whose architectural details are still evocative of the early 20th century. A few tables and red cafe umbrellas on the terrace out front lend a European flair that's hard to resist. All crepes ($5 to $10) are made to order, and in addition to the traditional egg-and-flour batter, there are gluten-free, vegan, and buck-wheat batters available. On the list of savory crepes, the Le Franco is delightful (caramelized green apples with spices, toasted walnuts, fig compote, and brie), as are the vegetarian-favorite Le Jardin (spinach, artichokes, sautéed mushrooms, caramelized onions, and provolone) and the surprisingly successful Philly cheesesteak crepe. I tend to favor sweet crepes no matter what time of day, and you can't go wrong with the citron crepe (lemon curd with strawberries and whipped cream) or the European-archetype Paris crepe (Nutella and banana with strawberries and whipped cream). Berries, chocolate, custard, crème anglaise—they're all here and can be mixed and matched if you don't find exactly what you like on the printed menu. Early in the morning, many a Westsider fills up on the Monsieur breakfast crepe, with spicy chorizo, cheese, seasoned potatoes, eggs, and hollandaise. Chez Elle has also emerged as the West Side's premier coffeehouse (the espresso-based drinks and chais are great) and sees a lot of lively business from locals throughout the morning. If Chez Elle is not in your neighborhood, I'd suggest checking it out on a warm day when you can make it more of a lingering event and watch some West Side neighborhood action unfold from those delightful patio tables.

Füd, 813 W. 17th St., at Summit; (816) 785-3454; www.eatfud .com. Tues through Wed 11 a.m. to 3 p.m., Thurs through Sat 11 a.m. to 3 p.m. and 5:30 to 9 p.m.; $. Heidi Van Pelt-Belle's West Side hole-in-the-wall is proof that organic, local, and 100 percent vegan don't have to mean holier-than-thou, bland, and hippy-dippy food that might as well have come from a livestock feed store. The pixieish Van Pelt-Belle is something of a wizard, conjuring cheese out of cashews and "barbecue" out of jack fruit. The bottom line is that while Füd pulls all the vegan foodies in Kansas City who know about it, even nonvegetarians will find plenty of appetizing choices—if they open their minds to it. Hey, there's even a cha-lupa on the menu. In the Jack Reuben ($8, served with organic sauerkraut on local rye bread), tropical jack fruit takes the place of pastrami and is seasoned liberally with juniper berries, cinnamon, allspice, cloves, garlic, and onion. The nachos ($9) use organic corn chips, topped with either Wild Mild (rice, portobella, and spice mixture) or Jack Phish (a riff on "tuna" made from jack fruit and infused with ocean flavor) and smothered with cashew goji cheddar, dressed with cashew lemony cream, salsa, scallions, and limony guac. Yum! Ingredients are always seasonal and local whenever possible, and gluten-free options are available. In line with the whimsical, fantastical creations on the menu, Füd is decorated in crayon-bright colors, orange being the most dominant. Give it a try!

Genessee Royale Bistro, 1531 Genessee St.; (816) 474-7070; www.genesseeroyale.com; Mon through Sat 8 a.m. to 4 p.m., also Fri 4 to 7 p.m.; $-$$. As of this book's press time, this cool little converted gas station restaurant was the latest foodie arrival in the redeveloping West Bottoms. Opened in December 2010 by Todd and Tracy Schulte, the friendly husband-and-wife team behind the beloved **Happy Gillis** in Columbus Park (see Downtown chapter, p. 6), Genessee Royale does updated versions of American breakfast and lunch standards with a bit of French flair. Even though the vibe at their restaurants is the epitome of easygoing, Todd and Tracy are classically trained chefs and don't get lazy about cooking techniques. An early favorite on the breakfast and lunch menu is the creamtop buttermilk biscuit and fried chicken ($9, with sunny-side up egg and gravy), while the Boyle's corned beef sandwich ($9, with brussels sprouts, aged gruyère, and grained mustard) is the hottest seller at lunch. Other simple bistro plates with both comfort-food appeal and gourmet cred are the milk-braised turkey and cured ham Monte Cristo ($9), the chicken salad sandwich ($9, given lovely texture and taste with almond, tarragon, and watercress) and Philip's Soft Egg ($6, with bacon marmalade and "soldiers," or toast points for dipping). Selections on the concise drink list focus on breakfast cocktails (such as Bellinis, $8) and bubbles (Cava, Prosecco, and Champagne by the glass or bottle); the house red and white wines (Viognier/Chardonnay blend or Mourvedre, both $8 per glass) are from Kansas City's own **Amigoni,** whose tasting room is across the street. Genessee Royale is an intimate yet airy place, with one peach-toned dining room sparingly appointed with 8 or so wooden tables. A collage of antique wood and tin pieces, collected by Tracy from various architectural findings dealers around town, fills one wall, and a broad wooden bar takes up about a quarter of the space. In mild weather, the glass garage doors open, and dining area spills out onto a small patio facing the Live Stock Exchange building. Although Genessee Royale was conceived as mostly a daytime place, they have added a happy hour—on Fri only, from 4 to 7 p.m.—with drink specials and a limited bar snacks menu. The "royale" in the name is a sort of mash-up of West Bottoms history: The first settlers of the area, in the early 1800s, were the French, while the biggest tenant down here now is the American Royal livestock show and BBQ contest.

La Bodega, 703 Southwest Blvd., between Summit and I-35; (816) 472-8272; www.labodegakc.com. Mon through Thurs 11 a.m. to 11 p.m., Fri through Sat 11 a.m. to midnight, Sun 4 to 10 p.m.; $$–$$$. K.C.'s wildly successful tapas lounge is a no-brainer choice when you want a sort of Mediterranean-downtown outing and would like to take your taste buds for a ride among a young and fun-loving crowd. There's a lot to love about La Bodega: the colorful

Spanish tiles inside and the bistro tables outside, the edgy and cool urban location practically underneath I-35, and of course a seemingly unending menu of really, really tasty tapas. From the simple (*patatas bravas*—potatoes in spicy tomato sauce, $6) to comforting (*champinones a la plancha*—roasted mushrooms with garlic and white wine parsley sauce, $7) to the refreshing (*esparragos y salmon ahumado*—chilled asparagus wrapped in smoked salmon, $9) to the refined (*pintxos de higo*—roasted red peppers, goat cheese, and fig coulis on grilled bread, $7) to the downright addictive (*datiles con jamon y chorizo*—pancetta-wrapped dates stuffed with chorizo, $8), everything on the list of more than 20 cold and hot tapas is a savory delight. Eating this way—at least for those who, like me, get Jedi-mind-tricked every time by the whole notion of "small plates" and use it as justification to sample everything—can get expensive (and plain-old gluttonous) in a hurry. So, a key strategy for La Bodega is to come in a group of like-minded, adventurous eaters (leave your picky, no-shellfish friends at home), so that you can go haywire with the ordering and not feel the wallet burn quite as much as the end of the outing. The atmosphere here, with noise and light ricocheting off the glossy tiled surfaces, is better suited to loud and jovial gatherings anyway than to couples looking for intimacy and romance. La Bodega also serves good ensaladas, sopas (soups), paella, and Spanish entrees, but I can't imagine coming to La Bodega and not gorging myself on just the upper half of the menu—that is, the tapas section. Of course, all of this must be washed down with copious amounts of good-time beverages, like the house sangria ($6 glass/$28 pitcher) or mojito ($8). The fun and interesting wine list (with lots of choices by the glass, $6 to $10) is heavy on Spanish and Argentinean offerings you won't find anywhere else in town. In late 2010, La Bodega expanded to the upscale One Nineteen shopping center in Leawood. The Johnson County incarnation of the restaurant is sleeker and more polished, all the better to woo the well-heeled suburbanites for tapas and sangria after a hard afternoon of shopping at the Apple Store or Crate & Barrel. The red-tinged room and dim lighting are enough to make any harried soccer mom unleash her inner Penelope Cruz.

Los Alamos Market y Cocina, 1667 Summit St.; (816) 471-0450. Tues through Sun 6 a.m. to 2:30 p.m.; $. Ask around among the food cognoscenti in Kansas City about where to find the best Mexican, and—in a hushed tone, looking around to make sure no one overhears—they'll invariably give you the name Los Alamos. It's the password to truly transcendent south-of-the-border *sabor* in a town overstuffed with bland burritos and Americanized tacos. Los Alamos, as my husband puts it, restores your faith in Mexican food. None of these mind-blowing flavors, which are seared blissfully in your taste buds' memory after your first visit, is dumbed down for the masses. Los Alamos, which is a sort of Mexican general store with a kitchen along the back wall, is only concerned with making good

Mexican food the authentic way, so you won't find anything drowning in cheese or sour cream. What you will find, in a completely open and exposed kitchen where the day's selections beckon from steaming table bins, are lovingly prepared, beautifully seasoned, lick-your-plate-clean-delicious dishes, from *carnitas* (fried-then-braised caramelized pork chunks) to *costillas* in salsa verde (chopped pork ribs in green sauce, an addictive concoction that I may need to seek treatment for), not to mention stupendous refried beans that belie the simplicity of this Mexican staple. Nothing on offer is labeled—and there's no printed menu, because it changes daily—so just chat with whomever is serving that day, and they'll be glad to tell you what's pork or chicken or beef tongue, and what's spicy or not. A fancy dining establishment it's not—only breakfast and lunch are served, and in Los Alamos's "market y cocina" setup, you'll eat alongside shelves displaying wrought-iron burros and statuettes of patron saints of Mexico. The whole thing is very spit-and-sawdust, zero-pretense, and, I repeat, not "Mexican" (i.e., Tex-Mex) as most Americans know it. Hospitality comes naturally to husband-and-wife owners Agustin and Ana and their extended family, who are often here to help out. You're always made to feel welcome and appreciated (even if you wander in at 2:45 p.m., as I once did, and they still graciously served me a heaping *plato*). On Saturday, crowds line up for Los Alamos's renowned *menudo* (beef tripe soup, with hominy, chile peppers, spices, onions, and garlic). My only complaint is that if you get food to go, the take-out containers do not stay closed under the deforming weight of the food they contain, so unless you are very careful, you are liable to lose some of that precious sauce en route.

R Bar, 1617 Genessee St.; (816) 471-1777; www.rbarkc.com. Tues through Wed 5 to 10 p.m., Thurs through Sat 5 to 11 p.m. Bar opens at 4 p.m. Tues through Fri and closes at 1 a.m. Thurs through Sat; $$–$$$. When ultracool R Bar opened in the old Sutera's space in 2009, it announced the West Bottoms as K.C.'s latest frontier of stylish redevelopment. Seeing R Bar's major focus on mixology and its menu, full of ambitious, molecular gastronomy that belies the "bar" moniker, foodies citywide let out a collective cheer. With its sophisticated food and cocktails and especially its pseudo-patinated Wild-West-saloon-by-way-of-Paris look, R Bar would be an "it" spot anywhere, but there's something about its location here in the heart of the old stockyards that makes it even more inviting. Rising-star Chef Alex Pope's cuisine is inventive and eclectic, rigorously seasonal and local whenever possible; most plates are essentially upscale comfort food but with innovative ingredient pairings and modern cooking techniques that have earned accolades for the R Bar kitchen. On the "First" half of the menu, the organic chicken lettuce wraps ($10) are made with sweet potato, tamarind, peanuts, mint, and yogurt; the braised bacon ($10) comes with apples, sprout leaves, rosemary ranch, and (most intriguing of all) porcini oatmeal crisps. Tempting "Second" dishes on a recent winter menu included a braised turkey pot pie ($19), with brie, black truffles, celery root, grapes, and truffle sauce;

or bourbon-glazed pork cheeks ($19), with parsnip tart, collard greens, apples, roasted garlic, and curry–goat cheese sauce. Pope's cooking style is perhaps best expressed in such creative entrees as butter-poached skate ($18) with crab, turnip tamale, carrot jus, cranberry, capers, and tequila. No trip to R Bar would be complete without one of their signature cocktails, whose names are as sexy as the spirits they contain—an Aviation for me, if you please, bartender; the lady will have a Japanese Slipper. The Corpse Reviver No. 2 ($9.50) is a gin martini with Cointreau, Lillet, lemon juice, and absinthe, while the Burning Bush ($13, with Bookers, syrup, jasmine, and ginger beer) is described as a "strong drink, order at your own risk." The highfalutin mixology here is on par with K.C.'s premier drinks den, "speakeasy" **Manifesto** (see Crossroads chapter, p. 86), and is just so . . . classy. A short but compelling wine and beer list supplements the cocktail offerings. R Bar also has live music on Friday and Saturday nights, which makes a weekend dinner here that much more memorable—try to catch frequently returning act Grand Marquis, whose classic speakeasy sound evokes Prohibition-era Kansas City, 1930s Paris, and New Orleans.

The Westside Local, 1663 Summit St.; (816) 997-9089; www .thewestsidelocal.com. Tues through Sun 11 a.m. to 10 p.m. (kitchen open 'til 11 p.m. Fri through Sat); $$. It could easily be in Brooklyn or Berkeley—the exposed brick walls, the modern aesthetic, the indie music on the stereo. The Westside Local is K.C.'s favorite gastropub, and it's an address that hipsters—or anyone craving some coast-inspired, laid-back sophistication in their local eatery—frequent with familial devotion. The place is very neighborhood oriented, and in fact its name sums up its ethos: It was conceived as a place where locals could come, eat, drink, and hang out, all the while supporting local farms and businesses. The Westside Local is clearly very cool, but it's also very comfortable. As for food, the kitchen turns out farm-to-table American bistro fare with a bit of a creative twist—but not too much of a twist; there's nothing earth-shatteringly "chef-driven" here. The menu is short but changes seasonally and always includes several dressed-up salads (the arugula, $8 for a large portion, comes with apples, Maytag blue, pumpkin seed brittle, sour cherry vinaigrette, and roasted grapes); a few savory starters like PEI mussels ($13) with Spanish chorizo and cilantro, chile, and lime; and sandwiches like the gourmet Summit burger made from ribeye, served on a toasted **Farm to Market** brioche bun. (All the breads here come from K.C.'s always-delicious Farm to Market bakery.) Among the handful of entrees (salmon, quinoa, tenderloin), the local chicken breast ($17), with bacon-braised greens, Delmonico potatoes, and port reduction, is a soul-warming slice of heaven on a chilly night. The most popular items on the menu, however, are at the top, under the heading "Localities." These

TOP MEXICAN PICKS

... *on the Boulevard*:

Central American immigrants are the defining demographic of *El Westside*. Southwest Boulevard from about 23rd Street to 30th Street is chockablock with Mexican markets, taquerias, and money-wiring businesses. Food and drink are served or sold in almost all of them, but from this dizzying lineup where Daddy Yankee is blaring from every doorway, how do you know what's good? Boulevard regulars all have their own favorites, but here are a few of our top picks:

El Patron, 2905 Southwest Blvd; (816) 931-6400; www.elpatronkcmo.com.

El Pueblito, 810 Southwest Blvd; (816) 471-5442; www.elpueblitokc.com.

Taqueria Mexico No. 1, 910 Southwest Blvd; (816) 221-1399.

... *on Kansas Avenue in K.C.K*:

Even more authentic than Southwest Boulevard are the Mexican tortillerias, taquerias, and carnicerias of downtown Kansas City, Kansas.

Bonito Michoacan, 1150 Minnesota Ave. (at N. 12th Street), Kansas City, KS; (913) 371-0326; http://bonitomichoacankck.com.

El Camino Real, 903 N. 7th St. Trafficway (at Armstrong Avenue), Kansas City, KS; (913) 342-4333.

Los Amigos, 2610 State Ave., Kansas City, KS; (913) 281-4547.

Tortilleria San Antonio, 830 Kansas Ave. (at S. Mill Street), Kansas City, KS; (913) 281-6433.

are small portions of mostly local and regional cheeses, meats, produce, and house-made hors d'oeuvres (all $2 each), allowing you to build an appetizer or full meal (of roasted beets, goat cheese, braunschweiger, deviled eggs, sweet-and-spicy pecans, for instance) according to your own tastes. The Westside Local gets a lot of buzz for its beer garden—an open-air side yard with a long, handmade table that encourages socializing—but it's not all suds here; the classy, New Orleans–style cocktails are excellent, and there's a decent wine list. Happy hour (Tues through Fri 4 to 6 p.m.) features the Localities menu ($2 each), generous "snacks" ($3 to $8), and enticing drinks deals ($3 for select **Boulevard Brewery** beers, well drinks, and house wine; $5 Dark & Stormys). Tip: Pair your drinks with the house fries, studded with glistening chunks of salt and pepper and served with the most addictive and intriguingly seasoned house-made ketchup.

Old-Guard K.C.

The Golden Ox, 1600 Genessee St.; (816) 842-2866; www.golden ox.com. Mon through Tues 11 a.m. to 9 p.m., Wed through Fri 11 a.m. to 10 p.m., Sat 4 to 10:30 p.m., Sun 4 to 9 p.m.; $$$–$$$$. As the city's oldest steakhouse, which happens to be located right in the heart of the old stockyards district and shares a wall with the fabulous old Live Stock Exchange building, the Golden Ox is an institution and must be mentioned in any food guide to Kansas

City. The place oozes Cowtown history: As you walk in, there's a gallery of old black-and-white photographs chronicling what the West Bottoms looked like in the heyday of the cattle trade down here, before the flood of 1951 and other factors phased it out. The clubby dining room hasn't been updated in decades—a good thing in a steakhouse, I think—and there's a delightful Old West mural along one wall. All of this nostalgic atmosphere conspires to make you really want to love the Golden Ox.

By all rights, this venerable establishment should be a terrific steakhouse. Here comes the "but": You get the feeling that the place is still sulking about the collapse of the stockyards and booming business they brought, and while the steaks are good, they're not amazing. And at $30 and up for the premium steak cuts, they should be amazing. (As mentioned elsewhere in this book, $30 is a very high entree price in Kansas City—in line with the most upscale "splurge" restaurants in town—but consistent with most other steakhouses around.) The 16-ounce American Royal Ribeye ($32.95) is the best steak on the menu. Apps and accompaniments include usual steakhouse suspects like loaded baked potatoes, iceberg wedge salads with blue cheese, sautéed mushrooms, and lobster bisque, but the Golden Ox also has its own hickory pit, so you can get ribs and other smoked meats, and BBQ sides like pit beans. The wine list includes some heavy hitters like Silver Oak Cabernet Sauvignon and top Oregon Pinot Noirs, but offerings by the glass are uninspired. It's too bad that the Golden

Ox doesn't have superior steaks, because it's the kind of historic place you'd love to take out-of-towners to show off the stuff that made Kansas City world famous for beef. I do encourage everyone to visit the Golden Ox at least once, if only for the throwback Cowtown ambience. Go and have a drink at the bar (where admittedly your only companions may be the ghosts of 1920s cattlemen), or try it at lunch, when a wide selection of perfectly decent salads, sandwiches, and burgers will only set you back about $10. And if you like your lunch, come back for dinner sometime and order that ribeye.

Rosedale Bar-B-Q, 600 Southwest Blvd., Kansas City, KS; (913) 262-0343. Mon through Wed 10 a.m. to 7:30 p.m. (8 in summer), Thurs 10 a.m. to 9 p.m., Fri 10 a.m. to 10 p.m., Sat 11 a.m. to 10 p.m., Sun 11 a.m. to 8 p.m.; $–$$. It's one of the older BBQ joints in town ("fired up since 1934," as the menu says) but known as a "sleeper" for being underrated among the field of bigger and more famous establishments in Kansas City. Though it draws mixed reviews, it's a place that anyone doing an exhaustive BBQ tour of K.C. will want to see and evaluate personally. Rosedale, which is a spacious, free-standing restaurant on the Kansas side of Southwest Boulevard, is as plain and stripped down as can be, as far as atmosphere, but the reassuring smell of hickory-smoked meat hangs heavy in the air. Fans of Rosedale give it high marks for the beef on bun sandwich ($4) and plenty of regulars swear by the tender ribs (in my experience, they've been excellent), but some critics claim that the meat at Rosedale is often dry. You certainly can't argue with the value vis-à-vis the competition—for about $10, you can get a heaping dinner of the BBQ meat of your choice plus 3 generous sides (the crinkle-cut fries have a cult following). On Monday and Wednesday, all rib slabs are $11.95 (normally $15.95 to $19). Note that Rosedale's house BBQ sauce is quite a departure from the middle-of-the-road, tomato-and-molasses-based K.C. sauces; it's a love-it-or-hate-it recipe that's similar to Asian sweet-and-sour sauce. While Rosedale may not be on the same level as other BBQ in town, it has its own workaday appeal; you can walk in at any time, grab a seat at the well-worn bar, and knock back a beer or four while gorging yourself on totally authentic K.C. BBQ for a great price.

Specialty Stores, Markets & Producers

Amigoni Urban Winery, 1600 Genessee, Suite 160; (913) 890-3289; www.amigoni.com/winery. Tasting Hours Wed, Thurs, Sat 11 a.m. to 6 p.m.; Fri 11 a.m. to 7 p.m. Grapes have been grown and wine has been made in Missouri for centuries. What Michael and Kerry Amigoni did, when they launched their "urban winery" in 2006, was make wine that connoisseurs and gourmets actually want to drink. In this handsome tasting room inside the Live Stock Exchange Building (built in 1910 and on the US National Register of Historic Places), you can sip their sophisticated bottles of Cab Franc, Mourvèdre, and many more. If your idea of Missouri wine is all sticky-sweet and food unfriendly, you're in for a major eye-opener here. The game-changing feature of Amigoni Wines (known as Inland Sea until the Amigonis bought out their partner in 2010) is that they're made from the same premium *Vitis vinifera* (literally, "wine-producing vine") grapes that are used in the production of the renowned wines of Europe and California. The overwhelming majority of Missouri wines are made from sweet but cold-hardy grapes like Concord that result in cloying, syrupy wines that a discerning wine snob wouldn't touch with a 10-foot pole. The challenge, however, was finding those vinifera varietals that could withstand the harsh Midwestern winter. The Amigonis' wine odyssey began in their Leawood backyard in the mid-1990s, when they attempted to grow their first wine grapes—Cabernet Franc—and produce a few bottles for themselves and their friends. Having learned firsthand what worked and what didn't, and having further researched what grapes could bear climates similar to the Kansas City area's (e.g., the Finger Lakes region of New York State), the Amigonis decided to ramp up this "hobby" and purchase 10 acres of farmland in Centerview, Missouri, about 45 minutes east of K.C.—mostly, they were doing it as an investment (or so they told themselves), but one acre would be devoted to vineyards. At first, the crops were harvested and sold to area winemakers, but by 2006, the single acre of vines had become 4½ acres, and the Amigonis were in business for themselves as a commercial winery. To this day—for an annual production of about 1,000 cases—nearly all the grapes for Amigoni wine come from their 4½ acres in Centerview (a small percentage is sourced from boutique vineyards in California to supplement the Missouri harvest), and the wine is processed at a warehouse on Southwest Boulevard, right in the heart of K.C. (Before they moved to that facility, the grapes were de-stemmed and crushed in the parking lot behind the Livestock Exchange building, and the wine was made in what is now Amigoni's tasting room.) Amigoni's Urban Red (Cabernet Sauvignon) and Cabernet Franc are particularly impressive, and their Mourvèdre (a dark red grape from the Rhône, known in Spain as Monastrell) is enchanting, with notes of pepper, spice, and earth and lots of nice tannins that perfectly complement the BBQ and grilled meats so prevalent in K.C. Amigoni also makes an Urban White (Viognier/Chardonnay blend) and released its first rose, made from Mourvèdre, in spring 2011. Bottle prices range from about $16 to $30. While Amigoni wines are sold at many fine area liquor stores, and found on the wine lists of top K.C. restaurants like **Justus Drugstore, JJ's, bluestem,** and **Room 39** (as well as neighbors **R Bar** and **Genessee Royale**), it's most fun to come for a free tasting at this location in the West Bottoms. Friday after about 4 p.m. is the best time to come: The atmosphere is like happy hour, and you can usually catch Michael and Kerry Amigoni hanging out and telling fascinating stories about life as Kansas City winemakers.

Bichelmeyer Meats, 704 Cheyenne, Kansas City, KS; (913) 342-5945. Tues through Sat 8 a.m. to 5:30 p.m. You gotta love this place. As a family-owned, soup-to-nuts operation that has its own ranch, slaughtering and meat-aging facilities, and retail case, Bichelmeyer represents the best of the carnivorous American Midwest. Bichelmeyer is a landmark in this wastelandish part of K.C.K, and from the outside, you might expect to walk into a supermarket-size meat store. However, only a tiny section on the south side of Bichelmeyer's large plant is dedicated to retail sales (and don't be put off by the industrial to-the-trade look of it, because the public is most welcome). The rest of the real estate is taken up by remarkably spotless rooms where beef sides hang, whole pigs are roasted, sausages get made, and brisket is smoked. (Those areas aren't visible unless one of the Bichelmeyers, like friendly son Matt, takes you for a behind-the-scenes tour—but be warned, even to die-hard meat eaters, the sheer quantity of largely intact animal flesh in this place can be sensory overload.) In Bichelmeyer's refrigerated display cases, expect to find every cut of beef and pork imaginable and some of the best-tasting whole chickens in the area. The family's extensive experience in the meat business, as well as their commitment to quality and transparency with customers, ensures that anything you buy here will be a superior meat product. If you've got some time and want to learn more about different cuts of meat, the cases at Bichelmeyer can be an educational tool—staff and especially family members are all too happy to take you step-by-step through beef and pork anatomy, explaining for instance where the ribeye is located in the animal and why that position makes it a premium steak, or why a smaller chicken is preferable to a plump one. (I, for one, always find this information fascinating.) No matter what you end up taking home, they can give you cooking tips. They also cater and do more than a thousand Hawaiian-style pig roasts in the Kansas City area every year. (Where are these luaus and why haven't I been invited?) Looking at Bichelmeyer's "bundle list" of bulk meats, you'll want to invest in a second freezer if you don't already have one: There's a half beef bundle ($650 to $900), a half hog ($140 to $190), and more real-world options like the value beef and pork combo ($95), for about 21 pounds of premium steaks, roasts, chops, sausage, bacon, and ground meat.

Boulevard Brewing Company, 2501 Southwest Blvd.; (816) 474-7095; www.boulevard.com. Tours (reserve online) Wed 3 p.m.; Thurs 1 p.m. and 3 p.m.; Fri 1 p.m. and 3 p.m.; Sat 10 a.m., 11 a.m., 12 p.m., 1 p.m., 2 p.m., 3 p.m., and 4 p.m.; Sun 1 p.m. and 3 p.m. Kansas Citians love their beer, and they also love their hometown. So when Boulevard Brewery opened in 1989 as Kansas City's first specialty beer producer, it enjoyed almost immediate success. (Another substantial reason to celebrate was that drinking Boulevard meant not only supporting a local enterprise but taking at least some business away from behemoth Anheuser-Busch in cross-state rival St. Louis.) Boulevard started out making 6,000 barrels per year; it now makes 600,000 annually. Boulevard's signature beer, Unfiltered Wheat, is a refreshing American pale ale with a trademark cloudy appearance and is normally served with a slice of lemon to highlight its underlying citrus notes. Unfiltered Wheat is pretty much the official beverage of Kansas City, on tap in every bar in the metro area, and has become the top-selling craft beer in the entire Midwest. But Boulevard also makes dozens of other beers at its brewery (its only production facility) on Southwest Boulevard. Some, like Lunar Ale, Single-Wide IPA, and Bully! Porter, are available year-round, while a handful of others are seasonal, like Irish Ale (a red ale released every February as a lead-up to St. Patrick's Day), ZON (the Belgian-style Witbier is heavenly in summer), and Nutcracker Ale. The so-called Smokestack Series—larger bottles, higher alcohol content, more complex brews—is where Boulevard gets creative. Smokestack beers include year-round offerings like Long Strange Tripel (a Belgian Tripel ale) and the very popular Tank 7 Farmhouse Ale (a delicious fruity-to-peppery *saison*), and many more limited releases like Chocolate Ale (a collaboration with local chocolatier Christopher Elbow, and which sold out in its inaugural season, winter 2010–11, in about 8 seconds) and Bourbon Barrel Quad (a Belgian strong, dark ale with toffee and vanilla top notes, it's aged in oak bourbon barrels and flavored ever so subtly with cherries). Free group tours of the brewing facility, which was completely overhauled and enlarged in 2006, are offered 14 times per week; midweek tours are generally smaller and typically afford visitors the chance to see the brewing and bottling process in action, whereas weekend tours are large and less personal, and the shiny equipment you're expected to ooh and aah at is often turned off. (Boulevard Brewery also has a gorgeous event space if you ever need a unique, modern, and fully equipped private-party venue.) The best part of the tour, perhaps, comes at the end, when the taps in the tasting room are opened up and you can sample (again, for free) small draughts of about 10 diverse Boulevard beers. A gift shop sells all kinds of Boulevard branded merchandise, from T-shirts and glassware to dog collars to Pale Ale mustard. Boulevard beers are sold throughout the plains states and much of the Midwest and have limited distribution in more far-flung states like Texas and Washington.

Fervere, 1702 Summit; (816) 842-7272; www.fervere.com. Thurs through Fri 11 a.m. to 7 p.m. or until sold out, Sat 9:30 a.m. to 2 p.m. or until sold out. The super-artisanal loaves at this hole-in-the-wall West Side bread bakery have a cultlike following. Fervere is pronounced "fur-VAIR-ay," from the Latin root for "passion" and "fermentation," and with only a little imagination, the place feels like it could be a shop in ancient Pompeii, right down to the brick and lime-washed walls and old wooden beams overhead. The regular menu features 11 different breads (about $4.50 to $6.50), the trademark loaf being *pain au levain,* a slightly sour French bread. All doughs, made with all-natural, almost 100 percent organic ingredients, are mixed, folded, divided, and shaped on-site. The breads are baked in an Old World–style brick oven in which the heat source, having warmed the chamber to the correct temperature, is removed prior to baking. The polenta bread is *pain au levain* with coarse cornmeal and sesame seeds and tastes great with both sweet and savory toppings, while the aromatic olive rosemary loaf tends to disappear within minutes of being sliced open on your kitchen counter. (Try toasting it and dragging the pieces through olive oil for even more scrumptiousness.) Fervere also makes a number of nutrient- and fiber-packed whole grain breads, like the *pain complet* (a 10-grain bread with a hearty, nutty flavor—it's made with whole wheat and whole rye flours, amaranth, quinoa, flax, rolled oats, millet, polenta, sunflower seeds, sesame seeds, and sea salt). The amazing Cheese Slipper is a fromage-ified ciabatta (*ciabatta* means "slipper" in Italian) where bits of smoky cheddar are suspended in the crumb and the crust is topped with garlic cheese curds. Fervere is only open 3 days a week, and they close when they're sold out; so it's a good idea to come early and avoid hearing the sad news that the last cheese ciabatta just shuffled out the door.

Fresher than Fresh Snow Cones; www.ftfsnowcones.com. Mobile food vendor from Apr through Oct, check website for exact locations and hours; Sun in summer in the garden at 17th and Summit, noon to 8 p.m. The FTF Snow Cone trailer rolled onto the K.C. foodie scene in 2009. It's the brainchild of Lindsay Laricks, a K.C. advertising creative director and graphic designer who, after a visit to Austin, had come back home enchanted by the food truck culture in the Texas capital. She soon became fixated on the idea of starting her own snow cone truck, because snow cones were a popular street food whose standard formula could definitely be improved upon. Laricks never ate snow cones growing up because they seemed so artificial and full of weird chemicals, but they didn't have to be, she thought. The idea of a blank canvas of finely crushed ice, to be flavored and colored with natural ingredients that not only taste great but look great together, was too good for the design person and home gourmet in her to pass up. With her small-scale, all-natural production and flavors like watermelon basil, pineapple and serrano pepper, and lemon prickly pear, Kansas City's pioneer food truck definitely qualifies as gourmet. From a lightweight vintage trailer she bought on eBay, Laricks sells her generously sized snow cones for $3 (in compostable cups made from corn) from various locations downtown from Apr to Oct. In addition to core flavors—each with their own adorable Laricks-designed avatars—like blackberry lavender (mellow as a walk in the woods, a touch aromatic) and lime mint (crisp and tart relief on a sweltering August day), there's always a "Daredevil" option of more out-there flavors (e.g., clementhyme), which Laricks defines as "always adventurous, never gross." The whole concept and experience of Fresher than Fresh is just so nostalgic and happy—even the 1957 trailer is a throwback to the good old days. On Sun in summer, the trailer is stationed in the garden at 17th Street and Summit, and on **First Fridays** (see p. 77) in summer, FTF is open for business outside Hammerpress (Southwest Boulevard and Broadway) in the Crossroads. Lindsay's latest movements can always be monitored on the FTF website or via FTF tweets and Facebook updates. In the off-season, FTF addicts can buy packaged snow pops (ice pops made from the same caliber ingredients as the snow cones) for $2 each, at Hammerpress and possibly at area grocery stores in the future.

Krizman's House of Sausage, 424 N. 6th St., Kansas City, KS; (913) 371-3185. Tues through Fri 8 a.m. to 5 p.m., Sat 9 a.m. to 3 p.m. Krizman's sausage isn't sold in retail stores, not even in meat-specialist markets like McGonigle's. But if you're a frequent K.C. diner of the meat-loving variety, you've almost certainly had Krizman's sausage. Practically every BBQ joint in the metro area—including big-name ones like **Oklahoma Joe's** and **Arthur Bryant's**—gets its sausage from this tiny production plant run by Joe Krizman. Krizman is a third-generation sausage maker whose grandfather emigrated from Croatia and opened this business in 1939. Until the 1970s, the sausages were known by the name of Krizman's partner, Grsnic, and even though the business name officially changed more than three decades ago, scores of Kansas Citians still refer to Krizman's as Grsnic's. You don't have to be a restaurant account to buy the goods direct from the source. Krizman's counts plenty of private-citizen sausage devotees as regular walk-in customers, even though they may live a 45-minute drive away. When I first visited the House of Sausage (30 minutes from my house), I was there to pick up some kielbasa for my mother-in-law's Easter spread. My mother-in-law grew up in Strawberry Hill and has Slavic roots, and she had given me some bewildering, rapid-fire sausage-ordering instructions that might as well have been in Croatian. As much as I love pork products of all kinds, I didn't know my way around a mostly to-the-trade sausage factory, and I was a little intimidated. Well, I needn't have worried one bit. Krizman's is the friendliest, most helpful house of sausage you'll ever walk into. Oh, and the sausage is terrific. That kielbasa (Polish sausage) is extraordinary and is Krizman's top seller, but you can also choose from bratwurst, Italian sausage, BBQ sausage, andouille, chorizo, knockwurst (perhaps too "authentic" for some tastes), and blood sausage. Everything is made on-site by a taciturn team of Serbian workers and in a surprisingly small production facility. Counter staff can guide you through the many sausage types on offer and give cooking instructions—many do quite well on the grill, but others are best smoked. (The pork used in Krizman's links is 100 percent Boston butt, lean meat from the shoulder of the animal, which does particularly well smoked.) Prices are so reasonable (about $5 for a package that feeds 2 to 4) that you don't have to limit yourself to those two links of kielbasa—try the andouille and the bratwurst, too—and invite your neighbors over for a sausage fest. Krizman's is an old-fashioned place (they keep the Croatian traditions of Strawberry Hill alive by selling first-rate sauerkraut and *povitica*) and a K.C. treasure: I am so glad my mother-in-law sent me down here that fateful April day.

The Roasterie, 1204 W. 27th St. (just east of Southwest Boulevard); (816) 931-4000; www.theroasterie.com. Tours Mon through Sat 10 a.m. In the early 1990s, Iowa native Danny O'Neill was living in Kansas City and selling cardboard boxes when it occurred to him that this might not be his life's calling. Instead, he longed to do something about a passion for coffee he'd developed while studying abroad in Costa Rica in 1978. What started out as a boutique operation in the basement of

O'Neill's Brookside home has grown into Kansas City's premier specialty coffee roaster with distribution citywide, 2 highly successful cafes (in Brookside and Leawood), not to mention accolades from coffee reviewers around the globe. The Roasterie sources its coffee beans from 31 different growing regions—from Costa Rica to Ethiopia to Bali—and all the beans are specialty grade (the highest rating) beans, grown at the kind of high altitudes that make for better-tasting coffee, and culled from the top 2 percent of Arabica beans worldwide. When they arrive at the Roasterie's plant off Southwest Boulevard, the beans are air-roasted before being packaged for sale at your local supermarket. Air-roasting is an elite coffee-roasting process that only a handful of roasters in the United States employ: Think of it as akin to a hot-air popcorn popper, a method whereby the beans are tossed into the air and roasted by the hot air of a convection oven on all sides instead of being exposed to the hot metal of the roasting chamber for long periods of time during roasting (as is standard with most other specialty coffee companies). The whole operation, from the picking and drying of beans, to roasting, blending, and packaging, is fascinating, and the Roasterie welcomes the public for free hour-long tours of its plant. (You have to wear a hairnet as you walk around, but they do give you a free cup of coffee for your compliance.) You will learn a ton from the tour and introductory video—did you know that one coffee tree yields just 1½ pounds of coffee beans per year; or that it only takes 12 to 15 minutes to roast a batch of raw green coffee beans but an expert roaster's supervision to ensure that the timing is exactly perfect? Even if you can't make the scheduled 10 a.m. time slot, you can stop by anytime during business hours, and the staff is usually able to show you around. As with tours at **Boulevard Brewery** down the street, it's best to avoid weekends if you really want to learn something; go on a weekday morning and you'll likely get a one-on-one tutorial in all things coffee.

The Crossroads

In Kansas City, the word "Crossroads" is synonymous with the arts scene and hipsterdom. In fact, the full neighborhood name, according to community development types, is "Crossroads Arts District." Clunky name or not, this is about as cool as K.C. gets, and where an old-school American cityscape collides with dynamic exponents of modern culture. Down here (including the nebulous areas east of Southwest Trafficway and I-35, south of I-670, west of US 71, and north of the train tracks that cut through town around 20th to 23rd Streets), wonderful old brick warehouses and industrial plants have been requalified for use by contemporary galleries, architecture and design studios, housewares and clothing boutiques, and of course, some exceptionally vibrant dining and foodie shop fronts. The Crossroads, which features such iconic skyline elements as the Western Auto neon sign and the rocket-topped TWA building, is the most exciting part of town where food is concerned—all but a handful of the restaurants here are fiercely independent, style conscious, and adventurous. The James Beard Award–winning chef Michael Smith has side-by-side restaurants here, and some of the most flavorful Asian in town can be found at **Lulu's** and **Nara.** (Coastal transplants, or anyone who's experienced the more advanced restaurant scenes of cities like New York and San Francisco, will find the Crossroads a welcome pocket of sophistication.) Crossroads restaurants are also very well patronized by a cross-section of informed Kansas Citians and visitors, lending an urban buzz that can be hard to find in this spread-out city. The energy is especially electric on First Fridays (see p. 77), when the galleries of the Crossroads hold special exhibitions, and the streets are flooded with serious art gawkers, families, and revelers.

Proper restaurants are only part of the story in the Crossroads; this is also a neighborhood with a fabulous wine store (**Cellar Rat,** where you can also do tastings and eat small plates); a fancy boutique chocolatier, **Christopher Elbow;** a cave-like speakeasy, **Manifesto,** where cocktails are an art form; and Kansas City's beloved temple of greasy late-night burgers, **Town Topic.** Forming the southern boundary of the Crossroads district is the Freight House, a linear complex of beautiful old railway warehouses converted into restaurants; BBQ mainstay **Fiorella's Jack Stack** and the Austrian newcomer, **Grünauer,** are both exceptional places, reviewed here, that get extra points for atmosphere by virtue of their Freight House locations.

The dramatic new Kauffman Center for the Performing Arts will open, after five years of construction, in September 2011 on 16th Street between Broadway and Wyandotte, at the northwest corner of the Crossroads district. With its massive, undulating, skyline-changing architecture and state-of-the-art facilities, the $413 million, 285,000-square-foot, two-performance-hall center is bound to have a major impact on the surrounding area and its food options. In fact, as this guide goes to press, Jonathan Justus (of **Justus Drugstore,** p. 217) is planning to open a new Modern American brasserie called Universal, at 1700 Wyandotte, to capture those hungry arts patrons.

 Foodie Faves

Dog Nuvo, 1724 Main St.; (816) 474-8899; www.eatatdognuvo .com. Mon through Fri 11 a.m. to 2:30 p.m.; $. If the all-American hamburger can get a gourmet makeover at haute K.C. burger joints like **Blanc,** why not its brother, the hot dog? Elevating this everyman, street-cart staple to gourmet levels, Dog Nuvo is the brainchild of Marshall Roth, an executive chef with a bicoastal pedigree who, through the vicissitudes of chefdom, somehow ended up in Kansas City with the opportunity to open his own business. Instead of a hoity-toity culinary palace, Roth wanted something more approachable, more comfortable (outgoing and cheerful Roth is a hug in human form), more fun, yet still chef-crafted and unique, and—eureka!—the dressed-up-dog cafe was born. The dog menu features 8 selections, like the Chi-Town Dog ($4.50), "dragged through the garden," or loaded with fresh vegetables; the French-inspired Poodle ($6), with such snobby accoutrements as boeuf bourguignon, brie, and Pinot Noir mustard; and the decadent and decidedly Midwestern Blue Pig ($6), with Maytag blue cheese, applewood-smoked bacon, and crispy shallots. There's even a Thai dog ($6), which is a sort of pad thai chicken wiener with spicy peanut sauce, bean sprouts, cilantro, and mint. You can also design your own dog with your choice of house-made krauts (made with the *sous-vide* technique: vacuum-sealed to ensure maximum flavor fusion and intensity), mustards, and pickles. The 100 percent beef frankfurters are an artisanal product made with all-natural casings and grilled in Nuvo's secret brine. The specialty buns, like poppy-seed challah, are made fresh daily by **Farm to Market Bread** in Waldo, K.C. While dogs are pretty much the main attraction here, there's also a short and rigorously house-made "sides" menu with potato salad ($3), slaw ($3), farm salads ($5), and truffle-Asiago potato chips ($3). Dog Nuvo, a sleek spot just adjacent to the landmark red-and-silver TWA Building (in the old Souperman space), is a perfect fit for the trendy Crossroads; not only is it fun and affordable, but the "haute dog" concept has hipster written all over it.

Extra Virgin, 1900 Main St.; (816) 842-2205; www.extravirginkc .com. Mon through Thurs 11:30 a.m. to 10 p.m., Fri 11:30 a.m. to 11 p.m., Sat 5 to 11 p.m. Closed Sun; $$. The enormous mural reproduction of the movie poster for *La Dolce Vita*—a voluptuous

Anita Ekberg, a smoking and debonair Marcello Mastroianni—on the far wall of Extra Virgin just about sums up the ethos of this tapas offshoot run by prominent Chef **Michael Smith** (whose namesake restaurant, reviewed elsewhere in this chapter, is next door). Extra Virgin is lush, fun, and frequently decadent. It's where this James Beard Award–winning chef lets his culinary imagination run wild and gets a little bit rock 'n' roll. Favoring the more sumptuous sides of Spain, Italy, and France, the menu (average prices $7 to $13 for cold or hot tapas) is a loving romp through mostly Mediterranean cuisine, even venturing into Lebanese flavors with a vegetable salad and lamb kebabs, while Central and South American influences are also present (ceviche veracruzano, empanadas, Mexican grilled corn). Although Smith loves Asian food, he draws the line there: You won't find any attempts at sushi, nor any Thai spices, anywhere. Colorful, piquant, stylish sauces and condiments (strictly house made, always bearing Smith's flair for artistically employing the freshest, highest-quality ingredients) accompany just about every dish, though there are also some dressed-down choices, like the Marcona almonds ($4), or EV's top-selling chickpea fries ($4) on the "Bites" menu. There are entire sections of the menu dedicated to charcuterie (the Italian Meat Slicer, $7 to $9) and cheese ($7), but Smith also courts foodie pioneers with a robust selection of "For the Adventurous" tapas—these include creatures or parts of the animal that aren't perhaps for everyone, like pig ear salad, duck tongue tacos, braised snail ragout, but they deliciously reward your bravery. With its pleasant patio overlooking 19th and Main, and its big, buzzy interior dining room with wraparound bar, Extra Virgin's space is as successful as its kitchen. Extra Virgin can be mobbed on weekend nights, but it's a lot more relaxed at lunch and in the afternoon, when many items are half off (the generous happy hour runs from Mon through Fri 11:30 a.m. to 6 p.m.). Monday night is pizza and wine night—pizzas are $8 and wine bottles under $100 are half price. Perhaps the best endorsement I can give Extra Virgin is that it's a restaurant I return to more frequently than anywhere else in K.C.—off-duty, by myself to contemplate the Crossroads view from the patio, or inside with friends at the bar—because I know that Smith's kitchen will always serve me some sophisticated savory surprise. See Extra Virgin's recipe for **Chorizo & Fig Stuffed Chicken** on p. 262.

Grünauer, 101 W. 22nd St.; (816) 283-3234; www.Grunauerkc .com. Mon through Thurs 11 a.m. to 10 p.m., Fri through Sat 11 a.m. to 11 p.m.; $$$. In Vienna's artsy district of Neubau, there's a beloved historic *gasthaus* called Grünauer that is as popular with politicos and other Austrian nabobs as it is with neighborhood folk. The same family that runs Vienna's venerable Grünauer (led here by Executive Chef and veteran restaurateur Peter Grünauer) took a chance on Kansas City's appetite for Germanic food and opened this Midwestern outpost of Grünauer (in the cozy Freight House location formerly occupied by City Tavern) in 2010. If you're bewildered by the notion of "Germanic" cuisine, don't be. In fact, given Kansas City's ethnic heritage—many German and eastern European immigrants settled in neighborhoods like Strawberry Hill in the early 20th century—versions of several Grünauer dishes are already part of many families' home-cooking repertoire, even though the names of dishes, strictly in German, may be more foreign. What's schnitzel, you ask? That's just a fried pork cutlet (see, nothing crazy), but here, Wiener schnitzel (pork cutlet in the style of Vienna) is a thing of beauty, with a scrumptious, buttery breading and melt-in-your-mouth meat. (Tip: Order the off-menu jägerschnitzel, which is Wiener schnitzel with a creamy mushroom-mustard sauce that will send your taste buds into rapture.) All the entrees ($15 to $22) are expertly prepared, soul-warming masterpieces that feel right at home in the Midwest, and portions are accordingly generous.

In the cozy bar area, dubbed Wunderbar, the original stone tile is charmingly cracked in places, and the dark lighting is well-suited for first-date drinks or winter nightcaps. Or, you can employ it as I do—which is as an afternoon waystation where you can get one of Grünauer's specialty wurst (sausage) plates—the curried Berliner is the best—for the happy "auer" price of $5 (vs. $9 during normal service hours). For dessert (all $8), it's hard to resist the apple strudel (whose aroma, whenever it's sent out of the kitchen, is a siren song), but the Viennese sweet par excellence is Sachertorte (a unique type of chocolate layer cake with slick, dark chocolate icing on all surfaces). With high ceilings, cast-iron chandeliers providing warm light, and dark wood floors, Grünauer has an elegant, European feel yet is also intimate and inviting. High marks go to the staff—servers feel like a family (some are in fact Grünauers, some aren't) that genuinely makes you feel at home, and they're happy to honor just about any special request. It's certainly ambitious to open up a restaurant specializing in Austrian food alongside big corporate restaurants Lidia's and Jack Stack. I, for one, am very much pulling for Grünauer to become as much of a Kansas City fixture as its Freight House neighbors. And from the warm atmosphere I've always found at Grünauer thus far, it's well on its way.

Los Tules, 1656 Broadway; (816) 421-9229; www.lostuleskc .com. Mon through Thurs 11 a.m. to 9 p.m., Fri through Sat 11 a.m. to 10 p.m., Sun noon to 9 p.m.; $–$$. For some reason, the overrated Manny's is the Crossroads Mexican restaurant that gets the big crowds. Insiders know, however, that the best brick-and-mortar Mexican in this 'hood (see also Port Fonda, the hip and delicious new Mexican food truck operating in the Crossroads) is on a lonely (but soon to be much more lively—the Kauffman Center is opening across the street in Sept 2011) stretch of Broadway in a garish orange building. There is nothing trendy about Los Tules, but in a town where sickly tomatoes and shredded cheddar often pass as taco toppings, Los Tules is a breath of fresh, authentic air. Seasonings are bold and well-crafted, lending memorable flavor to enchiladas, burritos, tacos (the small, taco-truck kind—Salvador and Maria Tule operated a mobile taqueria before taking over this restaurant in 2003), and a variety of shrimp and meat *platillos* (entrees). The *asada* taco (with chopped steak, onion, cilantro, and a piquant tomatillo sauce on 2 soft corn tortillas) is delicious, and a steal at $2. The fish tacos (with tilapia, chipotle sauce, and cabbage slaw, $4) are also fantastic. Thanks to its tasty, good-value food and its friendly and quick service, Los Tules has a faithful cadre of regulars, including a lot of construction workers from the Kauffman Center "hole" across the street, and just as many downtown hipsters. Tabs are almost always very cheap (unlike the ever-inflating Manny's), especially if you stick to the a la carte menu, where most items are $3 to $4. Los Tules has a full bar, specializing in margaritas ($6 by the glass, $14 for a half pitcher, $24 for a full pitcher), and also serves horchata (a rice drink with cinnamon and other flavorings, $2).

Lulu's Thai Noodle Shop, 333 Southwest Blvd., between Broadway and Central; (816) 474-8424; www.lulusnoodles.com. Mon through Fri 11 a.m. to 3 p.m. and 5 to 10 p.m., Sat 5 to 10 p.m.; $. In a town where Asian often means a stale buffet of MSG-gorged stir-fries, Lulu's is vibrant and fresh, with flavors that zing, and it makes for a lively juxtaposition of far-Eastern flair among the historic and very American Midwest brick buildings of the Crossroads. The independently owned, urban "noodle and satay bar" was opened by Malisa Monyakula, who has had a lifetime passion for Thai food thanks to her Swiss-Thai father. Lulu's charms immediately with its funky decor of exposed brick, lashings of chartreuse trim paint, foliage, and a central babbling water feature, all in a room with 40-foot ceilings that makes for a high noise level during peak hours. (The restaurant is also a sort of hipster haven: Skinny jeans, tattoos, and ironic haircuts are the norm.) Lulu's menu is one of those that sends your saliva glands into turbo mode with its myriad choices of dishes—satays, Thai salads, wok specialties, curries, fried rice, soups, noodles—that all look tantalizing. It's a menu that makes you vow to become a regular so that next time you can try the spicy beef *jantaboon,* and the time after that the rainbow peanut noodles. Many first-timers and regulars alike opt for the perennial favorite pad thai or the drunken noodles, a spicy ensemble in which wide rice noodles are tossed with Thai basil, Chinese broccoli, peanuts, lemongrass, scallions, sprouts, bell peppers, and egg. I am personally smitten with the curried coconut shrimp and chicken, with rice vermicelli, red onions, and peas—it's a heavenly balance of flavors that manages not to be cloying despite the coconut milk broth. All ingredients are super fresh, and entrees, available in 4 levels of spiciness (up to "blazing"), are priced between $7 and $10. Lulu's is exceptionally popular at lunch, when you can fill your belly for $6.98 with one of 15 different entrees and a crab rangoon. The small but lively bar serves unique, Thai-inspired cocktails and Asian beers (Singha, Sapporo, and Tsing Tao) in addition to domestic beers, premium spirits (including tropical fruit–infused vodkas), and house wines. If those fiery noodles don't make you feel toasty on a cold Kansas City winter's day, a hot sake most definitely will.

Nara, 1617 Main St.; (816) 221-6272; www.narakc.com. Mon through Thurs 11 a.m. to 10 p.m., Fri 11 a.m. to 11 p.m., Sat 4 to 11 p.m.; bar and robata/sushi open 1 to 2 hours later; $$–$$$. Sleek and comfy Nara, a self-styled *robata* (Japanese open-flame grill) and sushi bar, is one of the trendier places for a bite in the Crossroads. The room is sexily lit with custom Japanese-inspired fixtures and features shiny modernist seating, lacquered surfaces, and red floral accents that all conjure a cool Asian feel, but a big exposed brick wall warms it up and reminds you we're still in all-American Kansas City. Fortunately, the food at Nara is just as compelling, if not more so, than the aesthetics. When I first ate here, I was fully expecting Nara to be all style and little substance, but I was very pleasantly surprised at the quality and flavors coming out of the kitchen. The menu is overwhelming at first glance, with sections for small plates, *robata,* large plates, and of course comprehensive sushi offerings. No one else in K.C. does *robata*—Nara even flies in special Japanese charcoal to guarantee the authenticity of this grilling method—so if you're undecided, start with an item off that list, such as the delectable and marvelously tender *yaki gyu* (beef sirloin satay), spiced with chimichurri and served with a drizzle of addictive and tangy orange sauce. Sushi (2 pieces, $5 to $7 on average), sashimi (5 cuts, $12 to $16), and makimono (rolls, $6 to $16) are beautifully presented and always fresh. Entrees ($12 to $26) on the "large plates" part of the menu are more interesting than your typical

Japanese steakhouse or sushi bar fare, with dishes like the Kobe beef sliders trio ($16), with teriyaki and quail egg, spicy Asian mustard, lime yuzu, and lotus root chips, as well as classics like negi-maki, teriyaki, sukiyaki, and tempura. Nara definitely has a young and image-conscious feel, especially during happy hour when 20- and 30-somethings from nearby offices get off work and unwind in the front lounge, and it can be loud, but the staff is super friendly and welcoming of everyone.

Pizza Bella, 1810 Baltimore Ave; (816) 471-3300; www.pizza bellakc.com. Mon through Thurs 11 a.m. to 10 p.m., Fri 11 a.m. to 11 p.m., Sat noon to 11 p.m., Sun noon to 9 p.m.; $$. The hip and modern Pizza Bella pioneered the whole gourmet pizza trend in K.C. Originally opened in 2007 by ambitious K.C. restaurateur Rob Dalzell (whose overextended empire of downtown eateries—Souperman, Chef Burger, and 1924 Main—all ultimately crumbled), Pizza Bella changed ownership during the Dalzell restaurant group collapse of 2010 but still serves essentially the same fare now as then, and in the same inviting space, with clean lines of contemporary wood and brick. The tasty wood-fired pizzas are made with premium ingredients; the crust has a nice, not-too-thin texture (but not chewy and charred like Neapolitan-style pizza, which Pizza Bella does not purport to be). The menu includes such canonical offerings as the cheeseless marinara (tomato, garlic, and basil, $9), the red-white-and-green Margherita (the marinara plus fresh mozzarella, $10), as well as more boutiquey creations like the *biancoverde* (a "green and white" pie with fresh mozzarella, ricotta, Parmesan, and arugula, $12) and the egg (eggs, pancetta, sun-dried tomato pesto, roasted onions, ricotta, and arugula, $14). But you don't have to get pizza at Pizza Bella: On the antipasti menu you'll find the best brussels sprouts in Kansas City (with pancetta vinaigrette, almonds, and dried cranberries, $8) and an excellent *salumi* plate (with prosciutto, speck ham, soppressata, and chorizo, $12). As handsome as the contemporary restaurant is, it's also perfectly child friendly and is popular with Crossroads families and their young kids.

Port Fonda, (816) 645-0483; www.portfondakc.com. Mobile food vendor, location varies, but usually in the parking lot of the Rieger (Main & 20th St.) on Fri and Sat 7:30 p.m. to 2 a.m. Call or check website for exact opening hours and days. Airstream trailer with seriously tasty regional Mexican street food. Before settling back in his native KC to carve out a place in the local food scene here, Port Fonda owner/chef Patrick Ryan trained at many restaurants from coast to coast. His most influential experience was working under Rick Bayless at Frontera Grill and Topolobampo in Chicago— Bayless is the man widely credited with introducing authentic Mexican cuisine to the masses, so expect to see (and taste) a menu at Port Fonda that embraces street food like *tacos de chivo* (with goat, *pasilla,* radish, and grilled green onion, $3), amazing scratch-made sauces (like burnt orange for duck, or *mole amarillo*), and chef-driven flourishes like the Port Fonda *banh mi* (with Rancho Gordo beans, chicken liver pate, pork belly, pork rillette, pickled veg, cilantro, and hot sauce mayo, $7). On the often-changing menu, all tacos are $3 and *tortas* (sandwiches) are $7; mighty reasonable for these Midwest-sized portions. Port Fonda also does its own *horchata* (rice and milk drink with vanilla and cinnamon) and *aguas frescas,* in addition to serving authentic sugar-cane-based soft drinks like Mexican Coke and various fun flavors of the Mexicans soda *Jarritos.* But perhaps the most charming element of this Airstream trailer, which was custom-refitted by artist Peter Warren, is that you can actually dine *in* it. Well, six people can, anyway: Port Fonda has a single six-top table inside called *"El Comedor"* (Fri and Sat, seatings at 8:30 p.m. and 11:30 p.m.) that can be reserved for a set-menu meal of $250 for all six diners (a recent menu: first course of Rancho Gordo beans with grilled Crum's family radishes and turnips, basil, cilantro, mint, bean vinaigrette and chile; second course of *chicharrones al chipotle* with fried farm egg and crema; main course of a roasted, whole, bone-in, Berkshire pork butt with abundant fixin's; and dessert of ricotta donuts with tequila tres leches, strawberries, and rhubarb). El Comedor and Port Fonda have plans to launch lunch service during the week, and both can be booked for private events. See Port Fonda's recipe for **Ensalada de Ayocote Morado** (purple runner bean salad) on p. 274.

Tannin Wine Bar & Kitchen, 1526 Walnut; (816) 842-2660; www.tanninwinebar.com. Mon through Fri 11:30 a.m. to 1:30 a.m., Sat 4 p.m. to 1:30 a.m., Sun 4 p.m. to 1:30 a.m.; $$–$$$. Whether inside, sprawled out on the living room furniture or sitting at the bar or banquettes, or outside at the patio tables and canvas divans, this is one congenial place to sample a bit o' the vine. Tannin Wine Bar opened in 2011, seamlessly, in the space that had previously been JP Wine Bar. Not a whole lot changed with the switch over. The urbane decor remains, with exposed brick, leather upholstery, and the lively buzz of conversation and clinking crystal still functioning as the backdrop to the sophisticated and eclectic wine list with price points for every budget. The former JP's was well known for its wine flights ($10 to $16, for thematic tastings of, say, Argentine Red, Alsatian Varietals, Bubbles), while Tannin's has more of a DIY flight-construction approach. The extensive selection of wines by the glass (5 oz.) or "taste" (2 oz.) lets you craft your own tasting session, but staff can also help you choose. Oenophiles can become members of Tannin's wine club—different levels of membership come with various wine-related benefits and include a personal wine locker in the rear of the restaurant. To help keep you from leaving the place totally dizzy, Tannin also serves a surprisingly complete food menu. I prefer to nosh on the cheese flights ($15), La Quercia cured meats ($5), and attractive small plates (like grilled Beau Solais oyster mushrooms, $5; or jumbo lump crab dip with garlic cream sauce, bacon, Parmigiana Reggiano, and baguette,

$8), simply because they seem to go best with the wine and the bar atmosphere, but there are also full-fledged, foodie-worthy entrees ($9 to $13 at lunch, or $38 for a 4-course tasting menu at dinner) if you've got an appetite for something heartier. Happy hour, when all wines by the glass, beers, small plates and cheese are 25 percent off, is from 4 to 6 p.m. every day and from 10 p.m. to midnight Sun through Thurs. On Sunday and Monday, all wine bottles are buy-one, get-one-free (of equal or lesser value). And on a mild Sunday afternoon or Monday evening in spring or fall, sharing a few bottles of half-price wine with friends on the patio of Tannin reminds you of just how sweet life can be in Kansas City.

Old-Guard K.C.

Fiorella's Jack Stack BBQ, 101 W. 22nd St.; (816) 472-7427; www.jackstackbbq.com. Mon through Thurs 11 a.m. to 10 p.m., Fri through Sat 11 a.m. to 10:30 p.m., Sun 11 a.m. to 9 p.m.; $$–$$$. If you only have time for one barbecue meal in Kansas City, and you want a more atmospheric sit-down venue than the gas-station digs of Oklahoma Joe's or the Formica tables of Arthur Bryant's, Jack Stack at the Freight House is where you need to go. My fondness for this particular location of the venerable Jack Stack chain (aka Fiorella's) dates back to December 2006, when I had just flown in from NYC to visit my long-distance boyfriend (now my husband) for the first time. Upon picking me up from the airport on that cold and snowy evening, he took me to the Freight House for my first taste of Kansas City barbecue. I fell in love as soon as I walked in the door. The space, first of all, is amazing—one of the coolest rooms in Kansas City, and a very fitting introduction to this town's heritage. All brick and timber construction, it's a soaring barn of a place (indeed, a former freight house for the nearby railroad) with huge wagon wheel chandeliers casting warm, cozy light. The noise level is always set on "festive." And the heavenly aroma of wood smoke and meat, which you can smell even before you step inside, floats throughout. Jack Stack, unlike many BBQ joints in town, is a proper restaurant, where you tend to order full-fledged entrees, like a half slab of dinosaur-size beef back ribs ($14.75) or the outstanding lamb ribs ($16.95), as well as all manner of pork ribs, and any number of combination platters with BBQ chicken or sliced meats. (Out-of-towners unsure how to navigate the wild world of BBQ meats should ask the helpful staff for advice.) The "Signature Items" portion of the menu includes such specialties as Crown Prime Beef Ribs ($28.95) and New Zealand rack of lamb ($27.95), and steakhouse-style fare includes K.C. strip, filet mignon, and porterhouse steaks, salmon, trout, and jumbo shrimp. Of course, if you're not that hungry, you can order from the comprehensive sandwich menu ($9.25 to $13.50). Simply put, you can rely on Jack Stack to deliver expertly prepared barbecue and just about any other meat dish you can think of. Jack Stack's famous side dishes are as integral to the experience of eating here as the meat: all entrees come with creamy coleslaw and fries, but you can substitute their amazing hickory pit beans and their legendary cheesy corn bake at no extra charge, or order any of those sides a la carte ($3 to $5). The portions of everything are huge, and service is incredibly efficient. On weekend evenings, Jack Stack at the Freight House is always packed; they don't take reservations, so expect a wait of 20 to 45 minutes. But since there's so much parking here, it's an ideal place to start an evening of wandering the Crossroads, maybe having a drink or appetizer somewhere else, then heading back toward Jack Stack, once the crowds have subsided into their food comas, for some well-earned meat.

The Jack Stack company (which does a huge online business, shipping rib platters and such nationwide) has 3 other locations in the metro area (the original, in Martin City, is reviewed on p. 195), and the entire franchise is consistently rated by Zagat Survey as the Best Barbecue in the United States.

Town Topic, 2021 Broadway; (816) 842-2298. Open 24 hrs, 7 days a week; $. There is perhaps only one other neon sign in K.C. as familiar as that atop the Western Auto building. It's the Town Topic Hamburgers sign, a blue shark fin intersected by red block lettering, lashed to the roof of this matchbox-size diner by several haphazard strands of cable. Though it's no bigger than an Airstream trailer, with about 10 stools for counter seating, Town Topic is a Kansas City institution—for a certain late-night-noshing segment of the population, anyway. At this bastion of old-school Americana, the traditional standbys of the flat-top grill and fryer—burgers, onion rings, fries, you get the idea—reign supreme. The burgers are chock-full of their trademark grilled onions (onionphobes, give it a wide berth) and the grease-laden breakfast fare (try the truck stop omelet, a 4-egger with hash browns, toast, and choice of a meat) is enough to make a cardiologist apoplectic—though it might just make your hangover back down. In an artsy area like the Crossroads, where everyone's usually trying to outcool each other at gallery openings and tapas bars, Town Topic is a refreshing breath of artless air. The lights are fluorescent and unflattering, and most of the kitchen fixtures haven't been updated in decades. (Which, of course, makes it a darling with the ironic hipster crowd.) Despite the throwback feel, prices on the Coca-Cola-branded plastic-letter board menu seem to get more and more "modish" every year (the "bigger burger" with cheese is currently $6.15—not terrible, but given the zero overhead of this place, it seems high). Still, regulars return night after night for the classic burgers, patty melts, hash brown nuggets and pies, which change daily. Late evening—perhaps after a concert at the Sprint Center, or following a heroic night at the bars—is the most popular time to savor the Topic's unpretentious brand of greasy goodness. Your appreciation of Town Topic's no-nonsense diner fare may well depend on the hour, your hunger level, and how many cocktails you've had before stumbling into this fluorescent-

First Fridays

Once a month, the Crossroads Arts District really shows off its arty side in the form of **First Fridays.** On the first Friday of each month, all the galleries and exhibition spaces down here fling their doors open for a convivial encounter with painting, sculpture, photography, and other installations; often, wine and snacks accompany the shows. The atmosphere in the Crossroads on First Fridays—which are well attended year-round, regardless of weather—is fun, all-inclusive, and about as electric as Kansas City gets.

After visiting a few galleries and negotiating the crowded streets and sidewalks, it's fun to rest your feet at a Crossroads bar or restaurant. Pretty much all of the establishments listed in this chapter offer some kind of First Fridays special, but a particularly recommended place to take a load off and watch the pageant go by is the **Cashew** (2000 Grand Blvd., at 20th Street; 816-221-5858; www.thecashew.com; Mon through Sat 11 a.m. to 1:30 a.m., Sun 11 a.m. to midnight). It's one of K.C.'s most beloved bars for its huge garage-door windows on the corner of Grand and 20th, and three handsome, historic floors on which to drink in not only beer and cocktails but sweeping skyline views. Decent pub-style American fare is also served on the ground floor.

lit, dingy pod of midcentury nostalgia. Nothing like a little 2 a.m. camaraderie to make that BLT taste even better, right? Note that there is another location of Town Topic a few blocks away, at 1900 Baltimore Ave. (816-471-6038; open Mon through Sat for breakfast and lunch only), but the Broadway spot is the iconic one that's open 24/7.

Occasions

Michael Smith, 1900 Main St.; (816) 842-2202; www.michael smithkc.com. Tues through Fri 11:30 a.m. to 2 p.m. and 5 to 10 p.m., Sat 5 to 10 p.m.; $$$. James Beard Award–winning chef Michael Smith has an energy and fire that makes him a real standout in the culinary landscape of Kansas City, and his epony-mous restaurant is one of the top-five fine dining experiences in town. A meal here is always a three-cheers event. From the street, its sleek windows and bold modern graphics make you think this is another of the Crossroads art galleries or design studios, but inside is a warm and welcoming yet decidedly upscale restaurant that feels like it could be in Chicago or a sophisticated coastal city. Smith was trained largely in Europe, and in addition to an unwavering commit-ment to truly outstanding food, Smith has a weakness for European techniques and artisanal products. His contemporary American menu, though tight and well-honed, is a sumptuous tribute to the more decadent culinary contributions of Spain, Italy, and France.

There is hardly an entree without some appearance of cured pork, imported cheese, or rare mushrooms—sometimes all three—and everything comes with vegetable accompaniments, strictly seasonal and local whenever possible, that you can't wait to eat. Smith's formula, it seems, is not to add too many muddling flourishes that distract from the excellence of his *materia prima,* but he also doesn't leave things totally peasant: This chef is a man with a strong personality that always finds its way into his cooking, often in the form of unexpected flavor and texture combinations that rock your taste buds in the best way imaginable. On the menu, which changes seasonally, starters may include roasted beet salad with pumpkin dressing, pepitas, and goat cheese ($8) or seared *foie gras* with almond scone, white gazpacho, and grapes ($16), while the entree list always includes a mix of meat and seafood mains, like grilled rack of lamb with chorizo and semolina dumplings, crispy brussels sprouts, and huckleberry *gastrique* ($31), or pan-roasted barramundi with spiced carrot, shrimp, roasted garlic, and spearmint ($28). My favorite dish here is the braised rabbit with house-made gnocchi, shiitakes, leeks, and shaved Parmesan (either as an entree at lunch, $11, or a starter at dinner, $13). A wonderful selection of savory side items—sautéed garlicky spinach, scallion risotto—is also available, each $5. The well-edited list of wines by the glass or bottle is among K.C.'s best, and all bottles under $100 are half price on Wednesday nights. You can always expect personable, well-timed service. While the more ample Mediterranean menu next door at **Extra Virgin,** Smith's tapas concept, is quite tantalizing, Michael Smith is the original, the flagship restaurant with a capital R that offers the more cohesive, grown-up dining package and the sit-back-and-say-wow memorable food. Michael Smith also has the most exciting special event dinners in town—in 2010, he brought famed Tuscan butcher Dario Cecchini to his kitchen for a weekend of "carnirvana."

The Rieger Hotel Grill & Exchange, 1924 Main St.; (816) 471-2177; www.theriegerkc.com. Mon through Thurs 11 a.m. to 2 p.m. and 5 to 10 p.m., Fri 11 a.m. to 2 p.m. and 5 to 11 p.m., Sat 5 to 11 p.m. Bar open between lunch and dinner, and until 1:30 a.m. after dinner; $$$. As this book goes to press, the Rieger is Kansas City's "it" place to eat, drink, see and be seen. On the ground floor of the historic Rieger Hotel building (in the space formerly occupied by Rob Dalzell's old flagship, 1924 Main, which finally folded along with the rest of his downtown group of restaurants in early 2010), it's the cosmopolitan collaboration of hometown cocktail guru Ryan Maybee (whose speakeasy, **Manifesto,** is in the basement of the building) and Chef Howard Hanna, formerly of **Room 39** and the River Club. Hanna is one of the nicest, most talented guys in the K.C. restaurant business, and his food—upscale New American by way of Italy, with lots of lively spins on meat and vegetables—is reason enough to come to the Rieger. But as anyone who's ever been to Manifesto knows, the scratch-made drinks are just as compelling. Begin any trip to the Rieger with a trip to the bar: Here, Arturo and Valdes, who have both the appearance and the professionalism of 1940s movie bartenders, whip up seriously amazing cocktails like the Pendergast ($9, with bourbon, sweet vermouth, Benedictine, and angostura bitters) or the Chambeli ($10, with Beefeater gin, Gran Gala, Aperol, lemon, and rhubarb bitters). The wine list, too, is a thing of beauty, and an excellent range of Euro-centric wines are available by the 3-ounce glass ($3.50 to $6.50) or 6-ounce glass ($6 to $12). I love when restaurants do that. On the food side, much of what comes out of Chef Hanna's kitchen could be served at a progressive restaurant in Tuscany, and the menu is already packed with greatest hits. At dinner, order the charcuterie board appetizer ($11, with chicken liver pâté, head cheese, wild boar *rillettes*, Dijon, pickled vegetables, and all-you-can-eat triangles of toasted brioche). The Swiss chard *gnudi* ($10, with brown butter, pine nuts, and a spectacular ricotta salata) is the best pasta dish, but be aware that the pasta and risotto dishes are basically small plates. The star entrees are roasted beef tenderloin ($27, served with creamed spinach, sweet potato gratin, and roasted marrow bone), the crispy Berkshire pork ($21, 12-hour *sous vide* pork shoulder, whole-grain mustard sabayon, polenta, cavolo nero), and the rabbit pot pie ($19, peas, carrots, poached garlic, pearl onions, and the most amazing drop-biscuit crust). The outstanding Rieger Pork Soup ($7, with pork confit, garlic, gruyère, and *cotenna*) has already become a classic here. The Rieger is also open for lunch, with a different menu; a highlight is the *tagliata* ($10, sliced flank steak with salsa verde, rapini, and grilled bread), and there are also a number of salads (get the butter lettuce, $6, with sliced apple, buttermilk dressing, goat cheese, and Marcona almonds) and grilled sandwiches available.

The Rieger isn't just firing on its food and drink cylinders; the happening vibe and handsome ambience (dark woods, striped kitchen-cloth linens, splashy local art on the walls, and original cracked floor tiles for extra character) are also a major attraction here. Tip: Food-loving parties of 2 or solo diners should ask to be seated at the bar tables in the rear. Here you have an action-packed front-row view of the beamingly busy Hanna and his kitchen. See the Rieger's recipe for **Pork Soup** on p. 267.

Specialty Stores, Markets & Producers

Badseed Farmers' Market, 1909 McGee St.; (816) 472-0027; www.badseedkc.com. Fri 4 to 8 p.m., May through Feb. Badseed owners Brooke Salvaggio and Daniel Heryer have taken the locavore movement to the next level. At their farmers' market in the heart of downtown, they sell "beyond organic" heirloom vegetables, fruits, and more, much of it grown or produced at their 13.5-acre, off-grid farmstead, Urbavore, in Kansas City's East Side. Other metro-area vendors supplement Urbavore's offerings with locally grown or made

cheese; free-range beef, chicken, pork, and lamb; honey; preserves; pickles; baked goods; and mushrooms. The colorful shop front of Badseed Farmers'
Market is only open to the public on Fri evenings from May to Feb, when there's a festive "meet-your-farmer" atmosphere that gets even livelier when the market coincides with First Fridays in the Crossroads. There's also a weekly farmstand market at the Urbavore farm itself (about 8 miles away at 5500 Bennington Ave., off MO 350 and just west of I-435) on Sat from 2 to 6 p.m., June through Oct. Over 100 varieties of fruits and veggies are grown at Urbavore, including heirloom tomatoes, peppers, cucumbers, Swiss chard, kale, collard greens, carrots, beets, fennel, winter and summer squashes, lettuces and salad mixes, dried beans, fresh herbs, eggplant, broccoli, gourmet potatoes, turnips, apples, specialty onions, and garlic. In addition to being the picture of health from all that natural goodness they eat, Brooke—who worked at organic farms all over the world before settling back in her native K.C. to open Badseed in 2007—and husband Dan are passionate educators and avid sowers of sustainable food practices. They offer a range of accessible classes for the aspirational urban farmsteader—past courses (fees $30 to $50) have included Oyster Mushroom Cultivation (you will grow them on logs and must bring your own drill and drill bit!), Backyard Gardening: Growing Food for your Family, How to Raise Backyard Chickens, and Canning and Preserving Workshops. If you want to learn more, or find out how

to be an apprentice or volunteer, contact Brooke or Dan directly at brooke@badseedkc.com or dan@badseedkc.com.

The Cellar Rat Wine Merchants, 1701 Baltimore, at 17th St.; (816) 221-9463; www.cellarratwine.com. Closed Sun. It should come as no surprise that the coolest wine store in the city is in the Crossroads district. The wide-open, warehouse-like space, complete with tasting bar and classroom/event room, was opened in 2006 by a team of young restaurant-biz workers who saw a need in Kansas City for exactly what Cellar Rat has become: a fun, accessible portal into the world of wine, and a place where you can find tons of high-quality bottles, often from smaller, lesser known producers, no matter your price range. Of the more than 800 wines sold here, 75 percent are under $25, and the store is in fact merchandised with this budget factor in mind. The "splurge" bottles (over $25) are displayed in a small section to the right of the door, while the less expensive stuff (what staff refer to as "Monday, Tuesday, and Wednesday wines") takes up the majority of space, filling tall wire racks in the central corridor of the store. Selections are further organized by wine region and varietal. You won't find any mass-market stuff here, although there are still plenty of options for less than $10. But what makes Cellar Rat such a compelling place to buy wine (let's face it: Most of us will need to go out of our way to shop here) is the staff's firsthand knowledge of everything they sell and their passion for letting you in on it. Cellar Rat also has a robust education program, offering regular tastings (free or $5, at least once a week) and classes (Regions of Italy, or $10 vs. $100

Cab Sauv). There's a great sense of community at these well-attended, jovial events (where no one will bat an eye if you show up with your toddler), which have become just one more cultural entertainment option in this neighborhood. You can also come in anytime and have wines by the glass or flights, or drink any bottle sold here at the bar for a $5 corkage fee. (Owners had to lobby for a year with the city to obtain the permit to sell wine by the glass here, and you should be thankful they did, as prices are very reasonable.) Pair it with the store's artisanal selection of cured meats and cheeses—Cellar Rat is one of few merchants in K.C. area that sells such unusual pork products as *guanciale*. Dedicated oenophiles can join one of Cellar Rat's wine clubs and enjoy interesting, hand-selected bottles every month. Fun fact: Cofounder and behind-the-counter fixture Ryan Sciara was on season 2 of the PBS reality show *The Winemakers,* filmed in France's Loire Valley in 2009.

Christopher Elbow Chocolatier, 1819 McGee St.; (816) 842-1300; www.elbowchocolates.com. Tues through Sat 10 a.m. to 6 p.m. Super-artistic, often futuristic-looking (is it a truffle or a science-fiction show prop?), and exquisite-tasting chocolates have put Christopher Elbow on the map of Midwestern culinary luminaries, and the coastal foodie press has taken notice: He's been featured on the Food Network, and Elbow's No. 6 Dark Rocks was voted #1 chocolate in the nation by *Food & Wine* in February 2009. After chef stints under Emeril Lagasse and Jean Joho at Las Vegas hotels the Venetian and Paris, Elbow, a native Nebraskan, came to K.C. and began making chocolates as pastry chef at **The American.** His chocolate creations there became so celebrated that he opened this gorgeous flagship boutique in 2007. (He now has a shop in San Francisco, too.) With their delicate faceted tops, or flawless domes, or Miró-esque swirls of color, these chocolates are obviously handcrafted one at a time. Arranged in a glowing and warm modern store in the Crossroads gallery district, Elbow's creations are true masterpieces of art that appeal as much to visual aesthetes as to discerning

chocoholics. Taste Elbow's take on ice cream at **Glacé Artisan Ice Cream** (p. 154), which opened in the South Plaza district in 2010.

Manifesto, 1924 Main St.; (816) 536-1325; http://theriegerkc .com/manifesto/. Mon through Sat 5 p.m. to 1:30 a.m. If bars were celebrities, Manifesto, the brainchild of drinks guru Ryan Maybee, would be Humphrey Bogart. Kansas City's only speakeasy-style bar, which opened in 2009 in the cave-like cellar beneath the restaurant at 1924 Main (now the excellent Rieger Hotel Grill & Exchange), evokes a sexy early-20th-century boite, where the atmosphere is noir (literally—the only light is provided by candles on the bar and tables) and the cocktails are done the old-fashioned way. A small trifold menu is divided according to the base spirit—rum, gin, brandy, whiskey, bitters, vodka, tequila and mezcal—and everything they serve is a carefully hand-crafted work of art. All drinks—with names that evoke 1960s glamour (the cachaca-honey-cinnamon-lemon-butternut squash "Winter in Buenos Aires," or Pimm's-strawberry-ginger-lime "Anyone for Tennis") or gritty Americana (the bourbon-based "Ward & Precinct")—cost $11, for that you get a full glass plus the carafe of any leftovers (usually another almost-full glass) from the mixing process. Earn your cocktail aficionado stripes with the Smokin' Choke (applewood-smoked Four Roses, Cynar artichoke liqueur, maple syrup, and Peychaud's bitters), or try Manifesto's sublime spins on the margarita, like the Old Oaxacan (mezcal, agave nectar, angostura orange bitters) or the Port Fonda (silver tequila, cucumber, tomatillo, cilantro, serrano peppers, salt, and lime). Century-old civility is enforced at Manifesto: men must remove their caps, women may not remove their shoes, and obnoxious, loud behavior is not tolerated. Manifesto's official literature discourages men from hitting on uninterested ladies. "If you must, ask the bartender to send her a drink on your tab, and she will let the bartender know if it's OK for you join her." Naturally, all of this appeals wildly to nostalgic aesthetes as much as it does to swanky drinkers. Note that having a drink at Manifesto isn't usually as simple as showing up at the Rieger's back door and heading downstairs. Because the bar is tiny (48 seats), and because the operation strives to maintain a special atmosphere of intimacy, you must text message your name and party size in advance to make reservations or get on the waiting list. All of this may sound kind of snobby, but it really doesn't feel that way once you're there (there's no cover, and there's no "VIP" priority). However, on busy weekends, the wait can be several hours, so try a slower weeknight if the concept of waiting to get into a bar bugs you. The vibe downstairs will be the same—dark and classy, warm and inclusive—no matter which night you pick.

Midtown: From 39th Street to Crown Center

"Midtown" is a nebulous geographical description in Kansas City. Most people would include the Plaza and Westport (both of which have their own chapters in this book) in the description of midtown, but whatever midtown is, it's not a neighborhood with a core. So for our purposes, midtown is the diagonal swatch of central Kansas City that begins in restaurant-packed 39th Street, continues north and east through the fairly bleak 30s, across to progressive Union Hill and up to Crown Center (Hallmark's headquarters and mall, with attached high-rise hotels) and Union Station. Westport is midtown's neighbor to the south, while the Crossroads begins just north of the train tracks at Union Station.

39th Street between State Line and Wyoming is known in Kansas City as "restaurant row" for its plethora of dining options that almost feels like . . . a real city! Here, a wide spectrum of eateries—seasonal and local American, New York–style pizza, Greek, Vietnamese, dim sum, vegan bakery, Cajun, sushi, Moroccan, smoothies (not all reviewed here)—and a vibrant (for K.C. anyway) sidewalk energy make 39th Street a no-brainer when you find yourself in midtown and hungry. But aside from the food gauntlet that is 39th Street, most mention-worthy food businesses in midtown are spread out and isolated. Those listed here include out-of-the-way places like **You Say Tomato** or **Browne's Irish Market;** niche places like **Ambrosi Brothers** cutlery; and Kansas City's legendary splurge, **The American,** in a panoramic fourth-floor dining room within Hallmark's corporate complex.

Foodie Faves

Aladdin Cafe, 3903 Wyoming St.; (816) 531-5982; www.aladdin cafeonline.com. Mon through Sat 11 a.m. to 10 p.m., Sun 11 a.m. to 9 p.m.; $. Opened in 2007 at the eastern end of restaurant row as a sister to the restaurant of the same name in Lawrence, Kansas, Aladdin Cafe is the coziest of Kansas City's half dozen or so catch-all Mediterranean eateries. (It's also a sit-down place, whereas some other gyro places are cafeteria-style counter-service only.) The menu is more abbreviated than at most other Middle Eastern joints in town, as the Jordanian-born Iskandari family who owns and manages Aladdin has chosen to focus on Arabic and Greek dishes for the most part. Still, all the usual suspects— hummus, falafel, kebabs—are represented, the portions are huge, and the pitas are moist and fluffy. It most definitely hits the spot when you're craving Middle Eastern. The menu  is also *Aladdin*-themed, and some of the best items are named after characters in the Disney-fied version of the Arabian Nights tale: the Raja dip ($5.99), after Jasmine's tiger, is a decadent molten pot of feta, Parmesan, cream, and walnuts; Jasmine has her own vegetarian combo ($8.99, with hummus, falafel, baba ghanoush, *dolmathes*, Genie dip, feta, and olives). But it's Aladdin's lentil soup ($2.99 cup/$3.99 bowl; free with some entrees) that is the real magic-carpet ride of flavors, with red lentils, carrots, and corn seasoned with saffron curry, cumin, and lemon. If you think lentil soup sounds boring, Aladdin's version really is . . . a whole new world. The perfect counterpoint to all those assertive spices and seasonings is the house saffron-rosewater lemonade ($2.99), which fans describe with such gushy superlatives as "godly nectar," "heavenly elixir," and "the stuff that dreams are made of." Aladdin Cafe also has few patio tables in front, which is where you can smoke a hookah. They do not have a liquor license, but you can BYOB for a $5 corkage fee, which is sometimes waived.

Friends Sushi & Bento Place, 1808 W. 39th St., between State Line and Bell; (816) 753-6666. Mon through Thurs 11 a.m. to 3 p.m. and 5 to 9 p.m., Fri through Sat 11 a.m. to 3 p.m. and 5 to 10:30 p.m.; $$. In a casual way, it feels like it could be in San Francisco, New York, or Chicago—not an overblown and theme-parky Morimoto-style Japanese, just your subtly stylish go-to neighborhood sushi joint . . . the kind of sushi joint that urban hipsters and sushi-newbie Midwesterners can all hang with. The nigiri, sashimi, maki, and special rolls are consistently higher quality than almost anywhere else in town, and the room has a cool and relaxed vibe that's as suitable for groups as for dates. (True to its name, you could totally picture Ross and Rachel and the gang here). Among the maki rolls, the crunchy spicy salmon is a top seller ($5.95), and on the special roll menu, it's worth splurging on the dragon roll (mango-wrapped eel avocado roll, $9.95). Sushi and sashimi are $3 to $5 for 2 pieces, but sushi devotees will want to mark their weekly planners for Friends' happy hours—Mon 5 to 9 p.m. and Sat 11 a.m. to 3 p.m., when selected sushi and sashimi are only $1 and selected rolls are $3.99. At lunch, the bento boxes are a great deal. For about $8 ($10 at dinner), you can choose from hot and savory entrees like teriyaki, *tonkatsu,* or shrimp tempura with a bevy of sides (soup, salad, spring roll, cheese cracker, rice). Friends is not cutting-edge Japanese, so if you are looking for some of that nightclub atmosphere along with your *unagi,* seek out Nara instead (which will be more expensive). But if you're looking for a place that'll fairly closely replicate how you once did sushi night in other big cities you've lived in or traveled to, check out Friends.

Po's Dumpling Bar, 1715 W. 39th St., between Bell and Genessee; (816) 931-5991; www.posdumplingandnoodle.com. Sun through Thurs 11 a.m. to 9:30 p.m., Fri through Sat noon to 10 p.m.; $–$$. You might think its location next to Blue Koi—K.C.'s other, flashier dumpling and noodle specialist (not reviewed here)—would be a hindrance, but Po's actually outshines its neighbor more often than not. It's also one of few viable options for dim sum in town—though it's not advertised as such, and there's no stainless steel cart. The signature dish is the Emperor's Dumplings ($5.99 for 6), pan-fried pockets of wonder (choose chicken, pork, shrimp, or veggie filling) that take 10 minutes to arrive because they're always made to order. Just as many diners go slack-jawed for the cha su buns ($2.99 for 2), steamed buns filled with savory-sweet roast pork; to me, these epitomize all that is glorious about dim sum. The sweet red bean "peach" buns ($2.79 for 4) and the jade dumplings ($3.29 for 4), filled with steamed shrimp and chives, are also very satisfying and a bit different from other Chinese offerings around Kansas City. Po, for the record, is a real person, and grew up working for the family noodle business in Taiwan. He and his Taiwanese-born wife of almost 40 years, Rita, opened Po's after various restaurant stints around the Midwest and South. They're a lovely couple with a great love story, and their warmth is palpable at Po's. The kitchen makes everything from scratch, and you can tell—the fresh ingredients are always recognizable in the dishes here; they're never a mushy, MSG-packed mess. Soups are also a strong suit, and a light but soul-warming favorite is the tofu vegetable soup ($2.95 cup/$4.95 bowl). But the menu is much deeper than just dumplings, noodles, and soups; they've also got all the Chinese-American classics you might be craving—General Tso's chicken, orange beef, kung pao chicken, and the like ($9.95 to $11.95 at dinner). Recently added is also a short list of more, ahem, adventurous "new Chinese authentic dishes" like stewed sliced flounder with black bean sauce ($10.95) or spicy pickled sour mustard with pork intestines ($11.95). Whether there are enough daring Asian food eaters in K.C. to keep those items on the menu remains to be seen, but I hope so, because the flavors really are excellent and so different from your average Americanized Chinese. At lunch from Mon through Fri, many of Po's dishes are priced $6 to $8, including crab rangoons and soup. Po's has a full bar as well as a full line of kitschy rum-based tropical cocktails (from $6.75), like the Scorpion, the shareable Volcano, and the Zombie (limit 2 per person on this potent blend topped with 151-proof rum!).

Saigon 39, 1806½ W. 39th St., between State Line and Bell; (816) 531-4447. Mon through Thurs 11 a.m. to 2 p.m. and 5 to 9 p.m., Fri 11 a.m. to 2 p.m. and 5 to 10 p.m., Sat noon to 3 p.m. and 5 to 10 p.m.; $. Next time you throw a party where you need Asian hors d'oeuvres, do yourself a favor and order about a hundred of Saigon 39's spring rolls. These cool, plump morsels of rice noodles, cilantro, and shrimp wrapped in perfectly gummy rice paper are delicious simplicity on their own, but Saigon 39's justly famous peanut sauce takes them into the realm of addictive Asian appetizer bliss.

At this spunky little Vietnamese joint, run by a hip and helpful family, distinctive flavors run deep. Wisely (and uncharacteristically for so many Asian restaurants around), Saigon 39 limits its menu to fewer than a dozen meal-size soups and entrees (most priced at around $6 to $7 for lunch and $8 to $10 for dinner), ensuring that everything they make is spot-on as far as seasoning and cooking time. (They also don't do a lunch buffet—another sign of quality, generally speaking!) Mouth-watering broths are a specialty here: both the beef and chicken pho are fantastic, but the lemongrass-infused *bun bo Hue* (noodle soup with sliced steak) is even better. Among a handful of non-soup entrees (you choose your protein), there's a classic yellow curry with coconut milk, potatoes and carrots, and a mouthwatering—and very virtuous, given Vietnamese food's lack of heavy oils and starches—vegetable stir-fry. While most Vietnamese-food lovers in K.C. pledge allegiance to Vietnam Cafe downtown, I have consistently found the food at Saigon 39 to be tastier. Saigon 39 is small (there are maybe 12 tables), but the feel is airy and sunlit, with lofty arches separating the entrance and raised dining area. They even have a makeshift library that solo diners may wish to peruse, with such titles as the handy *Fish Mounts and How to Make Other Fish Trophies* and *Dante's Inferno,* probably sourced from Prospero's bookstore down the block.

You Say Tomato, 2801 Holmes St.; (816) 756-5097; www.ystkc .com. Mon through Sat 7 a.m. to 3 p.m., Sun brunch 8 a.m. to 2 p.m.; $. Combining vintage, artsy atmosphere with hearty and seasonal yumminess that'll have you rubbing your tummy and grinning blissfully for weeks to come, You Say Tomato in Union Hill is a Kansas City gem. For memorable homestyle breakfast and brunch stuff—that, let's face it, you will never get around to making at home—it's one of the best in town. Think of the cuisine here as "Midwest Modern": the foundations are 1950s American house-wife staples (biscuits and gravy, sausage and egg casserole, fruit pies baked daily), but there are just enough contemporary twists (including the fact that everything on the menu is seasonal, fresh, and, for the most part, local) that make the food here outstanding. While there are some menu staples (like the aforementioned B&G, casserole, and *bierocks*—more on them below), offerings can change from day to day, and in fact YST only posts its menu on a dry-erase board. Main dishes are normally priced around $7.50. By midday, you'll hear staff shouting (in the sonorous fashion of 19th-century sailors) that certain items have sold out, or there's only one left. If it's your first visit, you've got to try the biscuits and gravy, perfectly plump and floury-fresh and served with a magnificent sausage-mushroom gravy. Or equally representative of YST's heartier

fare is the sausage casserole, which is an enormous and rather dense brick (in a good way) of egg, sausage, and fresh herbs, and surprisingly piquant from the freshly ground pepper in it. Or try the quiche . . . you can't really go wrong. The place could probably stay in business on its *bierocks* alone—hard to find in K.C. restaurants, these are savory German-style pocket pastries (similar to pierogies) filled with beef, cabbage, onion, and cheese (or the veggie option, with curried lentils and potatoes) and served with spicy mustard. Lighter fare includes a variety of salads, flatbreads, panini, and hummus, but I can't imagine going to YST and not gorging myself on the kind of food the Eisenhowers might have enjoyed over Sunday brunch at the White House. You probably won't have room for dessert, but the pies are not to be missed, so just take a slice to go. Keep in mind that this is an order-at-the-counter place, so it's not fancy, but you could certainly impress your mom with a Mother's Day brunch here, or just check it out with friends. A mini specialty grocery takes up about one-third of the cozy, garage-sale-chic space, and while it's more an ambience thing than a real full-service shopping experience, they do sell splendid heirloom tomatoes in summer. Tip: On weekends especially, show up on the earlier side (before 11 a.m.) to ensure they haven't sold out of anything. Another tip: Walk off some of your calorific indulgence by exploring the up-and-coming surrounding neighborhood, which calls to mind aspects of SF's Mission or NYC's Williamsburg before they boomed.

Occasions

The American, 200 E. 25th St., 4th Floor (at Grand Avenue); (816) 545-8001; www.theamericankc.com. Mon through Sat 5:30 to 10 p.m. Reservations recommended; $$$$. When you decide to splurge on a meal at Kansas City's most formal restaurant, put on the fanciest clothes you own. Nowhere in K.C. but in the American, the Hallmark-owned crown of Crown Center, could you potentially get away with wearing an Oscar gown. The American was designed in the 1970s by architect Warren Platner (who also did the original Windows on the World at the World Trade Center in NYC) and its tiered, Art Deco dining room has that old Hollywood awards-show vibe in spades. Whatever you wear, be sure there's some elastic in it, because Chef Debbie Gold's progressive American food is not only decadent; it's so unrelentingly tasty that you will scrape up every last bit of it, from the opening *amuse-bouche* through the final crumb of pie crust. In between there will be savory vegetable-infused lamb jus to mop up, bread with goat's milk butter, and soup that will have you reel in amazement (get the white bean with *chicharrónes* if it's available). The dining room at the American may have a dated look, but the food is contemporary gourmet all the way. Chef Gold enjoys a no-expense-spared kitchen—there is no mushroom too exotic, no obscure seafood she can't airfreight in, no specialty meat she can't source. The result is a diverse and modern menu that is the ultimate showcase of all that Chef Gold, a James Beard Award winner for Best Chef Midwest in 1999, can do. And while some of the menu listings may seem daring, the

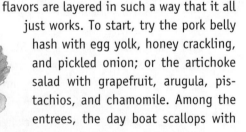

flavors are layered in such a way that it all just works. To start, try the pork belly hash with egg yolk, honey crackling, and pickled onion; or the artichoke salad with grapefruit, arugula, pistachios, and chamomile. Among the entrees, the day boat scallops with abalone mushrooms, leeks, and Meyer lemon are outstanding, as is the Piedmontese *côte de boeuf* with *socca* (chickpea flour pancake), spinach gnocchi, and Musser's white cheddar. The menu changes seasonally, and nothing is priced a la carte; instead, choose from a 3-course ($55), 4-course ($65), 5-course ($75), 7-course ($90), or 9-course ($104) meal, within which you may select any number of appetizers, salads, and desserts, but only 1 main dish. Some menu items carry an additional charge, from $6 to $30. General manager and wine director Jamie Jamison is your gracious host, personally attending to every table throughout the evening. He can design wine pairings on the spot or suggest a versatile bottle of wine for your table to share, such as a $200 Bordeaux or a $20 Chardonnay. Pastry Chef Nick Wesemann is nothing less than a wizard, whose whimsically deconstructed desserts are like plated flights on a loosely connected theme—like his Nickers Bar—chocolate torte, cashew caramel, bacon candy, nougat wafer, and sea salt ice cream. The American is an elegant place all around, but there are some old-fashioned aspects to the atmosphere that are worth knowing about before committing to a $100 dinner here. The spacing of tables and the high ceilings, compounded with the super discreet service, means that a dinner at the American is never a raucous event. Your focus will be on your tablemates, your food and wine, and on the skyline view out the floor-to-ceiling windows, not on any "hot scene" happening elsewhere in the restaurant. Even on a full night, the American feels hushed, except for the piano player tinkling out "As Time Goes By" from the mezzanine bar. All in all, it works best as a place for groups or families to come to celebrate something really special, less well as a spot for a romantic dinner à deux (couples will feel lost at those four-tops set for two).

Room 39, 1719 W. 39th St.; (816) 753-3939; www.rm39.com. Mon through Sat 7 a.m. to 3 p.m. and 5:30 to 10 p.m. Also in Leawood, KS, at Mission Farms: 10561 Mission Rd.; (913) 648-7639; $$$. The exceptionally warm and welcoming Room 39 is that rare restaurant that combines foodie all-star ingredients (house-cured meats, seasonal local produce, specialty cheeses, lobster, *foie gras*) and elegant preparations (ragouts, reductions, brittles, crisps) with a kitchen that actually delivers—with assertive and satisfying flavors—on the mouthwatering promise of what's printed on the menu. Room 39 does all of this in a convivial and inclusive space that really does feel like a room. It is everything I look for in a restaurant. (And I'm not the only one: Chefs from K.C.'s other top-notch restaurants come here when they're off duty.) Chalk it up to owners Ted Habiger and Andy Sloan, two pretty normal Midwestern guys who don't kill you with their chefly intensity (thankfully), but who clearly know a lot about hospitality and most of all, food. Executive Chef Habiger (a veteran of NYC's Union Square Cafe, Daniel, and Le Bernardin) and his team fully get the concept of sumptuous ingredients balanced with restraint, and it's evident in everything on the menu. From appetizers like the goat cheese gnocchi with lobster, oyster mushrooms, white wine tarragon cream, and pecorino Romano ($12) to entrees such as the pan-roasted half duck breast and leg confit with wild rice and *chana dal* pilaf, sautéed chickweed, roasted cauliflower and amarena cherry *mostarda* ($24), it all comes with unforgettable flavor, lovely texture, and refined, simple presentation. Room 39's veggie burger, made with bulgur wheat, black beans, and veggies, with red pepper aioli ($7 at lunch) has been voted "Best Fake Burger" by the local press. At lunch or dinner, fresh pastas are a mainstay, whether ravioli stuffed with caramelized onion–goat cheese in a sauce of mushrooms, Swiss chard, sherry cream, and fresh herbs ($20 at dinner) or house-made fettuccine with slow-roasted meat ragu ($11 lunch entree/dinner appetizer). For dessert, try the pistachio-lemon semifreddo ($7). At dinner, you can also do a 4-course tasting menu for $39, which gives you smaller-than-normal portions but is still an exceptional value. The restaurant is also a big supporter of local farmers; from April through early fall, all the produce, and most of the meat, comes from within one hour of 39th Street. (About once a month, the restaurant does a special lamb-three-ways dinner, with a baby lamb that comes from **Green Dirt Farm**—call for details.) Room 39 isn't just lunch and dinner, either: Habiger is passionate about breakfast—he believes in really good coffee (espresso is Italy's Danesi; coffee is a custom blend from K.C.'s own **Broadway Roasting Company**), really good farm-fresh eggs (from nearby **Campo Lindo**). A favorite on the breakfast menu is the smoked salmon scramble ($8), house-cured and smoked salmon, cream cheese, scallions, and soft scrambled eggs with breakfast potatoes and toast; but even better, perhaps, are the oven eggs ($8.50), 2 farm eggs baked in toast with gruyère and Genoa salami (add truffle oil for $2). Room 39 has a remarkably comfortable, lived-in feeling, with wall colors—crimson, buttercream, dusky blue—that could easily be from the Americana palette of the Ralph Lauren paint collection, and a nice noise level that makes it feel like the place to be. The pressed-tin ceiling, original to the 100-year-old building, and exposed ductwork add to the atmosphere. At lunch, the handcrafted wooden tables are left bare, but when Room 39 reopens at 5:30 p.m. for dinner, the tables are clothed with white linens and the lights are dimmed. At either mealtime, the effect is tonic—you'll want to linger for four courses. A lengthy wine list covers all bases, with plenty of choices under $50 and glasses for about $10. Well-informed waitstaff subscribe to the "it's all about you" school of service, minus the dreaded fawning and prolonged tableside discourses. Room 39 is special, and it's worth its $27 dinner entrees. Even if only for breakfast or lunch, treat yourself. Note: While Room 39 on 39th Street is the flagship, the restaurant has had a thriving second location at Mission Farms in Leawood, Kansas, since 2007. The menu is different and a bit longer at the Leawood restaurant (its larger kitchen permits such standouts as goat cheese beignets, which cannot be made at the 39th Street restaurant due to fryer limitations), and the roomier, slightly more formal dining room has a healthy bar scene. See Room 39's recipe for **Oven Eggs** on p. 264.

Ambrosi Brothers, 3023 Main St.; (816) 756-3030. Mon through Fri 8 a.m. to 5 p.m., 10 a.m. to 6 p.m. Sooner or later, all city cooks, whether professional or home chefs, end up here at Kansas City's excellent and only dedicated cutlery shop. In fact, I'm pretty sure that a big part of why my husband puts up with my kind-of-expensive kitchen-gadget habit is that it sometimes takes him to the temple of steel that is Ambrosi Brothers. While Ambrosi Brothers is a place where you can drop $100 on a Henckels *santoku*, it's not all "investment" level knives. There's a lot of fun and unique cutlery for around $20. But the real scoop here is that they also sell—for $3 to $10—refurbished commercial-grade knives. Look for these in the wooden drawers near the front door; they're no-nonsense knives with big, ugly handles and medievally substantial, sharp blades that have seen service in city restaurant kitchens. They may be a bit stained and worn elsewhere, but the cutting edges of these work-horses will cleave a chicken bone if you even breathe on them. And they're all displayed junk-drawer-style, so while you're browsing for that perfect parer to round out your collection, be careful not to slice open your wrist on that 12-inch chef's knife. You can also bring your own cutlery (even scissors) to be sharpened or repaired, for a very reasonable $3 to $5 on average. Before showing up with your dull blades, call to make sure they're doing sharpening that day; it usually can be done on the spot in less than 15 minutes. While you wait, browse the compact but interesting selection of specialty kitchen items, and let yourself be talked into buying (by your own conscience, not by the staff, who are helpful but not pushy) a 20-inch German-made, professional-grade mezzaluna for cutting pizza. Not that I'm speaking from experience.

Browne's Irish Market, 3300 Pennsylvania Ave.; (816) 561-0030; www.brownesmarket.com. Mon through Fri 9 a.m. to 3 p.m., Sat 10 a.m. to 2 p.m. Okay, remember the Mike Myers skit on *Saturday Night Live* about All Things Scottish, the store where "if it's not Scottish, it's crap!"? Well, this is the Irish version. It's been in business an impressively long time, since 1887, and is still run by members of the Browne family who founded it a century ago. In addition to being a store with Celtic gift items, shamrock-emblazoned knickknacks galore, and gimmicky packages of Irish dirt, Browne's also has a lunch cafe serving Irish staples like corned beef sandwiches ($6.50) and potato soup, while a small refrigerator is stocked with fresh soda bread ($9.95/loaf) and rashers and bangers (bacon and sausage, $9.95). Oddly enough, they do really amazing chocolate chip cookies ($1.75), too. On the six Saturdays leading up to St. Patrick's Day, and on March 17 itself, they offer traditional Irish breakfasts from 8 a.m. to noon. Browne's also sells boutique food items like lemon curd, trifle, Jameson's marmalade, and other pan-Britannic specialties. Browne's may not be uber-gourmet, but it's the only Irish-themed food market in town, with a historic feel that's an attraction in its own right. And for those legions of Kansas Citians brimming with Irish pride—even if they've never set foot in the motherland and couldn't locate Dublin on a labelless map, bless 'em—Browne's is definitely a place where they can come to load up on Irish vittles and all kinds of green, white, and orange heritage boosters. (And walk out smelling like bacon the rest of the day.)

The Filling Station, 2980 McGee; (816) 931-4335; www.filling stationcoffee.com. Mon through Thurs 6:30 a.m. to 6 p.m., Fri through Sat 7 a.m. to 6 p.m. You know how sometimes in the middle of a busy day, you find yourself in urgent need of a tall cup of hot caffeine and something for your plummeting blood sugar, so you stop into whatever your go-to gourmet coffee place is, and you end up dropping an unnecessary $7 on a so-so cappuccino and lackluster muffin? Well, the next time you find yourself in those circumstances, you will hopefully be within the vicinity of 29th and McGee. The Filling Station not only does coffee (and tea), pastries, and parfaits very well, but they also have a shockingly wide array of fantastic sandwiches, salads, and wraps, and creative fresh-squeezed juices—all served throughout the day. Coffee, you see, is actually the minority here, even though the skilled baristas can draw perfect rosettes in your first-rate cappuccino (at $2.40 for 8 ounces, the price is closer to Italy's than Starbucks'). In keeping with the progressive vibe in this neighborhood, the crowd is mostly cool and artsy (lots of tattoos and unflattering asymmetric hairstyles, but plenty of Joe Corporates, too), and food emphasis is on healthy and wholesome stuff, which in no way is mutually exclusive with the adjective "tasty." The ginger wrap (on wheat or spinach tortilla, $7.50) is a perfect expression of this: a mouthwatering combo of spring greens, cucumber, cranberries, almonds, and Mandarin sesame ginger dressing. Wraps in general seem to be the top sellers here. You can also get a little bit more decadent with sandwiches like the salmon club ($8), or cheese- and meat-filled quiches ($7, including side salad). An integral part of the Filling Station experience are the juices (from $3.75 for 12 ounces), like Liquid Sunshine (carrot, strawberry, orange, lemon, apple), Tasty Tater (sweet potato, pineapple, lime), the super-fibrous Stalker (cucumber, celery, broccoli), the refreshing Mint (cucumber, apple, mint) or the plain-dealing Just Friggin' Carrot (carrot and nothing). The place is located, as the name hints, in an actual former garage and service station, and the revamped modern interior has an open, buzzy feel, with modern furnishings and big potted plants in old oil drums. There's a nice-sized patio area, and in mild weather, the four glass garage doors are rolled up for a convivial alfresco vibe. Service is fast and really friendly, too. For the laptop crowd, the Filling Station is a viable place to get work done only if your machine has a good battery charge (outlets are few) and you don't mind a considerable noise level—steam from the espresso machine, downtown creatives talking shop, bass-heavy Girl Talk mashups—echoing off the high ceilings. But it's a great place to hang out, read the *New York Times,* and feel like the hip urbanite that you are.

Westport

What is now the entertainment capital of Kansas City was once a prosperous crossroads and outfitting center for wagon trains heading west. In fact, Westport is older than Kansas City itself. Visually, little remains of that frontier heritage (save the Conestoga wagon in the shopping center at Southwest Trafficway and Westport Road), as historic Westport over the years morphed into K.C.'s party zone. Before the Power & Light district opened downtown, with its corporate-planned bars and restaurants, Westport was the no-brainer choice in town for raucous nightlife. Festive Irish pubs and cheap, spit-and-sawdust bars (like McCoy's and Kelly's—still opposite each other at the corner of Westport Road and Pennsylvania) filled with college kids and 20-somethings used to be the norm in Westport (and still characterize much of the scene here), but more recently, the emphasis has shifted away from binge boozing to a varied and constantly renewed food and drink scene. You'll find James Beard Award nominees, farm-to-table acolytes, oysters at 1 a.m., and, yes, greasy burgers. Westport also gets huge foodie points for being home to my favorite kitchen store in the whole world, **Pryde's.** Allthough Westport lies immediately south of the tony Country Club Plaza, it has its own strong flavor and an artsy, collegiate vibe.

The main east–west artery of Westport Road is a gauntlet of inviting eateries and boîtes—whether you're in the mood for an exotic bite, a down-and-dirty bar and grill, a glass of wine or classic cocktails and small plates, or a five-star gourmet meal, Westport Road has you covered. The intersection of Westport Road and Pennsylvania is ground zero of the Westport nightlife scene, where you'll find many a reeling reveler on weekend nights, but some great foodie spots lie in this liveliest zone of Westport, too. Westport also has the unique distinction of being one of the few K.C. neighborhoods where you don't have to drive from place to place—most everything listed here is within walking distance from each other.

Foodie Faves

Boozefish Wine Bar, 1511 Westport Rd. (at Wyoming Street); (816) 561-5995; www.boozefish.com. Tues through Thurs 11 a.m. to 2 p.m. and 4 p.m. to 12:30 a.m., Fri 11 a.m. to 2 p.m. and 4 p.m. to 1:30 a.m., Sat 11 to 1:30 a.m. (kitchen closed from 2 to 5 p.m.); $$. In 2001, Kansas City didn't really have a dedicated wine bar. Maija Diethelm-Floyd—then barely out of college—gave winos a proper watering hole when she opened Boozefish. With its

cozy, European-inflected pub atmosphere, an
eclectic wine list, and comfy bistro food, it
became the place that it still is a decade
later—a neighborhood joint where you can
easily spend hours with good friends and
conversation. On the wine list, featuring
small boutique producers from California,

Oregon, Washington, France, Italy, Germany, Argentina, and
Australia, and some lesser-known varietals (especially among the
whites), 15 whites and 15 reds are always available by the glass ($8
to $10) or bottle ($30, $35, $40), while another dozen or so wines
are sold by the bottle only for $45, $50, and $55. The wines on
offer change slightly every season, and there are always sparkling
wines by the split (187 millilters), half bottle, and bottle. While
wine is the central theme and major seller to the predominantly
female, local clientele, Boozefish also has 15 single-malt scotches
and a respectable selection of beers. Equally tantalizing is the wine
bar's lengthy food menu, which is appropriately weighted toward
appetizers and sharing plates (like antipasto platters, $11 to $19,
with olives and hummus, or cheese and charcuterie, as well as brus-
chettas and dressed-up chips-and-dips) but also includes hearty and
wholesome cafe sandwiches ($9.50 to $11), classic European salads
($6 to $9), and soups, like the perennial favorite roasted green-
chile soup with pork ($7). The late-night menu is an abbreviated
version of their appetizer list, and happy hour deals include select
$6 glasses of wine and changing daily specials. On Tuesday, select
wine bottles are half off. Diethelm-Floyd is half French, and her

upbringing of summers in France certainly seems to have informed the approach to Boozefish, which is not overly designed or "cosmopolitan" in the manner of some American wine bars. Instead, it's all very down to earth and local feeling—she's nailed the casual-Euro vibe to a tee.

Cupini's, 1809 Westport Rd. (at State Line Road); (816) 753-7662; www.cupinis.com. Mon through Thurs 11 a.m. to 8 p.m., Fri through Sat 11 a.m. to 9 p.m., Sun 11 a.m. to 3 p.m.; $. What began in 2003 as a fresh pasta dough business didn't take long to explode into the all-purpose Italia-palooza that it has become. Now occupying three daisy-chained buildings near the corner of Westport Road and State Line, Cupini's fires on many foodie cylinders. It's an eat-in restaurant, a take-out deli and *tavola calda* (hot snack bar), a dessert case, a specialty grocer's, a coffee bar, and a caterer. All that's missing is *vino* (alas, city codes prohibit the sale of booze within 300 feet of churches, and Cupini's is 270 feet from Immanuel Lutheran). Cupini's is run by Franco and Eddie Cupini, a father and son who were both born in Rome. Franco has a background cooking in high-end hotels for dignitaries and heads of state, and Eddie grew up with the culture of the kitchen. As if you couldn't already guess by the folksy Colosseum mural on the patio, or the heady aromas of roasting garlic and simmering tomatoes wafting out the building, Cupini's does a lot of the kind of old-guard Italian fare that American palates love—red sauce, meatballs, and panini that employ the entire contents of the meat and cheese case. Lately, however, Cupini's has added more real Italian stuff drawn from Franco's Roman heritage, like authentic carbonara and amatriciana pasta, and my perennial seaside-Italian favorite, linguine with clams. Some items, like his secret-recipe artichoke brandy sauce, sold by the pint, reflect his previous life as a five-star hotel chef. Cupini's dine-in or carry-out menu of salads, pizzas (from $4.75 for the 6-inch size; 12- and 18-inch also available), pasta ($5.49 for *piccolo* portion, $7.49 to $9.99 for *grande*), and panini (about $5 for a 5-inch, around $7 for 10 inches) has an enthusiastic following among the lunch crowd (and early dinner—note closing hours). There's a banquet room for private parties, and they also cater. Cupini's freshly made pasta (i.e., you take it home, boil it, and sauce it) is how it all started, and it's still a fabulous resource, unique in K.C., and well-priced at $4.50 per pound for fettuccine, lasagne sheets, and a dozen different kinds of ravioli. Franco and Eddie's pasta is way more authentic and has much better texture than the gummy, yellowish stuff sold in the refrigerator section of the supermarket.

Pot Pie, 904 Westport Rd. (at Madison Avenue); (816) 561-2702; www.kcpotpie.com. Tue through Thurs 11 a.m. to 10 p.m., Fri 11 a.m. to 11 p.m., Sat 5 to 11 p.m.; $–$$. Chicken soup? For amateurs! When you really need your soul and palate warmed, step inside the door at 904 Westport Rd. for one of Kansas City's best-selling cold-weather dishes, Pot Pie's eponymous house specialty, the chicken-vegetable pot pie. Filled with moist chunks of stewed chicken, corn, onions, celery, and carrots in a white wine roux, the pot pie is served in a quart casserole (it could easily feed 2) and lidded with a football-sized sheet of the flakiest, most buttery-perfect pastry crust. To clarify, Pot Pie isn't a gimmick restaurant: It serves pot pie but doesn't, as the name has suggested to some, serve 18 varieties of pot pie to the exclusion of all other food forms. The 13-table (plus bar seating) Pot Pie is a warm and intimate bistro with a small menu of American cafe standards. It evokes your favorite no-nonsense neighborhood joint in New York or San Francisco—there's a simple open kitchen, exposed brick walls and beam ceilings in the dining room, and cartons of potatoes stacked by the rear entrance. Opened in 2003 by the laid-back husband-and-wife team of John and Sarah Williams, Pot Pie is best described as comfort food that gives a damn. It isn't trying to be a gourmet pioneer (the Williamses leave that to their neighbors Colby and Megan Garrelts, another husband and wife who run the epicurean temple **bluestem** literally next door), but it takes great pride and care in the quality of its small menu of American cafe standards. On that menu, which is written daily on a large chalkboard at one end of the room and changes slightly from lunch to dinner, expect to find a few beautifully dressed salads (spinach with fig and bacon dressing, $6), a handful of appetizers (steamed mussels, $6), and on the entree side, about a half-dozen savory main dishes and sandwiches ($8 to $16) that always include at least one seafood item (pan-seared scallops or grilled snapper), one poultry, pork, or beef, a pasta, and of course, that pot pie ($8). While chicken-veg is the clear customer favorite, the beef-mushroom pot pie is also

wonderful. The Williamses didn't set out to specialize in pot pie—the restaurant name started out as sort of a joke, but then stuck—but it is now, of course, what they're most known for. On your first visit, by all means order the pot pie, but then return to branch out into their delicious salads, sandwiches, and entrees. Pot Pie's approachable prices bring it a lot of regulars, but even first-timers will be charmed by the friendly vibe (there are family photos and kids' birthday invitations taped to the bar mirror).

Every pot pie—like everything else here—is made to order, and the Pot Pie kitchen is loving and meticulous in its preparation, so don't come here in a rush. But to watch John Williams assembling a chicken pot pie, an exercise he must do thousands of times per year, with as much patience and care each time as the last, never looking bored or annoyed, makes it worth the wait.

Sung Son, 4116 Pennsylvania Ave.; (816) 931-0670. Mon through Sat 11 a.m. to 10 p.m., Sun noon to 5 p.m.; $$. Sung Son is two kinds of restaurant in one—a Vietnamese bistro (how it bills itself) and a pan-Asian buffet that's several rungs above the competition. That's a smart split personality to have, because it courts both those on the hunt for the particular flavors and fragrances of Vietnam as well as the broader population of wagging-tongued seekers of General Tso's chicken and crab rangoon. With high, exposed concrete walls and dramatic blue-glass drop chandeliers over the tables, Sung Son is far more handsome than any buffet or noodle bar has a right to be. On the buffet line (a steal at lunch during the week, when $9 gets you unlimited refills plus 9 kinds of made-to-order pho from the noodle bar), standouts are the Vietnamese summer rolls (served at room temperature, with crunchy and flavorful veggies and shrimp or pork wrapped in translucent rice paper), spring rolls (crisp and not grease laden, with beautifully seasoned pork filling), and yellow chicken curry. You can also order off the menu, which is where you'll find the more interesting and authentic dishes like Vietnamese crepes and intricately seasoned shrimp and noodle plates. For a more full-on Vietnamese cuisine experience, you might prefer **Saigon 39** (p. 94) or **Vietnam Cafe** (p. 7), but for well-rounded Asian (with the added bonus of pho) in a clean and elegant setting, Sung Son is great.

Thai Place, 4130 Pennsylvania Ave.; (816) 753-8424; www.kcthai place.com. Mon through Thurs 11 a.m. to 10 p.m., Fri through Sat 11 a.m. to 10:30 p.m., Sun 11 a.m. to 9 p.m.; $$. I'll start by saying that K.C. still doesn't have a singularly amazing, knock-your-socks-off Thai restaurant. Nothing so well-executed and faithful that will send you into rapturous nostalgia for past meals taken in Bangkok or Koh Samui. That said, if you're anywhere in midtown and struck with an irresistible craving for that Southeast Asian blend of sweet-hot-sour-salty, Westport's Thai Place won't disappoint. Expect a reassuring selection of appetizers like chicken satay, noodles like pad thai (which is 2-for-1 on Tuesday), rice dishes and stir-frys, salads and soups (like *tom yum gai*—chicken in lemongrass and Kaffir lime broth) and red, green, *massaman*, and panang curries. There's also a robust selection of vegetarian and vegan items. If you're in doubt about the spiciness level, order milder than hotter, as most dishes' default setting is a sinus-clearing assault of chile heat. Though not as pretty as **Sung Son,** its Vietnamese noodle bar/Asian buffet neighbor up the street, Thai Place is attractive and cozy and has a bustle, especially at lunchtime, that makes it feel like an event.

Westport Cafe & Bar, 419 Westport Rd. (at Broadway); (816) 931-4740; www.westportcafeandbar.com. Mon through Fri 11 a.m. to 1:30 a.m., Sat 10:30 a.m. to 1:30 a.m., Sun 10:30 a.m. to midnight; $$. Owner-manager Aaron Confessori admits to kind of idolizing Keith McNally, the NYC restaurateur behind such popular eateries as Pastis, Balthazar, and Minetta Tavern. So when Confessori—a dapper Kansas boy who cut his culinary-world teeth both here in the Midwest and in the Big Apple—had the opportunity to open his own restaurant in Kansas City, he took inspiration from those Manhattan success stories, both in terms of the menu and the feel of the place. Granted, Westport Cafe & Bar, which opened in 2010 in the old Blanc Burgers space, is small and doesn't have the theatrical "wow" tableau of your typical McNally joint. But a canny remodel gave WCB a sexy and inviting 1930s-Paris look, with white subway tiles, black-and-white tile flooring, dark wood wainscoting, bentwood chairs, and a big mirror on which cocktails and a small-plate menu is printed in handsome old-fashioned lettering. WCB's sophisticated yet simple bistro fare includes such French-casual classics as sautéed mussels (try them with bacon and blue cheese, $11), croques monsieur and madame ($9 and $10, respectively), and steak frites (their signature dish, made from center-cut sirloin—a must at $19). You can also wander the Mediterranean a bit with such Italian-inflected plates as ravioli with goat cheese and caramelized onion ($9). Confessori is particularly proud of his bar hamburger ($10, add gruyère and sautéed onion for a buck), but you can also get a lighter bite here, like the arugula, Parmesan, and lemon salad ($6) or elegant cup of curried carrot soup. The menu at WCB is partitioned, as at New York's Pastis, with an emphasis on smaller sharing plates; there are only a handful of entrees (pastas, seafood, and meat) on offer. Nothing on the food menu is over $20, and the wine list, while curt, is fun and covers all bases. Only the Sancerre, at $12, tops the $10 mark, and even it sells like mad. Cocktails (all $8) are a strong suit, too, and you can belly up to the 10-stool bar and imbibe in style—perhaps an old-fashioned or a West of Rio (cachaça, lime, and blackberries). And did I mention the *fruits de mer*? WCB sources the best daily oysters available ($2 per piece) and even serves them late night. How civilized, K.C. Brunch items ($10 to $12, Sat and Sun from 10:30 a.m.) like eggs Benedict and brioche French toast with honey lavender cream come with a Bellini, mimosa, Bloody Mary, or coffee. From 3 to 6 p.m. daily several hors d'oeuvres, including smaller portions of those mussels and ravioli, are only $5, select wines are $5, and select bottle beers are $3. Nice Euro touches, like clear glass bottles for water and bistro-dainty glassware, round out the lovely and intimate ambience of the place. WCB is a place that truly feels like an old-fashioned cafe, where you might come to write or read (there's free Wi-Fi) or otherwise pretend to be artsy and intellectual (grab a copy of *Dwell* from the communal magazine rack), and encourages lingering.

Old-Guard K.C.

Westport Flea Market, 817 Westport Rd. (at Clark); (816) 931-1986; www.westportfleamarket.com. Mon through Thurs and Sun 11 a.m. to 11 p.m., Fri through Sat 11 a.m. to 11:30 p.m.; $. Don't let the dingy blue-and-white awnings or the giant burger-shaped truck stationed out front, or the spit-and-sawdust atmosphere inside fool you: The Westport Flea Market is a pillar of the Kansas City dining scene. One menu item has made this no-frills bar and grill legendary: the Flea Market burger. There's nothing fancy about it—it's not made from hand-massaged Kobe beef, nor is it topped with antelope *foie gras*, or artisanal cheese made by leprechauns. Instead, the Flea Market burger is the most traditional iteration of this American staple in all its greasy, juicy goodness. And while myriad other restaurants in town do burgers more or less like this, the Flea Market has risen to cult status. Maybe it's because the Westport Flea Market actually *is* a flea market, with about 4 indoor booths that actually sell their wares on weekends, and that ambience of '80s bric-a-brac gives eating here some oddball cache. Maybe it's the weird service system, whereby you order food from the cashier but drinks from a waitress, and then pick up your food from a separate counter. When your order is ready, one of the cooks will shout your name (or, more often, belt it out like an Otis Redding ballad), and then you can dress it as you like from the toppings bar. Or maybe it's because the burgers ($7.99 for the 10 ounce; $6.49 for the 5.5-ounce Mini Market) are made with ground chuck from K.C.'s best-loved meat market, **McGonigle's,** and left undoctored to allow that beefy flavor to shine through. The menu, I should note, is more than just burgers, so you can also come here for a wide variety of American standards, from bar-food apps to sandwiches to loaded salads and daily-special entrees (Monday is steak night; on Friday, sample the beer-battered catfish; both, served with generous sides, are $9.99).

The Flea Market enjoys a broad following, from business suits to raucous sports guys to families with preschoolers and infants, and everyone looks and feels right at home. Happy hour is a huge draw, with 44 different beers for only 99 cents from 2 to 5 p.m. Mon through Fri. Though its old-school, rib-sticking American fare may be simple, and the ambience unvarnished, Westport Flea Market is an archetype of Midwestern hospitality.

bluestem, 900 Westport Rd. (at Roanoke); (816) 561-1101; www .bluestemkc.com. Tues through Sat 5:30 to 9:30 p.m., Sun 10:30 a.m. to 2:30 p.m.; $$$$. Combining top-tier and unique ingredients, preparations that require the skill and artistry of highly trained chefs, and an all-around fine yet unfussy dining experience, bluestem is one of few exponents of progressive American cuisine in Kansas City and has single-handedly done a lot for the town's growing reputation as a well-kept foodie secret. Bluestem is the creation of husband-and-wife chefs Colby and Megan Garrelts, a pair of Midwesterners who cooked all over the country—gaining experience at places like Tru in Chicago, Las Vegas celebrity-chef restaurants, and acclaimed smaller kitchens in L.A.—during their early careers before landing back in Colby's hometown of K.C. to open their dream concept restaurant. Bluestem opened in March 2004, and the name comes from the common prairie grass that happens to grow both in Megan's native Illinois and on Garrelts family land in Kansas. Since opening bluestem, Colby has been a three-time nominee for the James Beard Award for Best Chef in the Midwest. The refined, all-lowercase menu reads like an exclusive tour of food-dom: "aerated *foie gras,* brandied apple butter, stout ice cream, pecan;" or "scottish salmon, indian rice, pearl onion, crispy sweetbreads, tarragon fumet." The preparations always reveal Colby's flair for haute culinary technique. That cooking style, often involving foams and gelées, isn't everyone's cup of tea. Plating is uber-artistic, and portions are, well, minimalistic. (In this manly town, where bounty and value are often cited as deciding factors in a restaurant's appeal, bluestem may offend traditionalists.) But the flavors are exquisite, and the atmosphere lovely. With plantation shutters, exposed brick, and accents of blue and red, the dining room is clean and American in feel, yet still a warm and convivial theater for what is bound to be a wonderfully leisurely meal. The dinner menu is a tiered prix fixe—$60 for 3 courses including dessert; $70 for 5 courses; $80 for 7. The biggest bang for your buck at bluestem is the 12-course (!) meal: $100 per person gets you chef's choice of dishes from all over the menu and must be ordered by your entire table. Those dollar figures may not shock out-of-towners, but as Kansas City restaurants go, bluestem is known as a once-a-year treat that any epicure nevertheless owes himself. But while a full-fledged meal in the dining room can be tough on the wallet, the lounge part of the restaurant—an alluring and lived-in space with patinated mirrors all over the walls—has its own, more approachable menu (like the La Quercia meat platter for 2, $15; a fancy mac and cheese, $8; or Prince Edward Island mussels, $14) and happy hour specials from 5 to 7 p.m. Tues through Fri. Bluestem is famous for its Sunday brunch (with reasonable a la carte items like smoked salmon with fennel, red onion, and creme fraiche on a bagel for $8; or the Wagyu corned beef hash with spicy tomato sauce and sunny-side eggs for $11) as well as its holiday teas (see their website for dates and details), during which Megan's tea sandwiches and pastries are served along with a selection of specialty teas. Bluestem isn't necessarily a place you'd go when trying to show off K.C. to your coastal-snob friends—big city chefs have been doing the Garrelts' style of food for a while now, and some diners are over it—but bluestem has nevertheless been a pioneer among K.C. restaurants, and the Garrelts' commitment to quality and style are a shining example of culinary accomplishment and sophistication in a town whose foodie star is most definitely on the rise. See bluestem's recipe for **Chocolate Truffle Cookies** on p. 276.

Specialty Stores, Markets & Producers

The Broadway Cafe & Roastery, 4106 Broadway (at Westport Road); (816) 531-2432; www.broadwaycafeandroastery.com. Daily 7 a.m. to 9 p.m. In 1992, owner-founder Sara Honan, who'd cut her teeth working at coffeehouses in Chicago through college, took a chance on Kansas City's taste for espresso and opened the Broadway Cafe & Roastery. Many a coffee snob is thankful she did, because this is arguably the best cup in the city. To start, the Broadway Cafe has that classic "coffee shop" vibe in spades—the wood-paneled bar area in front gives way to a hipster hodgepodge of diner seating where a Beat poet wouldn't look out of place; there's alt music on the stereo, and lots of boho-hippie types (fortunately the aroma of coffee all but neutralizes the patchouli and *nag champa*), free

Wi-Fi, a bulletin board, and big windows facing the human pageant of Westport weirdos up and down the sidewalk of Broadway. As much as it succeeds as an artsy hangout, what keeps the Broadway Cafe packed with customers is that it sells seriously good coffee. Baristas—thank heaven—subscribe to the purist, Italianate school regarding espresso, not the Americanized, venti-nonfat-cino approach, where overwrought "coffee drinks" usually trump high-quality, expertly prepared coffee. (Read partner Jon Cates's treatise on espresso on Broadway Cafe's website, and you'll know that they take it very seriously here.) Miniscule variations—from how much water is used to extract a shot, to grinding and tamping adjustments, to the all-important process of obtaining a layer of espresso crema—all affect the outcome of an espresso drink, but one taste of the Broadway Cafe's brew, and it's clear you're in masterful hands. In fact, Broadway's coffee has proven so superior to the national coffee chain standard that it drove a Starbucks, which opened next door some years ago, out of business in relatively short order. While most items on the coffee menu are espresso based, Broadway has excellent drip coffee and toddy drinks, too, and you can also buy their whole-bean coffee, lovingly roasted "in-house" at their facility at 40th and Washington, by the pound.

Jerusalem Bakery, 1404 Westport Rd. (at Terrace Street); (816) 931-8575. Mon through Sat 11 a.m. to 9 p.m., Sun 11 a.m. to 7 p.m. For anyone who's ever traveled in any Middle Eastern land (or seen movies about it), the Jerusalem Bakery will strike a familiar chord. Outside, it's one of Kansas City's more aggressively ugly strip-mall shop fronts; inside, it's a sleepy market/cafe that could be in any dusty town of Turkey or Jordan. All but a few lights are turned off (a classic!), and the tense wails of the high-pitched oud can be heard on a tinny stereo. But there are culinary delights to be found in this dingy oasis. Jerusalem Bakery (which is the more rough-and-ready parent of sit-down **Jerusalem Cafe**—and hookah joint—up the street at 431 Westport Rd.; 816-756-2770) is renowned for its buffet ($9 at lunch, $10 at dinner). Though it doesn't try to do too many things (a pitfall of other buffets around town), Jerusalem Bakery offers dishes from around the eastern Mediterranean, like falafel, kofta, dolmades, cold salads like tabbouleh, baba ghanoush and hummus, and exceptional moussaka. You can also order gyros and *shawerma* a la carte, but I recommend sticking to the buffet, and maybe taking some hummus to go. Jerusalem Bakery is also a grocery store stocked with Middle Eastern staples and, as its name suggests, a bakery: A small back wall is devoted to freshly baked pita bread.

Murray's Ice Cream & Cookies, 4120 Pennsylvania Ave, Suite 14; (816) 931-5646. Wed through Thurs noon to 9:30 p.m., Fri through Sat noon to 10 p.m., Sun noon to 8:30 p.m. Cash only. Westport's beloved homemade ice cream shop has a vintage parlor feel, right down to the intoxicating aroma of freshly made waffle cones wafting out to the sidewalk. Murray's flavors, however, have a decidedly more progressive profile than your grandma's chocolate and vanilla. Many of the inventive, addictive concoctions are based

LATE-NIGHT EATS THAT PASS FOODIE MUSTER

In addition to the open-late kitchens of **Boozefish** and **Westport Cafe & Bar** (both reviewed in this chapter), there are two Westport boîtes that are still serving solid fare after 11 p.m. Squaring off from each other at the corner of Westport Road and Pennsylvania Avenue, they are the venerable saloon Harry's Bar & Tables and the sleek but comfy newcomer, Beer Kitchen. With their attention to both good drinks and high-quality food, they have the palate of modern K.C. pegged.

The dark wood interior and serious line-up of liquor at **Harry's Bar & Tables** (501 Westport Rd., 816-561-3950; Mon through Fri 3 p.m. to 3 a.m., Sat through Sun 5 p.m. to 3 a.m.) harks back to a more stylish era. Where other pubs in Westport get bruised and abused every weekend and don't seem to care, Harry's has stayed handsome and kept its dignity. While it may be best known for its alcohol—the virtuoso bartenders can whip up all kinds of throwback New Orleans–style cocktails, and they stock 50 different brands of scotch—Harry's also has great food. The menu features a tasty range of small plates and gourmet pizzas. Furthermore, the patio, a private brick plaza shaded by mature trees and furnished with an antique phone booth, is one of this city's most congenial settings for alfresco eating and drinking. Harry's is a classic K.C. fixture with authentic retro polish that aesthetes appreciate, and it's a fun place to go with friends or a date, or even with your lonesome and something to read (provided it's not a weekend night).

Across the street at **Beer Kitchen** (435 Westport Rd., at Pennsylvania; 816-389-4180; www.beerkitchenkc.com; Mon through

Fri 11 a.m. to 3 a.m., Sat 10 a.m. to 3 a.m., Sun 10 a.m. to 4 p.m. Kitchen open until 1 a.m. Mon through Sat), the emphasis is on . . . you guessed it. Their beer list (whether on tap or by the bottle) is phenomenal. It's broken down into helpful categories like "Hop: Earthy & Dry," or "Smoke: Peat & Pepper" that makes navigating the menu, which is full of craft breweries both domestic and foreign and some obscure styles, a breeze even for non-beer aficionados.

They also make beer cocktails, classic and daytime cocktails (try the BK Mary, $5.50), and 9 wines by the glass. With all of that robust drinking, you might think food would be an afterthought. Not at all. That "kitchen" part of the name is there for a good reason. Everything, from bar snacks to burgers to entrees to the veggie sides, has a foodie flourish. Start with some Kobe meatball sliders, served with hand-pulled mozzarella, pesto, and aioli ($9), or try the rocket mix salad ($9), with goat cheese croquettes, beets, walnuts, shaved fennel, and sherry-orange vinaigrette. The gourmet burgers (like the tur-duck-en burger, $10) are on par with the tricked-out patties of **Blanc Burgers**, which left a void in the upscale burger market in Westport when it moved to the Plaza in 2010, and the classic entrees include such refined and hearty choices as Brown Shugga' Salmon ($15) and an excellent flat-iron ribeye ($18), served with chimichurri, garlic spinach, and buttermilk mashers. BK has only been around a little while (it opened in the old one80 location in 2010), but I hope it sticks around.

on traditional pies and cakes—grasshopper, French silk, carrot cake—or all-American flavors like root beer, but there are also dairy-free, tropical sorbets and such for a lighter treat. (For the most exotic and boutique-y gourmet ice cream in KC, however, go to uber-modern **Glacé**, p. 154.) The flavors on offer rotate throughout the season (Murray's is only open spring through fall) but a mainstay you can almost always count on finding is the legendary Chocolate Flake Fromage—a magical marriage of milk chocolate shavings and cream cheese that must be tasted to be believed. Ice cream cones and cups are what most people come for (and the ice cream is weighed before serving, which is kind of annoying), but Murray's also has a ton of baked goods as well as a kaleidoscopic array of toppings (melted Snickers is a favorite) that can make for heavenly build-your-own sundaes. Note that Murray's ice cream doesn't come cheap (single scoop runs about $3.50), and they accept cash only.

Pryde's of Old Westport, 115 Westport Rd. (at Baltimore); (816) 531-5588; www.prydeskitchen.com. Mon through Sat 10 a.m. to 6 p.m. In all my travels to cities bigger and more cosmopolitan than Kansas City, I have never seen a kitchen store more marvelous than Pryde's. It's the gourmet's mother ship, the epicure's mecca, the home chef's Shangri-La. Pryde's is a treasure trove of both fancy cookware and obscure inexpensive gadgets; it's a scavenger hunt through cramped shelves and dizzying wall displays (Williams-

Sonoma and Sur La Table look spartan by comparison); and it represents all that is wonderful about Midwestern culinary traditions. Simply walking into Pryde's is like taking a bite of warm apple pie: The old wooden floors creak, you're immediately enveloped by the grandma's-house approach to merchandising (i.e., there's stuff everywhere), and greeted by one of the kindly, aproned staff members who will probably offer you a cup of freshly brewed coffee. You'll need the caffeine to peruse the staggering quantity of wares at Pryde's, which takes up 2 floors—glassware, stoneware, and decorative items are downstairs (enter on Westport Road), while upstairs (enter on 40th Street) is the "work" floor with all the cookware and kitchen gadgets. This being the heartland, it's no surprise that there are huge inventories of baking, grilling, and roasting pans of every shape and size (and every imaginable accessory thereto). Big names like Le Creuset, All-Clad, and Emile Henry are all here, but there's also simple and sturdy stuff for a fraction of the price.

Where Pryde's really shines, and what makes it such a field day for cooks, is the specialty gear department. Need a turkey baster or a ravioli cutter? They have 8 kinds of each—only one may be prominently displayed, but dig deeper (or check the pie room—yes, there's a pie room) and you'll find one to suit your kitchen personality and budget. How about a green silicone spatula? Choose

from a canister filled with dozens of them. Pryde's has micro and macro colanders in every color, gnocchi paddles, stainless serveware from the basic to the bizarre, seafood crackers, an entire wall of cookie cutters, luxury dish detergents and hand soaps, and bin after bin of dish towels, tablecloths, pot holders, oilcloth, you name it. In the smaller downstairs section, a full range of Fiestaware is sold (every odd little piece, every color) as well as handsome and functional glassware (much of it from Italy), Lodge cast iron, and elegant tabletop items. For Kansas City brides, registering at Pryde's is practically a marriage sacrament. Pryde's also sells its own line of seasonings, rubs, sauces, and preserves, as well as gourmet condiments from other local and national producers.

I recommend allowing plenty of time to browse Pryde's—and given the hoarder aesthetic of the displays, it isn't so much browsing as burglar-like rifling—and leaving small children at home, as the store's narrow passageways are fraught with breakables. As an independent, family-owned business (open since 1968), Pryde's may not have the most competitive prices in the kitchen goods market, so if you need a new Cuisinart food processor or something else mainstream, you may be better off at Macy's or Amazon. But for the sheer joy that comes with finding an unusual tool for your kitchen arsenal or a unique addition to your countertop or tablescape (and knowing it didn't come from any old mall), Pryde's can't be beat. **The Upper Crust Pie Bakery** (aka heaven) is open on the ground floor of Pryde's on Fri and Sat from 10 a.m. to 6 p.m.

The Plaza & Around

With Spanish architecture, upscale shopping, impressive art museums, fountains galore, broad expanses of green, and a handsome water feature in Brush Creek, the manicured Country Club Plaza area is the showpiece of Kansas City, and for what tourism there is here, it's ground zero. The Plaza is lively, well-groomed, and packed with places to eat and drink. Within the outdoor retail and entertainment district—its unmistakable blocks consist of architecture drawn straight from historic buildings in Seville, Spain—that is the technical extent of the Country Club Plaza itself (from 46th Terrace to Brush Creek and between Jefferson Street and JC Nichols Parkway), the dining options are mostly chains that you can find in many other cities, but there are some noteworthy local, independent food businesses (Blanc Burgers + Bottles, Starker's, Fiorella's Jack Stack BBQ, and the Better Cheddar) amid corporate names like P.F. Chang's and Fogo de Chão. Anyone visiting Kansas City for the first time, or for a few days' business trip, will no doubt find themselves in the Plaza area at least some of the time, and here you'll find our top picks for eating and drinking among the sea of high-profile but often zero-personality restaurants that characterize much of the Plaza dining scene. Some of the best food-lover discoveries in this area, however, lie just a few blocks away from that core district, and those just-outlying food businesses are what we've focused most of our attention on in this chapter. So, be sure to read carefully to find those foodie treasures outside the confines of the Plaza's Sevillian architecture—like the fantastic New American fare at Cafe Sebastienne at the Kemper Museum of Contemporary Art, or the uber-gourmet ice cream at Glacé, or the zero-pretense deliciousness of the wings and BLTs at a century-old bar called the Peanut. Both Glacé and the Peanut lie along a stretch of Main Street, just south of Brush Creek, that has become a burgeoning culinary corridor where just about every address is a purveyor of food and drink of some kind. Enticing, also, are beautiful green spaces like Loose Park (51st & Wornall), the lawn in front of the Nelson-Atkins Museum, and Theis Park; these are some of Kansas City's best spots for a picnic and all within a stone's throw of the Plaza.

Because of their proximity to the Plaza (rather than to the rest of the Kansas/Johnson County listings in the book), a few Kansas-side restaurants and markets that lie almost due west of the Plaza, including beloved gas-station BBQ joint Oklahoma Joe's, appear in this chapter.

Blanc Burgers + Bottles, 4710 Jefferson St.; (816) 931-6200; www.blancburgers.com. Mon through Thurs, Sun 11 a.m. to 10 p.m., Fri through Sat 11 a.m. to 11 p.m. Also in Leawood, KS, at Mission Farms; $$. Pioneer of pimped-out patties, Blanc was opened by a couple of classically trained chefs who saw a need for upscale burgers in Kansas City. Blanc, which moved into this larger, higher-rent location at the Plaza after the original Westport hole-in-the-wall proved too small for its growing popularity, is a modern, subterranean space, done up in white (hence the "blanc") and orange that gives it the look of a Scandinavian disco. But that minimalist decor is just a foil for the baroque trimmings on every burger. Even the "classic" ($9) has gourmet toppings like aged white cheddar and house-made pickles, ketchup, and mustard, and is served on an artisanal sesame brioche bun. Of the 14 burgers on the menu, 6 are all-beef (Californian, corn- and grain-fed, and coarsely ground), while the remainder contain other meats (like the $8 pork "burger"—slow-cooked pork, pickles, mustard, and chipotle coleslaw) and vegetarian options, like the spiced lentil burger (curried lentils, spiced yogurt, cucumber and onion salad, avocado, and radish sprouts on a bun made with **Boulevard** Unfiltered Wheat beer). Their "inside-out burger" (stuffed with blue cheese, topped with smoked bacon, onion ring, lettuce, ketchup and mustard on an onion brioche bun, $10) was voted best burger in Missouri by *Food Network* magazine in 2009. On the supremely decadent side (where I tend to stray), try the "$100 burger": a steal at only $15, it's stuffed with red-wine-braised short ribs, smeared with *foie gras* butter and onion marmalade, and a balsamic glaze, while watercress provides a touch of green crunch beneath the rosemary focaccia bun. Or the "surf + turf" ($21) made with lobster and American Kobe beef, caramelized fennel, tarragon aioli, lobster butter, and asparagus salad. Blanc is as serious about its burgers as it is about its buns (most come from K.C.'s own **Farm to Market Bread Co.**) and its famous hand-cut, artfully seasoned fries, which are served in mini shopping carts. The truffle fries ($5) have become the signature side here, but you can also order delectable sweet potato fries and classic Russet potato fries (both $4). The "+ Bottles" part of the name refers chiefly to beers (although there is also a decent wine list). Sourced from the best domestic and international breweries, 150 lagers, IPAs, ambers, browns, whites, wheats, stouts, porters, Belgians, and more are served in bottles only (most between $4.50 to $8), and staff are happy to pair you up with a particular selection based on your burger order. Nonalcoholic beverages include 1950s soda pops like Nu-Grape, Bubble-Up, and Nesbitt's, Mexican Coca-Cola (made with cane sugar), and artisanal sparkling beverages from K.C.'s own **Soda Vie** (see p. 208). Blanc is now a mini-chain with a busy outpost in Leawood and an offshoot, B2 in Lee's Summit (slightly lower prices and different menu), as well as locations in Omaha and Little Rock.

Bo Lings, 4800 Main St.; (816) 753-1718; www.bolings.com. Sun through Thurs 11 a.m. to 9:30 p.m., Fri and Sat 11 a.m. to 10:30 p.m.; $$. The Plaza outpost of Bo Lings is the original location of what has grown into a beloved KC-only Chinese chain. In this restaurant, set amid the elegant apartment buildings on the south side of Brush Creek (and on the ground floor of the Board of Trade building), the atmosphere is classical Oriental (quite different from the modern urban feel of Bo Lings downtown, p. 3), with an open feel, lots of red and gold in the decor, and Chinoiserie on the walls. It also has the warmest hospitality chain-wide, often provided by the original Bo (Richard Ng) and Ling (Theresa Ng) themselves. In addition to the standard Bo Lings menu (see Bo Lings entry in the Downtown chapter for some of our top picks), you can also come here for dim sum on Sat and Sun from 11 a.m. to 3 p.m. For the uninitiated, dim sum (literally "touch the heart") style dining consists of dumplings, morsels, and snacks, to be ordered by the piece or small portion—the perfect way to assemble a custom lunch of a lot of different tastes and textures.

Cafe Sebastienne, at the Kemper Museum of Contemporary Art, 4420 Warwick Blvd.; (816) 561-7740; www.kemperart.org/cafe/. Tue through Thurs and Sun 11 a.m. to 2:30 p.m., Fri and Sat 11 a.m. to 2:30 p.m. and 5:30 p.m. to 9:30 p.m.; $$–$$$. In an airy, modern, bright setting that is a logical extension of the Kemper Museum's galleries, Executive Chef Jennifer Maloney turns out creative and above all soul-satisfying American fare that is hands-down some of the most brilliant food in Kansas City. And while the cuisine always employs high-end seasonal ingredients, Cafe Sebastienne is never fussy nor avant garde. Jennifer is a joyous, relaxed woman, and her personality shines in her food. There are no abstract platings, no confusing flavor pairings; nothing about this food is overwrought or pretentious. Expect spirited spins and comfort classics that carry Jennifer's loving touch, and that are made with fresh seasonal ingredients and local produce whenever possible. For starters, Cafe Sebastienne's warm spinach salad ($9.50) is the best I've ever had, with roasted mushrooms, parsnips, poached farm egg, and warm pancetta vinaigrette. The best sandwich on the lunch menu is the Cafe Reuben ($14, and with the most amazing house-braised red cabbage) but be sure to try Maloney's seasonal pasta (like *strozzapreti* with rock shrimp, fontina, Swiss chard, and roasted butternut squash-sage cream, $15) and risotto (lobster corn with tomatoes and basil, $15). A pizza du jour is always available, too, like the insanely flavorful one with fig marmalade, caramelized onion, goat cheese, fresh arugula, and balsamic reduction ($13). In the fall, do not miss a chance to try the pan-roasted chicken in cider-Dijon reduction with root vegetables ($23 at dinner, $12 at brunch). Cafe Sebastienne is a fabulous spot for brunch, and favorites on the a la carte menu are the heavenly brioche French toast with smoked bacon and Vermont maple syrup ($6 for half order, or $10 for full order) and the Cafe Benny (poached eggs on crab cakes, roasted potatoes, and lemon-Hollandaise, $15). The "outdoor" dining area is actually a courtyard with a transparent ceiling, and filled with light, greenery, and bold artwork—a wonderful choice for lunch or brunch in spring and summer. Or you can eat inside the main dining room, surrounded by the vivid colors of the room-encompassing cycle of oil paintings. *The History of Art* by Frederick James Brown was commissioned specifically for Cafe Sebastienne when it opened in 1994. Whether you dine in or out, you definitely know you're in an art museum. Luckily for us, Jennifer Maloney's simplified cooking style is one that translates well to home kitchens and avid home chefs, and you can pick up a copy of Cafe Sebastienne's cookbook, filled with gloriously pithy recipes, in the Kemper Museum bookstore. See Cafe Sebastienne's recipe for **Crab Cakes** on p. 273.

Cafe Trio, 4558 Main Street; (816) 756-3227; www.cafetriokc .com. Mon through Fri 11 a.m. to 11 p.m., Sat 5 p.m. to 11 p.m.; $$$. We'll get to the food in a minute, but first, that deck! Just off and uphill from the Plaza proper, Cafe Trio has a fabulous west-facing rear patio that overlooks the J.C. Nichols fountain and the Sevillian silhouettes of the Country Club Plaza. Like a treehouse-cum-sleek-beach-resort-bar, this is the spot in town for an alfresco drink and bar bites. But to focus on the deck alone is to sell Trio way short. It's a full-service, delicious American bistro with a jazzy food menu, strong drinks and heavy pours, and a big, sexy dining room that always makes you feel like you're in a more happening town than KC, while still preserving the warmth and friendliness of the Midwest—as was owners Christopher Youngers' and Tai Nguyen's vision. The red-toned room has an energetic vibe, with lots of space given to local arts (rotating exhibitions displayed on dining rooms walls; live and local music acts five nights a week). The menu here is huge (and it changes from lunch to afternoon to dinner), but one thing you can count on is liberal use of assertive and colorful ingredients. On a first visit, opt for one of Trio's house favorites like the Trio de Mare appetizer (fried calamari, scallops and clams with citrus aioli and spicy-sweet chili dipping sauce, $11), the Tuscan Shrimp cracker crust pizza (with crumbled bacon, Fontina, feta, artichokes and spinach, $11), a rich seafood entree like the scallops praline (encrusted in candied pecans and pan seared in Frangelico cream sauce, $27), or a steak. Trio's steaks, surprisingly enough, consistently earn raves as among the best in town (and they're priced a bit lower than those at stuffier steak-houses), and one that gets particularly glowing reviews is the steak Gorgonzola (16 oz. KC Strip with flamed blue cheese and roasted crimini mushroom and Port sauce, $29). But if there's a single signature dish here, it's the Mac Daddy, a luxurious interpretation of mac n' cheese with bacon, green onion, bell pepper, cherry tomatoes, bel paese, Fontina, and romano cheeses ($16, also available as a bar bite for $6). Trio is also famed for its drinks, and the cheeky cocktail menu (created by the much-lauded bartender Justin) features cocktails named for celebrities from Michelle Obama and Billie Holiday to Ricky Martin and Courtney Love. The wine list is also amusing: selections are grouped into such categories as "Easy Blondes" (fruit-forward and sweet whites like moscato), "Voluptuous Blondes" (mostly chardonnays), and "Crazy Mixed-Up Redheads" (red blends like meritage). Within each section are several options by the glass ($6.25 to $11). Come on Tuesday for the "half-corked" special—all wines under $50 are half price (by the bottle or glass). Trio is one of the most gay-friendly restaurants/bars in the Metro area, and it's equally popular with bachelorette parties, raucous groups of corporate suits, and everyone in between. On weekends, expect it to be busy and loud. On this stretch of Main, parking can be a challenge (as can be safely crossing Main on foot if you've parked a few blocks away), but Trio has inexpensive valet. Tip: At Christmastime, the view over the Plaza lights from Trio's heated patio is as holiday-romantic as it gets.

Go Chicken Go, 5101 Troost; (816) 361-6680; www.gochickengo .com. Mon through Thurs 10 a.m. to 12:30 a.m., Fri through Sat 10 a.m. to 2 p.m., Sun 11 a.m. to 11 p.m.; $. For the best fried gizzards and livers to be had from a drive-thru in Kansas City, look no further than Go Chicken Go. The lines of cars snaking around the UMKC-area location of this mini-chain (it began as a gas station that also served chicken in Kansas City, Kansas) are absurd. Fans can't get enough of this down-and-dirty, unapologetically greasy, cheap, and fast fried poultry. Just be aware going in that the neighborhood, and the whole experience really, feels a little dirty and sketchy, but that's why Go Chicken Go is such a beloved authentic K.C. institution. (That, maybe, and the adorable logo of the chicken on the lam, kicking up dust beneath his feet Road Runner–style.) Note that you can

also eat inside (typical fast food atmosphere), but most patrons prefer to go the drive-thru route, often taking their picnic of gizzards or what-have-you to one of the nearby green spaces like Theis Park or the lawn of the Nelson-Atkins Museum. While Go Chicken Go's especially flavorful secret hot sauce, G Sauce, is compelling enough to warrant a trip here, you can also buy a bottle of the stuff in many area supermarkets. But for those gizzards and livers, you've got to come to the source.

Grand Street Cafe, 4740 Grand Ave. (southeast corner of Brookside Blvd./Main St. and Emanuel Cleaver II Blvd.); (816) 561-8000; www.grandstreetcafe.com. Mon through Thurs 11 a.m. to 10 p.m., Fri through Sat 10 a.m. to 11 p.m., Sun 10:30 a.m. to 9 p.m.; $$$. Talk about not judging a book by its cover! Glancing over from your car window at 40 mph on Brookside Boulevard, Grand Street Cafe looks as anonymous as the copper-toned 1980s office building it's tucked into. But turn into the parking lot, and you'll see the much more inviting and urbane main entrance of the restaurant. Opened in 1991, Grand Street has become one of the most happening destinations for midtown dining—it definitely feels more special and insider than its national-chain brethren at the Country Club Plaza, just to the west. The kitchen, helmed by Chef Ian Hockenberger, has found a winning formula in eclectic and decadent American fare (the grilled salmon entree, $16 at lunch/$20 at dinner, is served with porcini risotto, mushroom ragout, fried leeks, and truffle oil), while a few "immigrant" dishes (a ceviche appetizer, or a Thai shrimp wrap, both $10) give the menu added interest. The dining room is done up in wallpaper of oversized botanicals and glass partitions—if you're nostalgic for 1990s Florida or California, this is your joint—past which the industrious waitstaff is always hustling; rarely in K.C. do you get such a polished and professional team of servers. Lunch gets very busy with the business crowd, when solo regulars grab bar stools for their meal-size salads ($9 to13) and midday Chardonnay. Yes, this is the kind of place where you can have a cocktail for lunch. It's also the kind of place where, while there's no dress code, you should at least wear your good jeans. Happy hour (Mon through Fri 3 to 7 p.m., Sat 11 a.m. to 3 p.m. and 9 p.m. to close, Sun 3 p.m. to close) is a great way to experience this upscale place, with $3 cocktails and glasses of wine and specialty appetizers priced from $4 to $9.

JJ's, 910 West 48th St. (between Belleview and Madison); (816) 561-7136; www.jjs-restaurant.com. Sun 5 to 10 p.m., Mon through Thurs 11 a.m. to 10 p.m., Fri 11 a.m. to 11 p.m., Sat 5 p.m. to 11 p.m.; $$$. On a steep, off-Plaza side street that evokes a bigger and more happening city than Kansas City (i.e., parking is a challenge), JJ's is like Cheers—if Cheers had an 1,800-bottle wine list and served lobster. In fact, JJ's has the distinction of having the best wine list in Kansas City (although some say it's tied with Starker's on the Plaza), and one that's on par with the most sophisticated coastal restaurants. Its museum-like collection of vintage ports

(28 available by the glass) alone is enough to impress the discerning drinker. Despite all the potential for pomp in the cellar and kitchen, JJ's manages to carry itself with the down-to-earth nonchalance of a broken-in yet classy neighborhood bar. The veteran bartenders, the lively noise level, the well-worn tables and stools that have acquired that olfactory patina of good liquor—all of this contributes to the warm atmosphere at JJ's. It also helps that owner Jimmy Frantze and his staff comport themselves with all the pretentiousness of Thomas Haden Church's character in *Sideways*. Never before has a $400 bottle of Joseph Phelps Insignia seemed so approachable! (Fear not, there are also tons of choices in the $20 to $40 range.) In my experience, JJ's works best as a wine bar—nearly 30 wines are poured by the glass ($7 to $18)—and bar-eats kind of place, but it is also very much a restaurant, with a serious menu of steakhouse-, French-, and Italian-inspired entrees ($24 to $42). The Petite Filet ($32), rubbed with porcini mushrooms and served with roasted garlic mashed potatoes, asparagus, and veal demi-glace, is glorious. The dining room is much smaller and cozier than at nearby Plaza establishments (a good thing), with beautiful lighting in the evening and a rustic elegance that perfectly nails the European bistro look. With its location between the restaurant-heavy districts of Westport and the Plaza, JJ's is known as a stomping ground for off-duty chefs and food biz professionals, who can often be found at the bar between or after shifts, sipping hard-to-find wines and

devouring the house burger (8 oz. of ground tenderloin, served on a Farm-to-Market onion bun, $10). If you're new to JJ's, give it a test-drive by ordering drinks and light fare at the bar, like their star appetizer, the bacon-wrapped Paco Shrimp ($14, with a divine white wine-Dijon dipping sauce), the artisanal cheese plate ($12), or the daily-changing pizza. One of the greatest things about JJ's is how versatile the atmosphere is: you can go there on a date, and it'll be romantic; you can go there with a big group, and it'll be fun and buzzy; and you can go there by yourself and contemplate it all solo without feeling like a loser, or, just as easily, you can strike up a conversation with one of the gregarious regulars at the bar. See? Cheers.

Osteria Il Centro, 5101 Main St.; (816) 561-2369; www.osteria-il centro.com. Mon through Thurs 4 p.m. to 10 p.m., Fri through Sat 4 to 11 p.m. Reservations accepted only on Valentine's Day and New Year's Eve; $$. In Italy, the word "osteria" traditionally refers to an informal, local tavern sort of place where the mood is convivial and the wine free flowing. On any given night, K.C.'s Il Centro certainly fits that description. Chalk it up to the location, in a strategic corner of the growing foodie mecca that is Main Street between Brush Creek and 52nd Street; or the space, a cozy and dark single room where you can easily elbow your neighbor but not necessarily hear him over the constant din of so many cramped tables. Either way, Osteria Il Centro always feels festive and lively, an important factor in a town where so many restaurants,

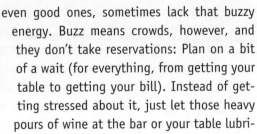

even good ones, sometimes lack that buzzy energy. Buzz means crowds, however, and they don't take reservations: Plan on a bit of a wait (for everything, from getting your table to getting your bill). Instead of getting stressed about it, just let those heavy pours of wine at the bar or your table lubricate the mood. The cuisine, when it arrives, isn't so much typical osteria fare (first of all, no restaurant in Italy would have this many chicken-based dishes) as something-for-everyone comfort food that includes elements of authentic Italian as well as Italian-American cooking. There's bruschetta, fried calamari, and a mixed cheese-and-meat plate on the appetizer menu, but if you can't decide, a generous sampler platter, perfect for sharing, comes with the calamari, bruschetta, a goat cheese and garlic spread with bread wedges, and red pepper hummus with pita. Favorites among the pasta and meat mains are the chicken walnut penne, in a heavenly Gorgonzola cream sauce, and the lamb chops, topped with an herbed brandy sauce and served with garlic-rosemary mashed potatoes. Many diners forgo full entrees and just order thin-crust "pizzettes" (of those, stick with the simpler ones like the Margherita, *quattro formaggio,* or prosciutto—the pesto shrimp doesn't work as well in reality as it does in print). Don't bring your hearing-impaired in-laws here: Il Centro is loud (yet somehow romantic at the same time—the dim lighting is certainly flattering), but the noise level and intimate room create an elevated sense of fun . . . or maybe that's the wine.

The Peanut, 5000 Main St.; (816) 753-9499; www.peanutkc.com. Mon through Thurs 11 a.m. to 1 a.m., Fri through Sat 11 a.m. to 2 a.m., Sun 10 a.m. to midnight; $. Down and dirty bar with legendary wings and BLTs. You gotta honor the classics. And cheap beer to go with 'em.

Rozzelle Court, at the Nelson-Atkins Museum of Art; (816) 751-1ART; www.nelson-atkins.org/welcome/restaurants.cfm. Wed through Sat 11 a.m. to 2 p.m. plus Fri 5 to 8 p.m., Sun noon to 2 p.m.; $–$$. Food lovers and art lovers are frequently the same folks, and they can marry both passions by taking a stroll through the world-class collections of the Nelson-Atkins Museum and following it with a meal in the museum's atmospheric Italianate courtyard cafe. The Rozzelle is not as ambitious as K.C.'s other notable museum dining, Cafe Sebastienne at the Kemper (see above), but the food definitely has its aesthetic principles, doing justice to its one-of-a-kind setting. Although the food is served cafeteria-style, with soup, salad, and sandwich displays set up in the lower arcades of the soaring Renaissance-revival space, the seasonal, high-quality ingredients are always combined creatively to wondrously flavorful effect—this is way more than your typical tourist-attraction concessionaire fare. The soups are excellent, and on a cold winter's day, there's nothing better than wrapping up a gallery wander with a nice bowl of the hot stuff. (If it's available, get the tomato basil.) Iron patio tables are set up in the sunken center of the courtyard, around a loudly gurgling fountain (the upper marble basin of which is from Hadrian's Villa near Rome), lending the feeling of an alfresco cafe—but with lots of echoes and year-round climate control. Fri is the only day the Rozzelle serves dinner, when you can either order a la carte or choose a $25 prix-fixe option. The evening menu features more sophisticated, Euro-tinged selections like an entree of pan-seared sea scallops with caramelized fennel and onion marmalade cream, whipped cauliflower, and French beans amandine. Many museum patrons come expressly for the exquisite desserts (also available from 2 to 5 p.m. on museum opening days, along with drinks and coffee), like the signature key lime pie. The Rozzelle Court kitchen team also prepares the food for Nelson Museum events and special exhibitions, often sourcing the menus from exotic and historical recipes to match a particular artistic theme.

SPIN! Neapolitan Pizza, 4950 Main St.; (816) 561-7746; www .spinpizza.com. Sun through Thurs 11 a.m. to 9 p.m., Fri through Sat 11 a.m. to 10 p.m.; $. Although this location wasn't the first of this hot local pizza chain to open, the South Plaza incarnation of SPIN! is the biggest and busiest and has quickly become the flagship of the franchise. Wildly successful SPIN! has earned hordes of devotees with its fun, modern vibe and pillowy Naples-style pizzas, topped with gourmet goodies like Gorgonzola, prosciutto, roasted eggplant, and onion-fig marmalade. The kaleidoscopic menu, posted next to the cashier where you place your order upon entering, is enough to make your head spin—in additional to all manner of pizza rossa, pizza bianca, flatbread, grilled panini, and deli sandwiches, there are some wonderful soups and salads (like the Sonoma with red leaf lettuce, spinach, grapes, raisins, apples, goat cheese, glazed pecans, and blood orange vinaigrette). The most popular item on the menu is the Pizza Mia combo ($8.25), which includes a 6-inch signature or 2-topping pizza with a side of any salad or a cup of soup. The main dining room is a lofty space with bright colors and exposed ducts (and a full view of the kitchen and enormous oven), with booths, tables, and bar seating, but in good weather customers vie for a spot under the umbrellas on the front patio, facing Main Street. Completing the whole grown-up pizza party atmosphere of the place is a respectable wine list (no White Zin here, folks), which always features a few interesting reds and whites being poured for $6.95 per glass. The clever marketing team has also come up with some cool events at this location, like premeal bike rides to help offset some of those pizza calories, or Ciao Bow Wow (your dog gets a gourmet pizza and dessert) that have enjoyed huge turnouts.

Old-Guard K.C.

Minsky's Pizza, 5105 Main St.; (816) 561-5100; www.minskys .com. Sun through Thurs 11 a.m. to 10 p.m., Fri through Sat 11 a.m. to 11 p.m. Also in downtown K.C. at 427 Main St.; (816) 421-1122; in Prairie Village, KS at 6921 Tomahawk Rd.; (913) 262-6226; see website for additional locations; $. Image-conscious, Neapolitan-style pizza restaurants (like SPIN!, across the street) may be the current rage in Kansas City, but sometimes you want to return to the familiar, classic genre of American pizza parlor. That's where Minsky's comes in. You already know the scene here: booths with shakers of pepper flakes and Parm on the tables, kids in their baseball uniforms, and the unmistakable aroma of rising bread, melting cheese, and roasting garlic permanently ingrained in the dark wooden walls. But Minsky's does better than just providing that comfortable old-school ambience: They prove that American-style pizza can still be a solid gourmet experience. Each pie is clearly assembled with care—toppings are always evenly distributed and there's always a generous load of perfectly melted (real) cheese and fresh meats and vegetables. Never do you look at your pie and think "ugh, how long were those olives sitting in the refrigerator?" Minsky's has several different dough choices, all of which are hand-rolled and tossed in plain view. Less hearty appetites can order the mini size (about 8 inches in diameter, from $6) or, on Mon through Fri, single slices of select varieties of pizza. A broad selection of apps, salads, and sandwiches also available. (Minsky's is a K.C. franchise with about a dozen locations throughout the K.C. area, but Main Street is where it all started back in 1976, and it's still the best.)

Oklahoma Joe's Barbecue, 3002 W. 47th Ave. (at Mission Road); Kansas City, KS; (913) 722-3366; www.oklahomajoesbbq.com. Mon through Thurs 11 a.m. to 8:30 p.m., Fri through Sat 11 a.m. to 9:30 p.m. Also in Olathe, KS, at 11950 Strang Line Rd.; (913) 782-6858; $. On a rainy Monday morning in March, it's 10:55 a.m. and there

is already a line out the door at Oklahoma Joe's. No other food purveyor in Kansas City has a following like this. OK Joe's has gotten a lot of mileage out of the fact that it's located in a gas station—which foodies who make a show of "slumming it" love. Anthony Bourdain named it among his "13 Places to Eat Before You Die," describing the food as not only "criminally good" but "the best barbecue in the world." But this energetic BBQ joint doesn't coast on its gimmicky digs and laudatory press. It is among K.C.'s most beloved for its dizzying menu of sandwiches, always-packed atmosphere, and above all, for the juicy, intense flavor of its meats. Chances are you will wait in line for the best part of a half hour to sink your teeth into one of Oklahoma Joe's signature sandwiches ($4.99 to $7.29); in a town where waiting for a table is practically unheard of, this may sound off-putting, but at least you're guaranteed a lively outing. Pulled pork is the best basic BBQ sandwich, but the Z-Man, a specialty sammie with brisket, smoked provolone, and onion rings the size of Saturn's on a Kaiser bun, is Oklahoma Joe's best seller. Of course, any self-respecting BBQ place must also serve heaping platters of plain old smoked meat, and OK Joe's certainly does a lot of volume in slabs of ribs, smoked chicken, meat by the pound (brisket, pulled pork, sausage, ham, and turkey), and combo BBQ dinner platters. The house sauce brand is Cowtown, whose spicy Night of the Living Bar-B-Q has won accolades in the most discerning sauce circles. Tip: Skip the crowds by phoning in your order; you'll be able to pick it up almost immediately, but phone orders are take-out only and may not be eaten in the dining room.

Occasions

Starker's, 201 West 47th St. (at Wornall); (816) 753-3565; www.starkersrestaurant.com. Tue through Sat 5:30 p.m. to 10 p.m.; $$$. For a special meal at a chef-owned, independent restaurant on the Plaza proper, there's only one place to go: Starker's. One of the most talented and passionate guys in the KC food world, Chef-Owner John McClure arrived at Starker's in 2005. Finding it a restaurant that had become stale, he immediately gave Starker's a jolt by revamping the entire menu on day one, trading tired steakhouse fare for farm-to-table, progressive American food and reenergized interpretations of Midwestern mainstays. McClure grew up on a farm and cattle ranch  in central Kansas, so he pays close attention to quality ingredients, knows where they come from, and most of all, believes wholeheartedly in taking good care of them. The Starker's dinner menu is divided into two halves: on the left side are the "classics"—more traditional dishes that are a part of Starker's history (the original restaurant, called Starker's Reserve, was a 400-seat bar, lounge, and restaurant that opened in 1972). Among these is the Bookbinder soup, a house classic with steamed fish in a rich sherry broth ($8) and the most outstanding fried chicken ($22) in town, made with Campo Lindo Farms chicken and served with mashed potatoes and green beans that are fresher and more exciting than they sound, and a sauce loosely called "gravy" on the menu that's one of McClure's secret weapons. Fresh local veggie sides available a la carte

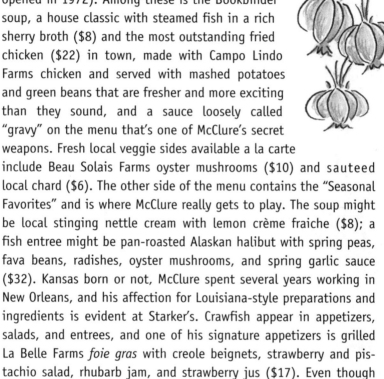

include Beau Solais Farms oyster mushrooms ($10) and sauteed local chard ($6). The other side of the menu contains the "Seasonal Favorites" and is where McClure really gets to play. The soup might be local stinging nettle cream with lemon crème fraiche ($8); a fish entree might be pan-roasted Alaskan halibut with spring peas, fava beans, radishes, oyster mushrooms, and spring garlic sauce ($32). Kansas born or not, McClure spent several years working in New Orleans, and his affection for Louisiana-style preparations and ingredients is evident at Starker's. Crawfish appear in appetizers, salads, and entrees, and one of his signature appetizers is grilled La Belle Farms *foie gras* with creole beignets, strawberry and pistachio salad, rhubarb jam, and strawberry jus ($17). Even though Starker's is definitely a bit pricier than average, it's less expensive than you might think for food of this caliber, especially at lunch. If you do go at lunch, it would be criminal not to order the burger ($9), a masterpiece that McClure is particularly proud of. The patty (strip, rib-eye, and filet all ground in-house) is stuffed with brown sugar bacon and Shatto cheddar cheese curds, then topped with housemade pickles, lettuce, onion; all of this contained in a Farm-to-Market egg bun and served with fries. The dining room, set one floor up from street level, isn't all that large, but it's light and airy with lots of blond wood and stucco-and-beam ceilings that evoke a French country living room—an effect that's compounded by the huge Oriental rug that runs underneath much of the space, and by the accents of blue and yellow in the china on the tables. The service here, too, is outstanding, striking a perfect balance of warmth and professionalism. Starker's is well known among oenophiles for having an impressive and remarkably current wine list (on par with the other major-wine-list restaurant in town, JJ's). The cellar boasts over 10,000 bottles, all of which are priced to sell, not sit and collect dust. Wine is front and center in the dining room, too: a rack of bottles occupies an entire wall. Starker's also does a lot of banquets and corporate events, with three spacious rooms for private dining. Tip: Many tables at Starker's have good views over the Plaza, but the prime table in the house is no. 9, a romantic two-top set next to a large window and looking northeast toward the splendid J.C. Nichols fountain.

Specialty Stores, Markets & Producers

Andre's Confiserie Suisse, 5018 Main St.; (816) 561-6484; www.andreschocolates.com. Tues through Fri 8:30 a.m. to 5:30 p.m., Sat 8 a.m. to 5 p.m.; also Mon during holiday season only, Thanksgiving through New Year's Day, 11 a.m. to 2:30 p.m. When I walk into Andre's storefront at 50th and Main, the heavenly aroma of molten chocolate, cream, and roasting nuts fills the air, and I am 9 years old again, reading *Charlie and the Chocolate Factory* and imagining what that chocolate paradise must have smelled like. (It probably smelled like Andre's.) The rich Swiss chocolate confections at Andre's honor old-world traditions that have been passed down through three generations of one close-knit family. The shop's namesake, master chocolatier Andre Bollier, immigrated to the US from Switzerland in 1955 and in that same year opened up his confiserie in Kansas City. Now run by his grandson Rene, Andre's still adheres to time-honored European methods and techniques; there's nothing trendy or contemporary about these treats. No bizarre flavor pairings like bacon, no weird ornamental dyes (patriarch Andre considered the color blue absurd when applied to chocolate, says Rene). Instead, in its large and ever-expanding combination production facility, retail store, and tea room on Main Street, Andre's makes truffles, barks, bars, and other candies of the utmost quality and decadence. One of Andre's most famous products (and to which I confess I have a troubling addiction) is its chocolate-covered almonds (from $5 for a 3-oz. bag) whose shape and texture evoke tumbled river rock—of thick bittersweet or milk chocolate, that is, and dusted with cocoa powder or confectioners' sugar. Another signature item is the Chocolate Orange Peel ($19.75 for 24 to 30 pieces), made with hand-picked oranges that are blanched and delicately candied before being dipped in bittersweet chocolate. Andre's is also well known for its exquisitely crafted holiday-themed chocolates, whether intricate chocolate Santas, pinecones, and wreaths at Christmas, or imaginative egg- and bunny-shaped chocolates at Easter. But as any veteran of the Kansas City lunch scene knows, Andre's isn't just chocolates and sweets: there's an adorable tea room in the back that looks for all the world like a Swiss Alps ski lodge. You can get a meal of hearty, authentic Swiss fare like *Croute Appenzell* (toasted French bread topped pears, melted cheese, bacon, and walnuts) or knackwurst and gruyère salad. The entrees on offer change daily and are posted in advance on their website (though quiche lorraine and cheese pie are available every day); lunch prices are fixed at a very reasonable $13.58, which includes entree, two sides, beverage, and dessert.

The Better Cheddar, 604 W. 48th St., between Pennsylvania and Jefferson; (816) 561-8204; www.thebettercheddar.com. Mon through Sat 9 a.m. to 9 p.m., Sun 10 a.m. to 6 p.m. Also in Prairie Village, KS, at the Prairie Village Shopping Center, #5 On the Mall

(71st and Mission Rd.); (913) 362-7575. Mon through Fri 9:30 a.m. to 9 p.m., Sat 9:30 a.m. to 6 p.m., Sun 11 a.m. to 5 p.m. The next time you're out shopping at the Plaza and feeling the need for a little foodie fix, don't go to Williams-Sonoma; come here! Kansas City's original gourmet shop is a real find amid the corporate retail landscape of the Country Club Plaza. As the name implies, cheese takes center stage, so whether you need mimolette, manchego, taleggio, or triple-cream brie, this is the best-stocked fromagerie in the area, and—here comes the really good part—there are little cubes of practically every cheese they sell out for tasting! (Try the delicious gjetost, a Norwegian goat cheese in which the milk sugars are caramelized during the production process, imparting an unusual caramel color and flavor.) The cheese cases wrap around the central checkout counter, behind which an outgoing and knowledgable staff can offer serving suggestions and tips about wine pairings (a corner of the store is devoted to wine). Endless varieties of mustards (Dr. Pete's Praline Mustard Glaze is a hot seller), tapenades, BBQ sauce, pickled vegetables, along with fine oils, vinegars, and olives, are packed into the shelves of the store, and you can also find all kinds of imported pasta, locally made compotes and spice rubs, and bulk bins of European chocolates. Browsing the Better Cheddar will make you want to host a dinner party ASAP—or at least the next meeting of your book club.

Glacé Artisan Ice Cream, 4960 Main St., between 49th and 50th Streets; (816) 561-1117; www.glaceicecream.com. Mon through Thurs 11:30 a.m. to 10 p.m., Fri through Sun 11:30 a.m. to 11 p.m. The cryo-genesis of high-end K.C. chocolatier **Christopher Elbow,** Glacé is ice cream with a bowtie and a PhD, not so much a welcoming shop as an icy lab—the interior is all chilly blues, whites, glass, steel and concrete—where the custard-style ice cream is given sterile surroundings. The flavors are outré (Thai Peanut Curry, anyone?) but scrumptiously smooth combinations like Goat Cheese with Honey, and the astonishingly good Farmer Bob's Sweet Corn, and are equally divided among fruity (sorbets include Pineapple Cilantro) and creamy (Blueberry Cream Cheese). For conservative palates, there are also a few fancy versions of classics, like Venezuelan Dark Chocolate. The best-selling confection in Elbow's chocolate business, fleur de sel caramel, makes an appearance here in frozen form. Forget cones—they'd interfere with Elbow's careful chemistry—but you can get small ($4) or large ($5.50) cups, with up to 2 flavors in the small and 3 in the large. There are a few tables and chairs inside and on the sidewalk facing Main. To-go pints of any flavor are $8, and select varieties of Glacé ice cream are sold at **Dean & Deluca** in Leawood (see p. 250).

Price Chopper of Roeland Park, 4950 Roe Blvd., Roeland Park, KS; (913) 236-6262. Mon through Fri 9 a.m. to 7 p.m., Sat 9 a.m. to 5 p.m. Elsewhere in the Kansas City metro area, Price Chopper is just your neighborhood grocery store, but in Roeland Park, epicenter of a thriving Latino community, Price Chopper is your connection for all things *cocina latina*. It's a gleaming, modern store, that just happens to be stocked with tons of bulk beans, dried chilis, and tropical fruits and vegetables that are hard to find in other places. An in-house tortilleria occupies the center of the rear of the store, churning out fresh flour and corn tortillas daily, and bakery cases are filled with Mexican cookies and cakes. In the meat section, you'll have no trouble finding beautiful cow stomachs for making menudo. Entire aisles are devoted to imported canned goods (again, who knew there were so many kinds of beans and peppers?), grains, sweets, sodas, and juices from Central America. In addition to all that, it's also a regular Price Chopper with all the expected super-market merchandise.

Stroud's, 4200 Shawnee Mission Pkwy., Fairway, KS; (913) 262-8500; www.stroudsrestaurant.com. Mon through Thurs 4 to 10 p.m., Fri through Sat 11 a.m. to 10:30 p.m., Sun 11 a.m. to 9:30 p.m. The iconic maison of fried chicken is perhaps not K.C.'s best anymore, but still a venerable institution and city tradition. No Kansas Citian can go through life without attending at least one birthday party here. Expect ginormous portions, old-fashioned family atmosphere, and cardiological guilt.

Werner's Specialty Foods, 5736 Johnson Dr., Mission, KS; (913) 362-5955; www.wernerswurst.com. Mon 9 a.m. to 2 p.m., Tues through Fri 9 a.m. to 6 p.m., Sat 9 a.m. to 5 p.m. Old World atmosphere awaits at this traditional sausage maker and deli in the heart of what used to be a predominantly German community. Werner's sell its own house-smoked bacon, pork chops, and turkey from its meat case, and on request, can get you fully smoked holiday hams or raw butcher-shop selections like steaks and roasts from the choicest cuts of meat available. They're also a deli with unique specialty sandwiches like the signature schnitzel (breaded and fried pork), German lunch meats like *schinken-wurst* and Alpine sausage, hard-to-find European cheeses like Tilsit, in addition to more mainstream sandwich components (roast beef, pastrami, egg salad, Havarti, white cheddar, etc.). Werner's also has a few grocery aisles with German and Scandinavian gourmet items.

Brookside & Waldo

Leafy, village-y Brookside, a district of greenways, parks, tree-lined streets, and handsome old homes south of the Plaza, is one of the most desirable residential areas in Kansas City proper. With a picturesque cluster of Tudor-style cottages forming its central business district, and a well-used bike and walking path, the Trolley Trail, serving as one of its main transit corridors, well-groomed and lively Brookside is a Rockwellian vignette of the most appealing all-American attributes of Kansas City—yet it's also one of few areas in Kansas City where you can hear foreign languages spoken at the sidewalk cafes. A strong sense of community pervades Brookside, thanks in large part to the neighborhood's dense concentration of restaurants, bars, and specialty food businesses. Brooksiders are some of the most open-minded and cultured Kansas Citians, a trait that manifests itself in hearty support of international cuisine, chef-driven menus (*The Next Iron Chef* season 3 and *Top Chef Masters* season 3 contestant Celina Tio's restaurant, Julian, is here), and top-notch ingredients. The result is a food scene that's several steps ahead of most of Kansas City. Residents don't mind paying a premium for that sophistication in their restaurants, but dining here doesn't have to break the bank.

Somewhere between Gregory Boulevard and 75th Street (the borders are blurry), Brookside becomes Waldo, which may be slightly less picturesque with its unsightly strip malls and obtrusive billboards straddling Wornall Road, but it's also a close-knit residential area and no less lively when it comes to eating and drinking. Waldo is perhaps best known for its Midwestern-stereotype bars with cheap beer and lots of TVs tuned into the Jayhawks' or Chiefs' latest endeavors, but Waldo does have its share of cherished, bona fide foodie shop fronts, too, like Kansas City's favorite meat market, **McGonigle's,** and 65-year-old **McLain's Bakery.** (As those two business names might suggest, this part of Kansas City is historically very Irish Catholic, which perhaps explains the myriad drinking options here—just sayin'.)

Brookside and Waldo are both fun-loving, unsnobby 'hoods, and no-frills bar-and-grills, pizza parlors, Tex-Mex places, and burger joints are as much a part of the local experience as artisanal cheese plates and truffles. A particular point of pride in Brookside and Waldo is that almost all of the restaurants here are independent, locally owned businesses, where your waiter probably lives down the street. If downtown and Westport are the domain of the 20-somethings, Brookside and Waldo are where young families and 30-somethings live and play. Funky, artsy, independent businesses are well-supported here, and the vibe is inclusive and unpretentious at even the more sophisticated restaurants.

As a rule, the dining is finer and more varied (and a bit pricier) in Brookside, but if you are a fan of the bar scene, the stretch of Wornall from Gregory (71st Street) to 85th is the heart of Waldo, and there is no shortage of inexpensive places where you can always find a burger, spinach dip, or chicken fingers to go along with those domestic drafts and well drinks. And everything, up till about 8 p.m. anyway, is family friendly.

Foodie Faves

Aixois, 251 E. 55th St., at Brookside Blvd.; (816) 333-3305; www .aixois.com. Mon through Sat 11:30 a.m. to 2 p.m. and 5:30 to 10 p.m. Coffee bar Mon through Fri 7 a.m. to 10 p.m., Sat 7:30 a.m. to 10 p.m., Sun 8 a.m. to 4 p.m.; $$-$$$. In early 2008, I was a recent transplant from New York City and in withdrawal from all its wonderful, stylish restaurants. Allured by Aixois's oh-so-pretty garden setting along this particularly verdant stretch of Brookside Boulevard, I longed to go for a meal here. It seemed so sophisti-cated and European, with its long covered terrace overlooking mani-cured shrubs and lawn. And really, is there anything better than a croque monsieur on a damp and chilly March day? But because my chief eating companion (my husband) never forgave Aixois for taking over the space (in 2001!) that used to be his favorite book-store, he refused to give this French interloper his business. So, it took me a while—way too long—before I ate at Aixois. Thankfully,

I found other people to enjoy Aixois with me, and in the process, I discovered one of K.C.'s loveliest low-key dining experiences. Eating at Aixois is an elegant yet unfussy experience all around, and owners Emmanuel Langlade (the chef and a native of Aix-en-Provence, hence the name of the place) and his American wife Megan Langlade have done a fantastic job of demystifying French bistro cuisine for the Midwest crowd (for whatever reason, Francophobia has been a problem for some K.C. restaurateurs) without dumbing down the recipes and flavors of Provence; that is, there are frog legs and escargots on the menu at all times. For lunch, that croque monsieur is devilishly delicious in its simplicity, and even the house salad is a chef d'oeuvre with perfect balance and amazing depth of flavor—a credit to traditional French technique as well as the utmost in quality ingredients used by Langlade. It's also tempting to order one of the specialty salads (I love the *salade de chevre chaud,* $9, with warm goat cheese on toast served with arugula, strawberries, and walnuts), the savory crepes ($8 to $8.50), or the quiche du jour ($7). At dinner, the refined

entrees include *Saint-Jacques grillées* ($24, grilled jumbo sea scallops sautéed with leeks in coconut vanilla sauce) and *magret de canard* ($19, grilled duck breast with shiitakes and black truffle sauce). It would be criminal, however, to skip an hors d'oeuvre of mussels ($9.50 to $11; choose from *marinière,* Provençal, or Roquefort sauces) or a dessert of profiteroles au chocolat ($6). Aixois feels more expensive than it is, especially at lunch and when you're on the patio, which abuts leafy Brookside Boulevard and the handsome shops of Crestwood. Furthermore, Monday "family nights" are a bargain, when a limited selection of simpler dishes is offered for $10.50 to $14.50. The attached coffee bar serves espresso drinks, drip coffee, and pastries, and is open on Sun, when the restaurant is not. Pick Aixois the next time you're feeling a little fancy, pair a meal with shopping at the boutiques of Crestwood, and pretend this is your everyday life: "Oh, you know, I always have quiche at Aixois after picking up cashmere sweaters, Tuscan antiques, and $8 greeting cards." And one of these days, I'll trick my husband into joining me at Aixois, and when he tries those mussels in Roquefort sauce, he'll bury that bookstore hatchet.

Avenues Bistro, 338 W. 63rd St., at Wornall Rd.; (816) 333-5700; www.avenuesbistro.com. Mon through Thurs 11 a.m. to 9 p.m., Fri through Sat 11 a.m. to 10 p.m., Sun 9 a.m. to 8 p.m. Also in Leawood at 10681 Mission Rd.; (913) 381-5678; $$–$$$. Want to impress out-of-towners with a show of how lively and sophisticated Kansas City can be? Take them to Avenues. With its dark and cozy room (one wall is almost boudoir-ish, done up in a bold harlequin pattern), where the noise level is just loud enough to make for an electric dining experience yet not drown out your tablemates, this culinary romp through European and American tastes is Brookside's most happening, most delicious restaurant. It seems an impossibility of mathematics that a place this size (26 seats) can offer such a lengthy and diverse menu (over 20 tapas choices, 20 entrees, plus soups, salads, and sandwiches—each more imaginative and tempting than the next) and execute each dish perfectly each and every time. Executive Chef Mario Galan, whose great gift is combining decadent ingredients with fresh seasonal produce while keeping it all light and letting individual flavors shine, is clearly kicking some serious butt back in the kitchen. It's fun to craft a meal from the tapas menu alone, which runs the gamut from surprisingly awesome ceviche ($10) to bacon-wrapped dates ($8) to seasonal offerings like glazed butternut squash with Serrano ham and manchego cheese ($10). Among the entrees, which include meat, fish, and pasta dishes and pan-European preparations, the lobster ravioli ($20) and the lobster and crab cakes ($17) are out of this world, and the steak frites ($22) is the restaurant's top seller. Avenues excels particularly at seafood mains ($18 to $21); pan-seared or grilled tilapia, sole, sea bass, halibut, and salmon are all served with wonderfully complementary sauces and fresh vegetable accoutrements. Service is spot-on—the unobtrusive yet friendly waitstaff possesses knowledge and perfect timing. A truly stellar list of wine, cocktails, and scotch and helpful sommeliers complete the very special experience of dining here. (The fact that they have my favorite white wine, the hard-to-find-outside-Italy Falanghina, by the glass, is an indication of the depth and uniqueness of their wine offerings.) Happy hour at Avenues runs every day from 4 to 6 p.m., but I prefer the reverse happy hour (Fri through Sat 8:30 to 10 p.m.); during either one, tapas are $5 with a drink purchase; and house martinis or house sangria are $5 each.

Blue Grotto, 6324 Brookside Plaza; (816) 361-3473; www.blue grottobrookside.com. Mon through Wed 3 p.m. to 1:30 a.m.; Thurs through Fri 11 a.m. to 1:30 a.m.; Sat 10 a.m. to 1:30 a.m.; Sun 10 a.m. to midnight; $$. When K.C. food biz veteran John Grier realized his lifelong dream of opening his own place, a Neapolitan-style pizzeria, nothing about the endeavor was half-hearted. The pizza oven was shipped, in multiple pieces, from Italy. Import accounts were set up to bring from Italy ultrafine Caputo flour for the pizza dough and San Marzano tomatoes, hand-picked from the slopes of Mount Vesuvius itself and canned within three hours, for the sauce. And not just any space would do: It had to be in Brookside, and it had to be cool, bringing to K.C. the aesthetics of eateries John had visited in more style-conscious coastal cities. Style infuses the menu, too; the core is artisanal pizzas but it has been expanded to let the chef's imagination run free, with the best local ingredients available, in the form of eclectic tapas. The pizza selection changes a bit throughout the year to reflect seasonal produce, but there are some always-available fixtures like the Margherita (the classic tomato, basil, and mozzarella, $11) and the quattro formaggio (ricotta, Gorgonzola, Grana Padano, and taleggio, $13). As enamored as he is with the simplicity of real Italian pizza, Grier and his chef can't resist a little gourmet flourish when it comes to their toppings. Beyond the traditional pizzas, you can also order such food-snob pies as the prosciutto (with wine-poached figs and goat cheese, $13), the funghi (with crimini mushrooms, roasted tomatoes, shallot confit, thyme, and Asiago, $13), and other fancy creations a traditional Neapolitan *pizzaiolo* would find extremely controversial. I find them delicious. Neapolitan crust, which should be light, moderately thin, and pillowy, yet stiff enough not to collapse under sauce, cheese, and toppings, is difficult to pull off, but Blue Grotto's pizza chefs do a very good job—the crust here is the most faithful rendition I've found in K.C. And in the true Neapolitan fashion, the pies are baked very quickly at a very high temperature (900 degrees F). (To learn all these techniques, Blue Grotto's *pizzaioli* spent 10 days training under the Italian-trained pizza guru who helped Grier assemble the oven.) As for the rest of the food menu, the chef does top-notch antipasti as well as riffs on Mediterranean fare: The tomato and goat cheese bisque ($6) is a thing of wonder, and the Moroccan lamb sliders ($12) are exceptional. Selections on the antipasti menu include house-cured meats (pork belly and duck prosciutto), olives, imported and domestic charcuterie (prosciutto Americano from Iowa's La Quercia; wild boar and *Genova salame* from Italy), and cheese plates featuring cheeses from Europe and Missouri's own **Green Dirt Farm.** Grier and his team have also worked hard to keep the wine list both interesting and within reach for regulars, with glasses priced from $6 to $9 and bottles from $24 to $30. All this decadence in a setting that very much achieves what Grier set out to accomplish: The minimalist, sexy architecture and fixtures throughout Blue Grotto speak the same language as hip restaurants in New York and San Francisco. (Who would have thought this used to be a sock store?) The long, sleek bar area is a fine place to meet a first date for wine and apps (lights are low and flattering); in the back, dark and roomy booths accommodate larger parties, while the upstairs tables (overlooking the bar and pizza oven) are less dramatic. The bar is definitely where it's at, so I'd recommend just eating your meal there if you don't mind the noise. Or go out to the rear deck—with built-in wooden booths, canvas cushions and pillows, and fire pits, it's like something out of a chic beach resort and one of the most congenial outdoor spaces of any bar or restaurant town. If it's above 45 degrees out and dry, the back deck is in full swing, and if you still feel the chill, Blue Grotto provides blankets.

Chai Shai, 651 E. 59th St., between Kenwood and Holmes; (816) 260-5203; www.chaishaikc.com. Tues through Sun 11 a.m. to 9 p.m.; $. Finally, an Indian joint that really reflects how most on-the-go Indians actually eat. (Hint: They're not sitting down to gut-bomb three-course meals of chicken tikka, biryani, and naan while on lunch break.) In Pakistani and Indian culture, the name "chai shai" roughly translates to "tea time"—impyling not only the service of tea but the snacks and socializing that go along with it. Nestled on a corner in this mostly residential pocket of Brookside near UMKC, Chai Shai is a hip and modern Indian cafe with a tight menu that has quickly become famous for its samosas (beef, chicken, or veggie, $4 for 2) and *chaats* (street food plates) and other "fast food" dishes. The cool, urban vibe—hey, there's free Wi-Fi!—is a world away from all the dated palace-style Indian restaurants around. Fully half the menu is vegetarian, but what meat products they do serve are halal. At lunch, try the pakora wrap ($6.50, with the spiced veggie and chickpea fritters in a flatbread roti, with a side of spicy mango). If it's available, the house-specialty omelet, packed with veggies and Indian spices, is a must try. After 5 p.m., they also serve a handful of entrees, like achari chicken korma ($9.50) and lentil dinner ($8.50). Chai Shai has a unique beverage list, with a variety of authentic south Asian teas (like hot masala chai, $3) and fruit drinks, like Pakistani-imported Rooh Afza, $3.50, a summery concentration of fruit syrups and rosewater, served with milk.

The Gaf, 7122 Wornall Rd.; (816) 333-1321; www.thegafkc.com. Mon through Sat 11 a.m. to 1:30 a.m., Sun 11 a.m. to 11 p.m. Kitchen closes at 10 p.m.; $–$$. Bars that serve food are a dime a dozen in this town, and especially in Waldo and Brookside, but the Gaf's ample, old-fashioned bar and its soul-warming pub fare have earned it a faithful following among the beer-sipping regulars of the neighborhood and comfort-seeking foodies alike. For what it is, the Gaf is a pretty classy place. It's like your own authentic Irish tavern, right here on Wornall and Gregory, and it's so warm and welcoming that it almost seems like there should be a few B&B guest rooms upstairs somewhere. (Alas, there aren't.) Dark, well-oiled wood gives the bar and dining room a venerable, homey feel (and without all the tacky neon and beer promo material that makes so many other bars around here look so cheap), and the hosts and servers are engaging and genuine every time. Plenty of people frequent the Gaf for the alcohol only before discovering just how good the food is (and that there's an entire separate room for dining in the back). About a quarter of the menu is Irish- and the British Isles–inspired, while the balance is American cafe fare. Do be aware that you will have to let out your belt a few notches after a meal here: Cheese, potatoes, cream, bacon, and puff pastry play a starring role in most dishes (and really, would you have it any other way in a dark and cozy pub?). For that reason, the Gaf tends to work best in blustery fall or bone-chilling winter weather and is a bit less recommended in bathing suit season. (In summer, however, the sidewalk tables make for a great hangout.) No matter the season, I can't set foot here without having the Gaf's famous and seriously habit-forming Curry & Chips ($4.99), steak fries served with about a pint of warm, creamy, piquant Irish-style curry dip (my husband has been known to stop and pick this up on the way home from work as an appetizer for our family, and between two gluttonous adults and a toddler who loves dip, it's tough to finish). The Gaf is also strong on hearty sandwiches ($7.99 to $10.99) like the classic Reuben ($8.99, with housemade kraut and gruyère), tuna melt ($6.99, with Irish cheddar), or French dip ($10.99, with provolone and fontina, caramelized onions, and horseradish aioli), as well as assorted burgers, wraps, and panini. The food-dare item par excellence (and reminder that we are in the big-eatin' Midwest) is the Irish Gut Bomb sandwich ($9.99), a huge breaded pork tenderloin topped with onion rings, bacon, cheddar, red onion (yes, in addition to the onion rings), 2 fried eggs, and BBQ sauce. All sandwiches and entrees come with a generous side—I prefer the beautifully seasoned, crispy-on-the-outside, smooth-on-the-inside sweet potato fries. As for the beverage-oriented side of the Gaf, a broad range of beers, spirits, and mixed drinks are served, as well as a limited selection of wines, from a handsome wraparound bar (with requisite TVs tuned to sporting events). As the line between the dining and drinking areas gets blurred later in the evening, the atmosphere is always lively.

Julian, 6227 Brookside Plaza; (816) 214-8454; www.juliankc.com. Mon through Tues 5:30 to 10 p.m.; Wed through Sat 11:30 a.m. to 2 p.m. and 5:30 to 10 p.m.; Sun 10 a.m. to 2 p.m. and 5:30 to 9 p.m.; $$–$$$. Among the most talked-about restaurants in town these days is Brookside's Julian, opened in 2010 by one of the brightest stars on the K.C. dining scene, Chef Celina Tio. From 2001 to 2008, Tio was executive chef at **The American** (see p. 97), and won a James Beard Award during her tenure there. In the fall of 2010, Tio finished in third place in season 3 of *The Next Iron Chef,* putting Kansas City on the radar of foodies—or at least Food Network junkies—nationwide. With all that acclaim, media exposure, and accomplishment, Tio might have opted to make Julian, her first proprietary restaurant, a high-end, high-price-point culinary showcase, but as she herself stresses, Julian was conceived to be a neighborhood joint with feel-good, memory-evoking food that's priced democratically (albeit a bit higher than Applebee's), where—the bottom line for Tio, an avowed people person—she could see some of the same customers visit from month to month. Moderate prices or not, Julian's menu is very much chef-driven, artisanal, and seasonal—and peppered with obscure ingredients and fancy foodie terms you might have to Google on your iPhone or risk embarrassment by asking a waiter. Still, Tio is serious about the comfort food factor—she does haute riffs on mac 'n' cheese, pot pie, burgers, pulled pork sandwiches, and eggs Benedict, and this aspect of her cooking personality really shines during Sunday brunch (mains $7 to $13): The woman makes her own English muffins, scones, and doughnuts, and even smokes her own salmon and cures her own bacon in house (though she doesn't brag about this on the printed menu). Because, as a former *Iron Chef* contender, why wouldn't she do that for her patrons? The lunch menu is without a doubt the most approachable way to experience Julian; it's a really, really good deal for food of this caliber. Any main dish is $9, but $12 gets you a main and a side or "ending" (dessert or cheese), and $15 gets you a veritable midday feast, with one selection from each menu section. On the dinner menu, which like everything here changes seasonally, expect inventive and sophisticated mains like crispy pork shoulder with sweet potato puree and tamarind pork sauce ($16) or seared halibut, roasted heirloom beets, greens, and lemon emulsion ($20). Chef Tio also offers customers a wild-card option for tasting her creations during the Sunday Family Meal—each Sunday evening (reservations recommended) you show up and get whatever she is making that day

($30 for 3 courses, $34 for 4); there's usually a unifying theme, like basil or Italian cuisine, and the dishes are never anything that's on the regular menu. Whenever you eat at Julian, the young serving staff is casual, friendly, and always timely. Tio herself often delivers dishes and will likely stop by your table at some point to ask if you're enjoying your meal, and she genuinely cares. Julian took over the old Joe D's Wine Bar space, and its outdoor patio tables in the heart of Brookside are the best seats in the house when weather permits. Though freshened with brushed metal fixtures and a modern grayscale palette accented with mustard yellow, the interior dining room (a bit sterile and bare, with stained carpet) is the one discordant note here; some revamping of the dining rooms would go a long way to complement Tio's inspired kitchen. At any rate, Tio's formula seems to be working: At the American, a "regular" was a patron you saw once a year, while at Julian, there's already an enthusiastic following of regulars who visit several times per week. See Chef Tio's recipe for **Carrot Thai Curry Soup** on p. 265.

La Cucina di Mamma, 6227 Brookside Blvd., between 62nd Terrace and 63rd St.; (816) 444-1138; www.kcbellanapoli.com. Mon through Thurs 11 a.m. to 9 p.m., Fri and Sat 11 a.m. to 10 p.m.; $$. Acquired during my past life as an expatriate in Rome in my 20s, my habit of being overly critical of Italian food establishments in the United States is admittedly annoying. I disparage "Americanized" Italian restaurants that drown everything in garlic, cream, and ersatz "Parmesan." I scoff even at New York hotshots like Mario Batali because they do not faithfully reproduce the typical dining experience that is such a beloved aspect of life in Italy, injecting too many flourishes of celebrity chef personality into their dishes. So what passes muster for me? Truly authentic places like La Cucina di Mamma, the restaurant attached to Jake Imperiale's **Bella Napoli Alimentari** (p. 177). It's unpretentious, comfortable, and tasty, with a kitchen that serves food very similar to what you find in restaurants today all over Italy. From the menu to inexpensive wine carafes to the atmosphere, this is as close as you'll get to a real trattoria *italiana* in Kansas City. Diners accustomed to the American version of Italian food will find plenty of familiar menu items—cheese-filled ravioli in tomato sauce, lasagna, pesto—but Imperiale does them the Italian way, stripped down to their basic but top-notch ingredients (as he was taught by his native Italian mamma). He also serves classic Italian trattoria fare that may be less known on this side of the Atlantic, like *spaghetti cacio e pepe,* a Roman standby made with pecorino Romano cheese and lots of black pepper ($11.99) or an antipasto of *bresaola e rughetta* (cured beef and arugula, tossed with olive oil, shaved Parmigiana Reggiano, and lemon zest, $9.99), and an array of *contorni,* or veggie sides ($3.99) like spinach with butter and Parmesan, or bean salad, that are also always ordered a la carte in Italy. A Neapolitan pizza menu gives you the option for something even more casual. Normally priced from $8.99 to $10.99, all pizzas are $5 on Monday nights; the other fabulous deal here is that all bottles of wine are half off on Tuesday and Wednesday evenings (bring a group for the most proper enjoyment of this Brookside bacchanalia). At lunch, you can also order any of the panini on the Bella Napoli menu and eat them in the restaurant for no extra charge.

Old-Guard K.C.

Charlie Hooper's, 12 W. 63rd St., between Baltimore and Main; (816) 361-8841; www.charliehoopers.com. Kitchen open Mon, Tues, Thurs 11 a.m. to 11 p.m., Wed, Fri, Sat 11 a.m. to midnight, Sun 11 a.m to 10 p.m.; $. At first blush, it's just another Brookside/Waldo bar and grill, but Charlie Hooper's extensive beer list (34 drafts and 150 bottled beers from around the world) makes it a blip on any brew aficionado's radar screen. The solid American pub fare is also better than average—while onion rings at other sports bars with kitchens are usually a soggy mess, the onion rings at Hooper's are a perfect, crispy, glistening gold. Daily deals (Monday is burger night, when $3 gets you a burger and fries; or beer flight Wednesday, when 3 beers and an appetizer are only $10) make Hooper's a boon for social folks on a budget. For all the beer that's served, you'll see tons of kids in here, especially on weekends, when families cram the joint, pig out on the tasty bar food, and watch whatever KU, Mizzou, or Chiefs game happens to be on. We love to stop in here on a wintry Saturday for the "dog day" special ($1.25 to $1.50 for all-beef hot dogs with specialty toppings) and join in the community atmosphere of all the moms, dads, and kids bundled up in their snow gear, fresh off an exhilarating morning of sledding on Brookside's "Suicide Hill."

G's Jamaican Cuisine, 7940 Troost Ave.; (816) 333-9566. Daily 11 a.m. to 9 p.m.; $–$$. Well, Troost Avenue may be a long way from the splendid beaches and turquoise waters of Jamaica (although parts of this rundown neighborhood might recall the outskirts of Kingston), but that isn't stopping G (George) from slinging tasty, authentic Caribbean street food specialties like meat pies and platters of jerk chicken ($10.25) and curried goat ($11.25). (Do yourself a favor and try the goat if you never have before—it's fantastic: For the meat, imagine a flavor somewhere between lamb and goat cheese, stewed with curry and all kinds of lively Jamaican seasonings.) The dirty rice, red beans, and cabbage are also amazingly flavorful. At lunchtime during the week, G's is usually packed with locals on their lunch break. Just be aware that when G's says hot, they mean hot, Hot, HOT! The atmosphere is always congenial, and when it's not too busy, G will sit down with you and talk about his food. On weekend nights they bring in live reggae and dancehall acts. A full bar is stocked with Jamaican beers, rum, and everything you need for tropical-inspired cocktails.

Governor Stumpy's Grill House, 321 E. Gregory Blvd. (between McGee and Oak); (816) 444-2252; www.governorstumpys.com. Mon through Tues 11 a.m. to 9:30 p.m., Wed through Sat 11 a.m. to 10 p.m., closed Sun; $–$$. Who cares if the dining room has only slightly more panache than a Holiday Inn breakfast room? Sometimes you just gotta go to Stumpy's. Spinach dip? Check. BLT? Check. Ribs combo? Check. We always make our way back here when we're not in the mood for anything too time-consuming or stereotypically "foodie," and we just want a reliable and well-priced all-American dinner from an independent restaurant. Stumpy's is basically your (idealized) grandma's kitchen—feel-good food, nothin' highfalutin, and heaping portions of burgers and hot sandwiches, dinner platters, pastas, pizzas, and hearty salads. With all due respect to the crop of upscale and trendy burger joints in the K.C. area, Stumpy's Frisco Burger ($7.45), a gluttonously, glorious, greasy affair with grilled onions, Thousand Island dressing, and American cheese on sourdough bread, beats them all. My husband is faithful, visit after visit, to RT's Chops ($11.25), 2 smoked pork chops served with cinnamon apples and garlic mashers. The Reuben is a house specialty ($7.25), but if you are Michael Phelps, try the Reubenator ($19.95), which weighs in at eight gajillion calories with a pound of corned beef, a half pound of sauerkraut, 6 pieces of rye bread, and 6 pieces of melted swiss, all awash in Thousand Island dressing.

Papu's Cafe, 604 W. 75th St. (between Jefferson and Pennsylvania); (816) 822-8759. Daily 11 a.m. to 9 p.m.; $. This listing should probably read "Shell Station Shawerma." Papu's is located inside a working gas station and convenience mart, and from the street there is practically no sign of it except for a generic GYROS sign in the parking lot. Some locals are calling it the Middle Eastern version of **Oklahoma Joe's,** due to the fact that, like the famous BBQ joint in Kansas City, Kansas, Papu's is located inside a purveyor of unleaded and diesel. It opened as a cafe with a short menu of made-to-order Middle Eastern favorites in 2010 and has enjoyed such success that they've had to extend their hours. As Papu's happens to be in my neck of the woods, it's quickly become my favorite neighborhood stop for fast and satisfying vittles. My go-to is the falafel sandwich ($4.50), which is huge and served on a pita slathered with hummus, but the *shawerma* ($5.99) is also fantastic: The meat is juicy and tender and dressed with a unique mix of Pakistani spices and sea-sonings. Any of the sandwiches can be made a "platter" (with extra pita, hummus, tabbouleh salad, and a small fountain drink) for just $1 more. Whatever you order, get it with hot sauce. In fact, Papu's hot sauce has become such an integral part of the menu that they even have a catchphrase, "Always say yes to the hot sauce." Papu's spicy condiment isn't the kind of hot sauce that makes you reach for water every other bite; it's just kicked-up, tangy-sweet peppery flavor that makes everything taste better. P.S. Don't let the gas-station venue notion scare you—this is a small, neighborhoody Shell with no vagrants about. The dine-in atmosphere—which is exactly as you might imagine dining inside a mini-mart would feel like—might be limited to displays of antifreeze, Funyuns, and a wall-length fridge with every soft drink under the sun, but the place is clean and bright (and they even have hand sanitizer on every table), and the friendly owners are always checking on customers to make sure you're happy with your food.

Waldo Pizza, 7433 Broadway; (816) 363-5242; www.waldopizza .net. Mon through Thurs, Sun 11 a.m. to 10 p.m., Fri through Sat 11 a.m. to 11 p.m.; $–$$. You can't write a chapter about food in Waldo and not mention Waldo Pizza. The topic of pizza, and what's your favorite and why, is about as polarizing for Kansas Citians as picking your favorite BBQ place. Waldo Pizza isn't fancy pizza. It isn't Neapolitan pizza. It's the pizza of your childhood, it's piping hot and tasty, and it's hugely popular around here. It's also one of few food-establishment phone numbers we have programmed into our home cordless—that should tell you something. Waldo Pizza's kitchen-sink approach to toppings, from additional cheeses (Gouda, goat, soy mozzarella) to meat and fish (burnt ends, salmon, smoked turkey, Spam) to veggies (almonds, roasted corn, avocado, eggplant) is truly encyclopedic, and they also offer 3 different crust styles—traditional hand-tossed; St. Louis–style thin crust, glazed with garlic butter; and honey wheat. Hand-tossed and honey-wheat pies get mozzarella and provolone, while St. Louis–style gets swiss and cheddar in addition to the other two. When we're here, my husband and I order, without fail, a sausage, mushroom, and black olive pie on honey-wheat crust, and it's a hit every time; that is the only pizza we ever order, but I can vouch for the crispness (even laden with heavy veggie toppings) and cheesy symphony of the St. Louis–style pie. The always-busy dining areas are your typical pizza parlor—wooden booths, a small bar area—and filled most often by families or groups of friends. Waldo Pizza also delivers pretty much anywhere (with extra charge for longer distances), but be warned that it can take up to an hour on busy evenings, so it's often easier to place an order for pickup.

Specialty Stores, Markets & Producers

Bella Napoli Alimentari, 6227 Brookside Blvd.; (816) 444-1138; www.kcbellanapoli.com. Mon through Fri 10 a.m. to 6 p.m., Sat 9 a.m. to 5 p.m., Sun 11 a.m. to 3 p.m. For me, whose five years living in Rome are seared into my identity, Jake Imperiale's authentic Italian deli and market makes Kansas City feel like home. Imperiale, a second-generation Italian-American whose mamma was from Napoli, used to sell pacemakers before he tossed in the corporate towel and started contacting importers about realizing his real dream, opening up his own *alimentari* (Italian for small grocery store). What I love about Bella Napoli is that it doesn't take the cloying mandolin on the stereo, raffia-wrapped Chianti bottle, or overwrought specialty sauce approach to being an Italian market.

This is current, basic Italian housewife stuff, with shelves nearly identical to the Roman or Milanese equivalent of Hy-Vee, albeit on a smaller scale and with a few more gourmet items, like artisanal pastas, thrown in. Everything is imported. You'll find jars of *cipolle borettane* (small, flat onions from Emilia-Romagna, in oil, amazing as appetizers), cans of Italian tuna, packets of dried porcini, and—a key item for any Italian kitchen—small shelf-stable cartons of *panna da cucina* (cooking cream, which is thicker than and totally different from American heavy cream). A deli case along one wall stocks premium cured meats (prosciutto di Parma, *bresaola*, capocollo, and more) and more than 15 fine Italian cheeses, including mozzarella di bufala. Bella Napoli also makes up deli sandwiches ($6.29 to $6.99) with fresh ingredients from the deli case. A room to the right of the market is a coffee bar with espresso drinks and lots of tables for lingering and conversation, while the room to the left, along with half the square footage of the market itself, become the restaurant incarnation of Imperiale's empire, **La Cucina di Mamma** (p. 170) at lunch and dinner.

Brookside Farmers' Market, 63rd St. and Wornall Rd. Sat 8 a.m. to 1 p.m. from Apr through Oct. From spring to fall, it's a fundamental Brookside Saturday morning ritual to pick up certified-organic and sustainable produce, meat, dairy products, and baked goods from this seasonal, manageably sized market in the parking lot of Border Star Montessori School, in the heart of Brookside's shopping and dining district.

Coffee Girls, 7440 Washington St., between 74th and 75th Streets; (816) 221-2326; www.kccoffeegirls.com. Mon through Fri 6:30 a.m. to 7 p.m., Sat 7:30 a.m. to 7 p.m., Sun 7:30 a.m. to 3 p.m. Occupying a large space in the very modern glass-and-steel building on the corner of 75th Street and Washington, Coffee Girls is a great caffeinate/hangout/work-on-your-laptop addition to Waldo. The espresso, specialty and frozen drinks, and drip coffee are all really nice, but Coffee Girls also does a lot of besides coffee. Most noteworthy are the flavorful combinations of fresh-squeezed juices (the Vagabond, $5 for 20 ounces, is strawberry, carrot, ginger, apple, and beet) and colorful, healthy smoothies (the Waldo, also $5 for 20 ounces, includes raspberry sherbet, blueberries, blackberries, banana, and fresh-squeezed apple juice). Vitamin up on one of these nutrient-packed babies the morning after a big night of Waldo barhopping. At lunch, go for one of the heaping sandwiches ($7), served on artisanal bread, and salads ($6.50) loaded with freshness and crunch. There's plenty of room inside and outside (in the breezeway between this shop and Kennedy's bar next door), to sit and read the paper, write your novel, meet with your life coach, whatever. Coffee Girls provides free Wi-Fi, but they close at 7 p.m.; if you need somewhere to work later, head up the the **Roasterie Cafe** in Brookside (p. 185).

Cosentino's Brookside Market, 14 W. 62nd Terrace, between Brookside Plaza and Main St.; (816) 523-3700; www.cosentinos .com. Daily 6 a.m. to 10 p.m. Foodies who appreciate the finer things won't find a more pleasant all-around supermarket in Kansas

FARM TO MARKET BREAD CO.

If you've ever had ciabatta, whole grain rolls, or sliced sourdough at a restaurant in Kansas City, chances are they came from Waldo's own **Farm to Market Bread Co.** (73rd Street between Central and Wyandotte; 816-363-3198; www.farmtomarketbread .com). This artisanal bakery, hands-down the finest in town and a real treasure for foodies, unfortunately isn't set up for retail sales or tours of any kind at the actual bread-making facility, but you can order online and of course buy Farm to Market Bread at most supermarkets and gourmet stores in the metro area. Farm to Market's retail breads (from $3 per loaf), sold in white paper sleeves at market endcap displays, include Grains Galore, challah, San Francisco sourdough, French Farm, and Asiago ciabatta.

City—Brookside Market is the one-stop shop for anyone who lives remotely nearby and whose daily grocery list calls for something a bit special. Attractively arranged gourmet items, specialty produce, an excellent selection of fine wines, and staples like Cheerios have made this market a cornerstone of this cultured, family-oriented community. It also draws food lovers from around the city for its huge deli area, where you can get pancetta and prosciutto sliced to order, or pick up premade entrees (orange-chipotle glazed duck breast, anyone?), salads, and nigiri combos. Whenever I have a recipe that calls for something a bit more niche (like arugula, grown at local farms), or that's critical to have fresh (like littleneck clams for my *linguine alle vongole*), I always go to Brookside Market and am never disappointed. Their invitingly merchandised cheese and antipasti departments alone are enough to lure me in for idle wandering (and, inevitably, indulgent purchases). While the prices here are higher for everyday goods than at other more mainstream markets like **Price Chopper,** Hy-Vee, and Hen House, those other markets can't compete in the specialty-item category. And among those area markets that do sell gourmet goods (Whole Foods, McGonigle's, and Dean & Deluca), Brookside Market generally has the lowest prices.

Foo's Fabulous Frozen Custard, 6235 Brookside Plaza; (816) 523-2520; www.foosfabulousfrozencustard.com. Sun through Mon 1 to 11 p.m., Tues through Thurs 11:30 a.m. to 10 p.m., Fri through Sat 11:30 a.m. to 11 p.m. Wedged in among the European-style shops of Brookside Plaza, Foo's is a Kansas City original and the only place to go when you need a frozen dessert. Like a fool, I wasted way too much money on shakes and other frozen treats at Baskin-Robbins up the street before I discovered Foo's. You might wonder, as I did, how and what do you order at a frozen custard place? Well, no sooner do you walk in the door of the earthy store (it could very easily be in Berkeley) than those questions are answered. Small handwritten placards reading "everything starts out as vanilla" (aha!) are posted strategically throughout, and a giant chalkboard displays, in colorful blurbs, all the mix-in or topping options. (Another Foo's educational placard explains that a "concrete" is a mix-in, while a sundae is just those add-ons on top.) You can't go wrong with the mint Oreo (crème de menthe and crushed Oreos), but the possibilities—with nuts, fruit, liqueurs, peanut butter, fudge, caramel, butterscotch, candy bars, cookie dough, coconut, and more—are pretty much endless. Foo's may be a one-trick pony and a simple concept, but that base custard has got to be some amazing stuff, because these really do taste fabulous. Look for me on summer nights on one of the benches out front. Concretes start at $2.82 for the mini size (big enough for one as a midday or post-meal treat).

McGonigle's Market, 1307 W. 79th St., at Ward Pkwy.; (816) 444-4720; www.mcgonigles.com. Mon through Sat 8 a.m. to 6 p.m., Sun noon to 5 p.m. McGonigle's is Kansas City's mecca for meat lovers, backyard grillers, and amateur BBQers citywide. With the feel of a great country market you might stop at for provisions on the way to the mountains or the lake, two-thirds of the store is dedicated to produce, basic and gourmet grocery items (including a vast array of grilling sauces and marinades), and liquor, while the far aisles on the right are all about the meat. The butcher counter is a feast for carnivorous eyes, stocked with the highest-quality beef, veal, Berkshire pork, lamb, poultry, and seafood in town, and always staffed by the most helpful and friendly meat experts. These guys are an amazing resource, so don't be shy: Pick their brains with all your meat-related questions, from what to do with different cuts of pork to how to get the juiciest lamb chops to how much rib roast you need to feed a holiday gathering of 12. Steaks are the house specialty, and although they'll cost more here than at the supermarket, the careful aging process and custom trimming at McGonigle's is well worth the extra expense for a special occasion. An aisle-length freezer case is chock-full of prepackaged meat and seafood like lamb kebabs, crab legs, or meatloaf mix, and specialty meats like buffalo, artisanal sausages, ostrich, wild boar, elk, venison, and more. They can also special order any seafood item. You can't drive by McGonigle's without inhaling the heavenly aroma of BBQ, produced on-site every day in the parking lot smoker. Brisket, pulled pork, and Italian sausage sandwiches, ribs, chicken, and fried pork tenderloin are sold steaming hot (and at reasonable prices) from a trailer in front of the store, along with such house-made sides as fries, cheesy corn, and baked beans. Eat at one of the picnic tables on the adjacent grass. (Trailer hours: Mon 10:30 a.m. to 3 p.m., Tues through Sat 10:30 a.m. to 5:30 p.m., Sun noon to 4:30 p.m.)

McLain's Bakery, 7422 Wornall Rd.; (816) 523-9911; www .mclainsbakeryinwaldo.com. Mon through Fri 7 a.m. to 2 p.m., Sat 7 a.m. to noon. I have met very few cakes that I won't scarf down like a rabid dog if they're left on my kitchen counter. I have been known to eat frosting straight up when struck by an urge for sweets. But my white, buttercream-frosted wedding cake from McLain's Bakery was something entirely different. Simple and straightforward, like our courthouse nuptials, it was the best white cake I've ever had, and though it was purported to serve 16, it ended up serving just one—the very gluttonous bride, whose morning, afternoon, and midnight nibblings made it disappear in about four days. This anecdote is just meant to convey just how sneakily delicious McLain's is. Nestled in a 1940s shop front amid the hard-drinking bars of Waldo, McLain's is one of the last remaining old-school fresh-baked-daily bakeries in the entire K.C. metro area. There's nothing innovative about it, and they don't sell anything that they didn't perfect decades ago; McLain's stays in business because patrons expect them to adhere to the traditions the bakery was founded on over 60 years ago. And because McLain's is absolutely meticulous about every step of the baking process (a careful chemistry where even the slightest shortcuts and imprecise measurements can have disastrous results)—from timing, order of mixing ingredients, and temperature—all the bakers here have been drilled in the correct, immutable, time-tested way to make pastries, cookies, and cakes. Generations of Kansas Citians have been making weekend pilgrimages to McLain's for such signature items as the Chocolate Cup Cookie ($0.85 each, a pecan sandy with a dollop of rich and velvety chocolate buttercream frosting in the middle), butter Danish ($1.75 each), and German chocolate coffee cake ($9.25). A wide range of cookies, Danishes, and coffee cakes is always available, but most cakes and large quantities of anything should be ordered in advance. However, McLain's is also expert at handling last-minute requests: If you show up at 10 a.m. on a Friday and need a special cake for an event for that evening, no problem; if you're hosting a big corporate event on Tuesday and need 400 dozen Danishes for the brunch, just place your order with McLain's by Saturday morning.

The Roasterie Cafe, 6223 Brookside Blvd.; (816) 333-9700; www .theroasterie.com. Mon through Thurs 6 a.m. to 10 p.m., Fri 6 a.m. to 11 p.m., Sat 7 a.m. to 11 p.m., Sun 7 a.m. to 10 p.m. A fixture in the daily lives of freelancers, as well as a favorite rest-and-refuel stop for parents out for vigorous stroller pushing on the Trolley Trail, the Roasterie Cafe is Brookside's biggest and best coffeehouse. You don't have to be a coffee snob to discern the superior quality of the Roasterie's sourcing and roasting model. A robust brew bar offers coffee fiends the option of having your cup brewed on the spot (you pick the bean blend, which can get pretty exotic) using one of 4 gourmet methods—Clover machine, pour-over, French press, or siphon. Even the machine-drip coffees (at least 2 varieties are on offer each day) are bursting with smooth, nuanced flavor, and the espresso-based drinks are executed with much more expertise and attention to detail than at certain other nationwide coffee chains that shall remain nameless. It's enough that the coffee here is out-

standing (the 100 percent Arabica specialty-grade beans are handpicked from small farms around the world and air-roasted at the Roasterie's facility downtown (see p. 55), but the sleek and spacious place is also an excellent hangout (and not in an overtly artsy/hipster way, like Broadway Cafe in Westport). Laptop-toting students and work-from-home types can set up shop in the cafe's many comfortable seating areas (electrical outlets are always nearby, and there's free Wi-Fi throughout), though you'll also find more animated tables where friends are catching up over tea and lattes, or where informal business meetings or job interviews are being conducted. The Roasterie Cafe is the kind of place where you can pop in for a to-go cappuccino and be out in 3 minutes, or you can stay for 3 hours and never feel jostled. The patio out front (where dogs are welcome—the cafe provides water bowls—but smokers are not) was enlarged in 2010 and is always well utilized in mild weather. Pastries, parfaits, and **Christopher Elbow** chocolates are sold from a case next to the register. You can also, of course, buy all range of Roasterie coffees in bulk, ground or whole bean, by the pound, as well as Roasterie-branded merch, with its cool retro aviation motif.

75th Street Brewery, 520 W. 75th St., between Pennsylvania and Washington; (816) 523-4677; www.75thstreet.com. Mon through Thurs 11 a.m. to 1 a.m., Fri and Sat 11 a.m. to 1:30 a.m., Sun 11 a.m. to midnight; $$. K.C.'s only brewpub, 75th Street Brewery is a big (yet cozy) bar and grill with a friendly atmosphere and familiar faces. They only serve their own beer, all of which is brewed on-site—the large beer vats are clearly visible in the middle of the dining and bar areas. Over 20 different ales and lagers, many of them seasonal specialties, are brewed throughout the year. Particularly recommended brews are Saxy Golden Ale and the Fountain City Irish Red, both available year-round. Besides what you might drink at the bar or with your meal, six-pack samplers are available to take home as are half gallon "growlers." The food here is a step up from the usual bar food offerings, but still with good personal size flatbread pizzas ($10.99) burgers (you won't even miss the meat in the black bean burger, $7.99), sandwiches (the vegetarian, $7.99, is heaped high with lots of colors and flavors and topped with roasted garlic mayo), and some notable appetizers like the moules frites (Saison-steamed mussels with crispy garlic pub fries, white truffle mayo, and baguette, $12.99), as well as scotch eggs ($5.99). Among the entrees, try either of the 2 styles of fish 'n chips (the classic recipe, "London's Best" is $10.99; the "Mt. McKinley," with Alaskan halibut and lemon-basil aioli, is $15.99); both are battered with wheat ale. If you want some fresh air, head out back to The Alley, which is 75th Street Brewery's smaller beer-garden type environment, adorned with hop plants to keep in line with the beer theme. Join the Mug Club and have your own mug stored at the bar for when you want a beer from your favorite stein. The staggeringly extensive (and tall) collection of members' mugs on shelves above the bar gives the atmosphere some nice Old World character. (Thanks to Bruce Cameron, 75th Street Brewery regular and decorated home-brewer, for this write-up.)

South Kansas City

South Kansas City, consisting of "everything else" on the Missouri side below 85th Street and east of State Line, is a mostly residential area with commercial pockets here and there, usually in the form of beige strip malls and drive-throughs. Yet there are also some longtime favorite restaurants down here, such as Jasper's and the original location of Fiorella's Jack Stack, insider finds like Olive Cafe, and hip producers like Soda Vie. Farther south along Holmes Road is a charming rural landscape with such working retail farms as KC Buffalo Co. and the Berry Patch.

Foodie Faves

Big City Hot Dogs, 10510 Grandview Rd.; (816) 437-7232; www .bigcityhotdogsonline.com. Mon through Sat 10:30 a.m. to 8 p.m.; $. The team at Big City Hot Dogs has scoured the mean streets of big cities from coast to coast, researching hot dog carts nationwide so that they could assemble, all in one place, a menu of fully-loaded, all-beef wieners that honor the traditions of Coney Island, Chicago, Detroit, Boston, and even Seattle. Each is piled high with a mixture of krauts, relishes, diced veggies, or cheese, or some sort of sauce, but none of them can be eaten without serious hazard to your clean shirt. Try the Detroit Coney Island (which the owners call "delicious yet controversial"), with yellow mustard, beef chili and diced onions, or the Seattle (cream cheese, dill pickle, mayo, and green onion), or for something really messy, the Atlanta Carolina dog (aka "Hillbilly Dog," slathered with creamy coleslaw). The pièce de résistance here, however, is the Kansas City BBQ dog, topped with pickle spear, bacon, BBQ sauce, diced onion, and blue cheese crumbs. They've also got a few non-dog menu items, like gyros, Philly cheese steak, and the increasingly popular Big City Tuna Wrap.

Olive Cafe, 9530 James A. Reed Rd. #B, at Bannister; (816) 763-0009. Mon through Sat 10 a.m. to 8 p.m. (closed from 1 to 2 p.m. on Fri.), Sun 10 a.m. to 7 p.m.; $. Insider find alert! In the culinary dust bowl of East Bannister Road, this is a well-kept secret that happens to have what regulars claim is the best Mediterranean/Middle Eastern food in Kansas City. Its location is so obscure and its shop front so well hidden in the back of a strip mall (where another more prominent shop bearing the name Olive Cafe is boarded up), however, that most people, even food lovers who live sort of nearby, have no idea it's there. Olive Cafe's primary vocation is as a mini-market serving the grocery needs of south K.C.'s Middle Eastern communities. The in-house bakery churns out fresh, fluffy pita

daily. Olive Cafe is a friendly but no-frills environment (which, of course, always adds to insider foodie cache) with a simple but clean dining area grafted onto the back of the market. The owners are Palestinian, so the cuisine is central Middle Eastern in style, featuring the typical flavors of Syria, Lebanon, and Iraq. They've built a die-hard lunch following with generous platters (try the chicken or mixed meat over hummus, with unlimited pita), juicy and flavorful gyros, kebabs, kofta, and particularly succulent *shawerma*. Lunch dishes are priced between $5 and $7. Vegetarians swear by their falafel sandwiches—the falafel is nice and crisp on the outside and soft and moist on the inside. In addition to the weird and wonderful grocery items sold on the shelves of the market—who knew you could get that many varieties of jarred grape leaves in the Midwest? Or, for that matter, such a broad range of apple malt-liquor beverage, bulgur wheat, and tahini?—Olive Cafe will also sell you their in-house dry falafel mix so you can try your hand at making the spiced chickpea balls at home. Note that Olive Cafe is open daily, but it closes from 1 to 2 p.m. on Fri, when staff attend prayer services.

Swagger, 8431 Wornall Rd.; (816) 361-4388; www.swaggerkc.com. Mon through Sat 11 a.m. to 1:30 a.m. (kitchen closes at 11 p.m.); $–$$. I lived just down the street from this place for years before I realized that Swagger isn't just your typical dive bar. Certainly it has all the attributes of a dive bar—the yellowish light, the '70s rec-room pool-table area, the "colorful" regulars. But Swagger also has a staggering selection of beer, including about 50 on tap ($2 to

$5) and 100 more in bottles or cans. The place is a beer geek's dream come true, with menu notes that indicate the style (e.g., Belgian Strong Pale Ale, Witbier, American Adjunct Lager, Hefeweizen, etc.), provenance, alcohol content, and even the glassware it's served in. Swagger is particularly deep in Belgian, Missouri, and specialty Italian beers. The food here is definitely superior to average bar fare, and in fact several dishes were featured on the Food Network's *Diners, Drive-Ins, and Dives*. Most famous is the Suribachi Burger (⅓-pound beef patty, grilled, tempura-battered, and fried, with Asian mustard, Sriracha hot sauce, Pepper Jack, and wasabi coleslaw). Swagger draws a very mixed crowd (including acclaimed local chefs who come here for late-night bites) and is always lively during weekday happy hours (3 to 7 p.m.) and on weekend nights.

Thai House, 9938 Holmes Rd.; (816) 943-1388; www.kcthaihouse .com. Mon through Thurs 11 a.m. to 9:30 p.m., Fri 11 a.m. to 10:30 p.m., Sat noon to 10 p.m.; $–$$. There's a puzzling lack of Thai restaurants in the otherwise restaurant-rich districts of Brookside and Waldo, south of the Plaza. But if you swing just a bit farther south, to 99th and Holmes, Thai House has very good food. Anchoring the corner of a rather bleak shopping center, Thai House is handsomely appointed with red-and-black Asian-style interiors (the booths are the best seats). It never really gets busy, so you can come and slurp your noodles undisturbed. Even if you don't stick around for the atmosphere, Thai House is an excellent take-out option. I love their mint beef salad ($7.95), pad thai ($8.95), and *massaman* curry (from $8.95), but they also have wonderful "home cooking" vegetarian entrees like spicy ginger tofu ($8.95) and basil bok choy ($6.95). Note that there's no lunch buffet, but entree prices at lunch are about $2 less than at dinner (defined as after 3 p.m.).

Old-Guard K.C.

B.B.'s Lawnside Bar-B-Q, 1205 E. 85th St. (at Troost); (816) 822-7427; www.bbslawnsidebbq.com. Tues 4 to 10 p.m., Wed 11 a.m. to 9 p.m., Thurs 11 a.m. to 10:30 p.m., Fri through Sat 11 a.m. to 11 p.m., Sun noon to 9 p.m.; $–$$. In 1990, local BBQ enthusiast and noted blues expert Lindsay Shannon came up with a natural pairing that, surprisingly, wasn't anywhere else in K.C.: a BBQ joint with live blues. He found a vacant restaurant space with a granite pit that had been built in 1950, he lined up local, regional, and national blues acts to play 6 nights a week, and B.B.'s Lawnside was born. It's the kind of place where after one visit, you'll want to become a regular. The classic roadhouse layout of the place alone is a treasure: A great old wooden bar lines one end of the room, while the band makes a makeshift stage of the other end. Playbills and photos of blues musicians (and especially harmonica players, for whom Shannon has special admiration) with an evident patina of wood smoke and good times line the walls. In between are long communal tables where patrons dive into hickory-smoked meats cooked slow and low, Louisiana-style home-cookin', and drink beer (premium bottles include Louisiana's Abita Jockamo IPA and Dixie

Blackened Voodoo Lager). The ribs (from $8.95 for a 3-rib platter with 2 sides) are truly outstanding, and so moist and tender that they don't need sauce, but it's hard to resist the house BBQ sauce, sweet and smoky with an underlying secret ingredient (I can't tell if it's apple or cherry, and Shannon demurs when I ask) that differentiates it from the pack. Deal alert: Check out the Thursday rib special—a full slab with 2 sides is a steal at $14.95 (a half slab with 1 side is $9.50). Rib tips ($8.99 for the Smokey Hogs platter with B.B.'s delicious battered fries) are another house specialty and unique among K.C. BBQ offerings, as they are more part of the inner-city barbecue tradition, much of which has disappeared in downtown K.C., than the more widespread suburban style of BBQ around town. Many dishes are named after blues musicians, such as the Yardbird Combo ($11.95), a quarter chicken with ribs and fries, in honor of Charlie Parker, or Memphis Minnie's smoked catfish ($11.95), another menu favorite. All in all, Lindsay and his wife Jo have come up with a lot of original plates that you won't find at other BBQ places in Kansas City: How about burnt end soup ($5.25), or a brisket-based BBQ meatloaf ($8.95), or a bar-b-cue "sundae" ($6.59) of pulled pork, pit beans, and coleslaw served in a mason jar? But rest assured it's all down-home, rib-sticking, flavorful and filling. The only time you won't find Lindsay and Jo here is when they're on one of their roadtrips to Louisiana—undertaken as pure research, of course, for good food and music. Note that a cover of $3 to $6 is charged if you come to B.B.'s and stick around for the live entertainment; Tues through Thurs and Sun, the acts go on between 6 p.m. and 7:30 p.m., while on Fri and Sat night the music starts at 9 p.m. Fans of Blues Brothers–style, horn-heavy Chicago blues should check out regular act 4 Fried Chickens and a Coke. Check the website for monthly show schedules.

Gomer's Fried Chicken, 615 E. 99th St. (at Holmes); (816) 942-0030. Tues through Sat 7 a.m. to 9 p.m., Sun 7:30 a.m. to 5 p.m.; $. Sometimes, you just need fried chicken. Or an unapologetically large and cholesterol-filled breakfast platter. Sometimes you just need to stuff your face with the kind of classic American diner fare that makes cardiologists blanch. When that craving hits, you could do much worse than Gomer's. As the name suggests, fried chicken is the main event here, and the menu offers all kinds of ways to order, whether you want a dinner ($5.09 to $7.69) with sides (like mashed potatoes, green beans, spicy apples, mac and cheese, or cold salads) or just chicken à la "part" (2 thighs and a leg for $4.19; 6 wings, legs, or thighs for $6.29; you name it). No matter what, you can always specify exactly which parts of the bird you want, which is nice. Gomer's chicken is crispy and not too greasy, and many return customers come just for the livers, gizzards, and hearts ($5.79). On the breakfast menu are your typical egg and meat plates with some extra Midwestern gluttony thrown in for good measure—such as a pork chop with eggs ($7.79), buttermilk biscuits and gravy (from $4.79), and of course, fried chicken with eggs ($7.79). Gomer's is a mom-and-pop place with a simple country dining room that is totally congruent with the kind of food served here. You can also get any food to go, such as a 20-piece chicken family pack with 4 large sides ($38.99), but to take advantage of Thursday night's All-You-Can-Eat chicken deal (only $7.99, folks!), you have to eat in.

Fiorella's Jack Stack BBQ, 13441 Holmes Rd.; (816) 942-9141; www.jackstackbbq.com. Sun 11 a.m. to 9 p.m., Mon through Thurs 11 a.m. to 10 p.m., Fri through Sat 11 a.m. to 10:30 p.m.; $$–$$$. Kansas Citians may disagree on where to find the very best BBQ in the city, but Jack Stack is, if not number one, among the top three on just about everyone's list. That's saying a lot. So is the fact that Jack Stack consistently ranks as best barbecue restaurant in the United States by the Zagat Survey. This rambling, low-ceilinged, saloon-like location in Martin City is where Fiorella's Jack Stack all started—long before corporate expansion and a nationwide shipping program. Though the menu is the same here as at Jack Stack's three other locations around town, the restaurant here in Martin City feels a whole lot more authentic. And for some reason, which no doubt involves the age of the place and its cooking equipment, the food just tastes better here. Count on superb pork ribs (get the small end spare ribs, $16.25), BBQ chicken ($9.95 for a quarter-chicken dinner), lamb ribs ($16.95), sliced meats, burnt ends, and smoked prime rib (from $24.95 for 12 ounces). As at its other locations, Jack Stack excels at side dishes; creamy coleslaw and fries come standard with every entree, but you can substitute, at no extra charge, hickory pit beans (IMHO, the best rendition in K.C. of this classic BBQ accoutrement), cheesy corn bake (also amazing), or potato salad. Whereas you might put on a nice-ish outfit when you eat out at **Fiorella's Jack Stack BBQ** at the Freight House (see Crossroads chapter, p. 73), this much more casual location (in what used to be pure countryside) is frequented by contractors in their overalls and work boots and families fueling up post baseball game. The restaurant has an ample patio open in mild weather; otherwise, dine in one of the interconnected dining rooms, done up in dark woods and red upholstery—the palette of BBQ itself.

Jasper's, 1201 W. 103rd St. (at State Line); (816) 941-6600; www .jasperskc.com. Mon through Fri 11:30 a.m. to 2 p.m. and 5 to 10 p.m.; Sat 5 to 10 p.m.; $$$. Jasper J. Mirabile Jr.—"JJ" to those who know him—may be the hardest-working man in the Kansas City restaurant business. He's certainly the most PR-savvy. Whether doing cooking demonstrations at Hen House markets, radio shows (11 a.m. Sat on 710 AM), or chef/instructor stints at the Culinary Center and the Broadmoor Bistro in Overland Park, and broadcasting his every move on Facebook and Twitter, the guy is everywhere. (And if he can't be there in person, a life-size—and unnervingly lifelike—cardboard cutout of JJ stands in for him.) His public profile notwithstanding, JJ is passionate about food, and he dedicates himself heart and soul to continuing the work begun by his father, who opened the original Jasper's in Waldo in 1954. The Watt's Mill incarnation of Jasper's has been here, overlooking Indian Creek, since the late '70s, when the restaurant was reinvented as a less formal trattoria-style place. (The atmosphere still feels special, and a dress/conduct code prohibits tank tops, do-rags, and cell phone use.) Jasper's is still going strong today as a beloved fixture in the K.C. dining scene, and it's the best classic Italian this town has to offer. It's also become a bit of a celeb haunt: Personalities such as Overland Park's own Paul Rudd can't miss Jasper's jovial hospitality and delicious food when they're in town. Jasper's is, for the most part, old-world Italian—there's a lot of butter and cream in these dishes, a lot of red sauce and garlic, and a lot of cheese—but all of the aforementioned ingredients, handled by an expert in the kitchen, tend to add up to bliss on your taste buds. JJ does his best to honor real Italian cooking traditions as opposed to American modifications, and he makes at least one food pilgrimage trip to Italy every year to bone up on regional recipes, or to scout out a contemporary dish to add to his Kansas City menu. The Mirabile family is a long line of food lovers and food students, with an insatiable curiosity about recipes and ingredients. A prime example of JJ's adoration of real Italian food, and his commitment to bring it to his K.C. customers, is his table-side mozzarella preparation (summer only). From a wooden cart custom-made by his cousin, JJ hand-pulls a ball of fresh mozzarella from a bowl of hot water and milk curds right before your eyes. The spectacle, complete with lively and educational narration, takes all of two minutes, and the warm mozzarella is divine. As for what else to order on the extensive menu, it's hard to imagine going to Jasper's and not having pasta, as the sauces are superbly flavorful and authentic, and the egg-pasta dough is made in-house. Try the exquisite Capelli d'Angelo alla Nanni ($17.95, angel hair with mushrooms, prosciutto, peas, cream, tomato, and Parmigiano-Reggiano). The tomato-and-garlic-based seafood pastas are heavenly and the closest you'll get in K.C. to what an Italian beach vacation tastes like. Jasper's also does a variety of meat (osso buco, veal Marsala) and poultry (chicken saltimbocca) entrees, and seafood dishes, as well as rotating seasonal specialties (e.g., pumpkin ravioli in nutmeg cream sauce in the fall). Almost everything on the menu is excellent, but the *scampi alla livornese* ($10.95 as an app; $22.95 as an entree) is Jasper's ace in the hole. The shrimp are marvelously succulent, and the sauce (a secret blend of cream, wine, and garlic not printed in the Jasper's cookbook, alas) is nothing short of addictive. Once you run out of the *livornese* sauce but not the desire to keep mopping it up with warm rolls from the bread basket, you can ask your server to bring you more sauce, sans shrimp. (We did this once, and sure enough, more sauce arrived in a gravy boat within minutes; we weren't the slightest bit embarrassed about our gluttony, because it's that good.) JJ's earnest commitment to high-quality ingredients and elegant preparations are evident on every visit. That, combined with the elevated level of professionalism among servers, makes this more of a special event restaurant than other institutions of "Italian" food in Kansas City. The prices, too, land Jasper's in the splurge category. But unless he is in Italy or at his niece's wedding, JJ is there every night, the jolly captain of his staff of 50, cooking your food and making the rounds of the dining room in his chef's coat, chatting up customers and making sure you're having an enjoyable meal. See Chef Mirabile's recipe for **Osso Buco Milanese** on p. 266.

Jess & Jim's, 517 E. 135th St. (just west of Holmes); (816) 941-9499; www.jessandjims.com. Mon through Sat 11 a.m. to 10 p.m., Sun noon to 9 p.m.; $$$–$$$$. A giant black statue of a bull presides over the building, and the rear of the restaurant overlooks the rails along which Burlington Northern–Santa Fe freight trains rumble daily. You can almost imagine that at one time, cattle cars might have rolled right up to deliver Jess & Jim's its meat. Founded in 1938 by the Van Noy family who still run it, Jess & Jim's lies firmly in the pantheon of old-school Kansas City steakhouses, and it gets extra points for being in the tiny enclave of Martin City, which, for its 2-block extension, still has a little bit of that Old West feel to it. Inside, Jess & Jim's is nothing fancy, nor is it dripping with nostalgic atmosphere; on a good night, it's sort of lively. Steak, not ambience, is what Jess & Jim's spends its time and energy on. When you walk in, you'll see a helpful museum-type glass case of the various steak cuts on the menu, from filet mignon (from $19.99 for the 5-ounce) to top sirloin ($22.99), ribeye (from $21.99 for 12 ounces), T-bone ($29.99), porterhouse ($41.99), K.C. strip (from $20.99 for 10 ounces), and Jess & Jim's most famous steak, the

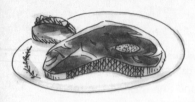

25-ounce Playboy Strip ($41.99). What's especially helpful about this meat-on-ice display, at least for the metrically challenged like me, is that you can see what 10 ounces vs. 18 ounces really looks like. All steaks are exclusively hand-cut Angus, and consistently juicy and tender—as far as a tasty red meat meal, you get your money's worth. Note that all steaks are served unseasoned (it's not a bearnaise kind of joint), and do pay attention to Jess & Jim's steak temperature chart, as their version of medium-rare (dark red center) is closer to some others' idea of rare. (If in doubt, ask your server.) Jess & Jim's will also sell you completely raw or frozen steaks in case you'd rather take them home to grill yourself; inquire about availability and pricing. Most everyone is here for the steak, but the menu also includes an extensive list of other big-belted, all-American beef, chicken, pork, and seafood main dishes and sharing plates, even frog legs (breaded and fried, $16.99 for a pound), and a standard lineup of Midwestern appetizers from $6.99. The wine list is a pleasant surprise, with several interesting and affordable bottles. As at most other Kansas City steakhouses, there's no need to dress up: Even as you rack up a bill of at least $50 a head (high for K.C. as a whole, but on par with other steakhouses in town), you'd look completely appropriate in a T-shirt and shorts.

Snead's Bar-B-Q, 1001 E. 171st St. (at Holmes), Belton, MO; (816) 331-9858. Wed and Thurs 11 a.m. to 8 p.m., Fri and Sat 11 a.m. to 9 p.m.; $–$$. In business since 1956, Snead's is an old-time landmark on the rural stretch of Holmes past Martin City. It may not have the most succulent ribs in K.C., but the BBQ is pretty good, and there's lots of country atmosphere. It's definitely worth a stop if you're out this way to visit the **Berry Patch** or **K.C. Buffalo Company,** or if you're out shopping for Fourth of July fireworks at one of the many Black Cat tents set up around here. Snead's menu is concise by BBQ restaurant standards but features some Southern-style dishes as well as traditional K.C. smoked meats. Starters (all $2.95) include fried okra, corn nuggets, and Texas toothpicks (onion and jalapeño straws). Their coleslaw is also excellent, and though a small portion comes with sandwiches and entrees, you might want to order a side of it ($1.75), or a pint to go ($3.25), if you're a slaw lover. A Snead's BBQ sandwich original, the Log Meat Sandwich (from $5.75), is a chopped blend of hickory-smoked meats on a bun and much more delicious than it sounds. You can also get larger plates of sliced BBQ meat ($5.75 to $6.95, beef, ham, pork, turkey, or sausage), "brownies" (burnt ends, $9.95 to $11.95), and of course ribs ($8.75 for a small order, $11.95 for a half slab, $17.95 for full slab). The big, open dining room, with hardwood fixtures and tables set like your great-aunt's rural house, has the feel of a Missouri lodge. The rear section has a pretty view through windows that overlook a grove of trees and a bicentennial bur oak.

Tasso's, 8411 Wornall Rd.; (816) 363-4776; www.tassosgreek restaurant.com. Mon 11 a.m. to 3 p.m.; Tues through Thurs 11 a.m. to 3 p.m., 5 to 10 p.m.; Fri through Sat 11 a.m. to 3 p.m., 5 p.m. to midnight. Live entertainment Fri 7 p.m. and 9:30 p.m., Sat 9:15 p.m.; $$.

On a proper night at Tasso's, you will utter "Opa!" more times than you may care to admit the next day. In addition to being K.C.'s best Greek restaurant (a category with little competition), Tasso's is also K.C.'s best campy dinner experience. While the food on its own really is great, you can't come here expecting a quiet meal à deux of spanakopita and souvlaki. Instead, you come in a group—the bigger, the better—and you go for the loosely Greek live entertainment on weekend nights (a belly dancer makes the rounds of the dining room and gives an impromptu lesson to the less inhibited patrons, and a Neil Diamond look-alike sings and plays a keyboard), the dark lighting and looping videos of Santorini, the plate-breaking bouzouki interlude, and being festive with friends and family. If you're picturing something out of *My Big Fat Greek Wedding,* you're not too far off the mark. Patriarch Tasso and the rest of the Kalliris family have been feeding Kansas City Greek food and entertainment since 1976, when the original Tasso's opened as a tiny bar and kitchen in Brookside. They later moved the restaurant to Waldo and then again to this current location, which underwent a face-lift in 2009 to better resemble a Greek tavern, with a more Mediterranean facade and some patio seating. As for the menu, start with the Tour of Greece appetizer ($8.50), which comes with tzatziki, hummus, skordalia (garlic dip) and *melizane salata* (eggplant dip) and lots of warm pita triangles to drag through it. They also have good *dolmathes* (grape leaves stuffed with ground beef and rice and topped with lemon-egg sauce). For the entree,

I invariably order the "house favorite" *Arnaki* Tasso (roasted and thinly sliced leg of lamb, $17.95), but other Greek classics like moussaka ($15.95) and kebabs ($13.95 to $18.95) are also excellent. A few well-executed steakhouse standards (K.C. strip, pork chops, swordfish steak, and salmon) are available should anyone in your party not care for Greek seasoning. Tasso's also has meal-size salads (smaller portions of these come with entrees) tossed with Tasso's special house-made Greek dressing. Let me repeat: As dependably tasty as Tasso's food is, what you'll really remember about the place (because cheesy or not, it is memorable) is the customer-participation entertainment and clapping your hands along to that bouzouki a little too vigorously. Blame it on the ouzo.

Specialty Stores, Markets & Producers

The Berry Patch, 22509 S. State Line Rd., Cleveland, MO; (816) 658-3663; www.theberrypatchonline.com. Mid-June through mid-August (blueberries and blackberries), Tues through Fri 7 a.m. to 9 p.m., Sat 7 a.m. to 3 p.m. Mid-August through mid-November or first hard freeze (blackberries), Tues and Sat 7 a.m. to noon. Year-round (frozen blueberries) Tues and Sat 8 a.m. to noon. Call ahead to be sure they're open. **Nothing says "summer in Kansas City" like heading down to Cleveland, Missouri, for some pickin' at the Berry Patch, the state's largest blueberry grower. Cleveland is about a half-**

hour drive from central K.C., and even a short excursion here gives you that tonic day-in-the-country feel. From June to Aug, pick blueberries ($2.65/pound), and blackberries ($2.85/pound) from summer through fall's first freeze. But before you start Googling recipes for the gallons of berry preserves that you will make with your harvest, call ahead to see what is open and available for public picking. The calendar for berry picking is sensitive to weather issues, and the dates given above are based on annual averages. Additionally, patches of the overall property open to the public are controlled to ensure thorough picking of the fruit in each area. So be sure to call ahead for the most up-to-date picking report (the website is not as accurate). Once you're in, the crop is huge and the berries plump and juicy. It doesn't take long to fill up a bucket, and it'll cost you far less than what the supermarket charges. Expect to sustain a few scratches as you navigate the brambly berry bushes, and to come home with stained hands from berry juice. If you just fancy a drive to the country, but you don't want to mess with the whole U-pick process (or if they're not open for picking that day), you can also buy baskets of picked berries (and frozen berries year-round) from the Berry Patch. They also have some kids' activities, like the "berry train" and a hay-bale maze, set up during the summer.

K.C. Buffalo Co., 2201 E. 203rd St. (just east of Holmes), Belton, MO; (816) 322-8174; www.kcbuffalo.com. Wed through Fri 10 a.m. to 6 p.m., Sat 10 a.m. to 5 p.m. Places like this make me love living in Kansas City. Just 20 minutes from my front door, there's a real working ranch where the buffalo roam—free ranging, USDA inspected, and hormone-, stimulant- and antibiotic-free. Mere feet from the ranch fence where the shaggy animals loll, anyone can walk into K.C. Buffalo Co.'s tiny store and buy fresh or frozen bison meat, whether it's a pound of burger patties ($7.25), bratwurst ($8.25/pound) or jerky (from $2.75 for 1 ounce), brisket ($8/pound) or steaks ($10 to $17/pound), a 20-pound variety pack ($145), or an entire side of the animal ($1,270). They even sell 100 percent bison-meat dog food. American buffalo (aka bison—they're the same thing) meat is most similar, among mainstream red meats, to beef—there's nothing weird or gamy about its flavor and texture—and when prepared correctly, it's simply delicious. It's also much healthier than beef as it provides more protein, vitamins, and minerals with fewer calories and less fat. Buffalo meat is rich in iron, calcium, potassium, and vitamins B6 and B12. Less fat, of course, can mean less juiciness after cooking, so in general you need to reduce standard beef cooking times to retain bison's moisture and tenderness. Peter and Susan Kohl, owners of K.C. Buffalo Co., can give you cooking tips when you visit; they also sell a buffalo meat cookbook and have posted some bison meat guidelines on their website. K.C. Buffalo Co. meats are also sold at **McGonigle's** (p. 182) and at some farmers' markets in season, but it's so much more authentic to get the goods here at the source (and the rural drive out south on Holmes, once you're past 135th Street, is lovely).

Marco Polo's, 1201 W. 103rd St. (at State Line); (816) 941-6600; www.jasperskc.com. Daily 10 a.m. to 9:30 p.m. This casual Italian market and deli is an extension of the more formal **Jasper's** restaurant (p. 196). Marco Polo's menu has little in common with its more elegant sibling; instead, it specializes in loaded (read: Americanized) Italian sandwiches ($6.75 to $7.25) like muffuletta, heros, meatball subs, and the Fat Marco Polo, an over-the-top panino served on a third of a loaf of Italian bread and heaped with mortadella, capocollo, Genoa salami, black olives, garlic butter, onions, and cheese. Perhaps the most famous menu item is the Italian sausage sandwich ($3.50), whose charcoal-grilled aroma can be smelled for several blocks around. There are always several entree options ($5.75 to $10.25) on offer, including various pastas, ravioli, lasagna, eggplant Parm, and chicken saltimbocca, as well as gourmet Mediterranean salads (marinated artichoke, olive, tomato) and Jasper's own Caesar ($6.25). They also make pizza by the slice ($3.50 to $3.95), but the bulk of Marco Polo's business is in sandwiches and take-out deli items. As it's located right along the Indian Creek bike trail, Marco Polo's is also a great spot to provision up for a picnic at one of several parks westward along the route in Johnson County. The market side of things is sparse (nowhere near as well stocked as **Bella Napoli** in Brookside), but you can find a small range of specialty pasta sauces, oils, vinegars, and imported Italian sweets. Order your food to go or eat in at one of the congenial wooden tables inside the shop.

Royal Liquors, 1301 W. 103rd St. (at State Line); (816) 942-8888; www.royal-liquors.com. Daily 7 a.m. to 1:30 a.m. From the outside, Royal Liquors just looks like a glorified gas station convenience mart. You'd never know there were $100 bottles of Barolo inside. Its entrance marked by fuel pumps and garish neon signs, this alcohol superstore may not have the aesthetics of a fine spirits purveyor, but venture inside and you'll find that Royal Liquors consistently has Kansas City's best array of wine, beer, and hard liquor, from the highbrow to the bargain basement. Fancier drinkers might prefer a prettier store with oak shelving and classical music instead of Royal's fluorescent glare and squeaky linoleum, but this is nevertheless the discerning K.C. drinker's Shangri-La. The wine section is as big as a Kansas wheat field, with 12 lengthy aisles divided according to varietal and region. Royal's wine merchants do a fantastic job of bringing interesting, quality labels in the $10 to $15 range to the shelves, but there are plenty of choices under $10 (and a wall of box and value wines) and many splurge bottles at $50 and up. The beer section, too, is exhaustive, with imports from every country, tons of domestic microbrews, and shelf upon shelf of craft beers sold by the single large-format bottle. The staff tends to be well-informed and can steer you toward a new stout you might have otherwise overlooked. Whiskey and scotch are strong suits here, too, but pretty much every mainstream spirit and obscure liqueur can be found in the booze maze that is Royal Liquors. There's also small area stocked with mixers and snack foods. Royal also has locations in

Brookside and downtown, but those stores are much smaller; for the full effect of Royal's inventory, go to the 103rd Street flagship.

Soda Vie, 10510 Grandview Rd.; (816) 437-7232; http://sodavie .com. Mon through Sat 10:30 a.m. to 8 p.m. KC's own local producer of artisanal sparkling beverages makes sodas (packaged in beautiful, hefty blue glass bottles) with flavors like the refreshing strawberry mint or cucumber, or more palate-jolting citrus chili and Thai basil clove. Some flavors are seasonal, like Spiced Apple in the fall. All beverages are meticulously brewed and carbonated naturally from real food—no weird chemicals, no high fructose corn syrup. They can also craft custom flavors for events (and for other restaurants, like **Dog Nuvo** [p. 60], whose signature soda is Soda Vie's blueberry-tarragon). You can find all the Soda Vie flavors here, at their lab/retail store in the back of Big City Hot Dogs, or find selections at gourmet stores like **The Better Cheddar** (p. 152), and **Dean & Deluca** (p. 250). Restaurants serving Soda Vie include **Blanc Burgers + Bottles, Beer Kitchen, Dog Nuvo,** and **Glacé Artisan Ice Cream.**

Trader Joe's, 8600 Ward Pkwy., in Ward Parkway Center; (816) 333-5322. Daily 8 a.m. to 9 p.m. The boutique grocery store that began on the West Coast in the '60s and won legions of fans nationwide with its funky vibe and unique foodie finds is finally coming to Kansas City. When those of us who've shopped at T.J.'s elsewhere saw the banner reading TRADER JOE'S COMING IN 2011 go up at a Ward Parkway mall in late 2010, we all let out a collective whoop of joy. As this book goes to press, the grand opening is scheduled for July

15, 2011. (Trader Joe's is also slated to open in Leawood, Kansas's One Nineteen shopping center, at 119th and Mission, 913-327-7209, about the same time.) For those not familiar with the chain, think (very loosely) of a cross between Whole Foods and Aldi. The foodie items are there, and usually at eye-poppingly low prices. All stores have cedar-planked walls, to give it that trading-post look, and the crew wears Hawaiian shirts. Trader Joe's keeps costs down by doing everything in-house, with its own branding, and by being kind of secretive about its sources and operation. Their buyers scour the globe for interesting international foodstuffs and there's an amazing variety of frozen and ready-made meals and health food/healthy lifestyle items. T.J.'s sells its own Asian simmer sauces, its own brand of cookies (from chocolate chip to more obscure ethnic varieties), and gourmet cheeses for much less than at other fancy grocers. They're especially strong on premade apps and party food (e.g., mini brie bites, teriyaki short rib party skewers). Despite the tantalizing packaging, not everything Trader Joe's sells is a home run, but the selection is so much fun and the prices so low that you won't mind experimenting a little bit to find your can't-live-withouts.

A major draw at Trader Joe's in other states is its wine section (and its famously affordable, fairly drinkable Charles Shaw, aka Two-Buck Chuck); how that will be organized given this store's location in a mall remains to be seen, but so far the legal liquor hurdles have been cleared.

The Northland

Kansas City's Northland—the sprawl north of where the Missouri River runs through downtown K.C.—may not come to mind as a foodie mecca. It's better known for its humongous outdoor malls like Zona Rosa, chain restaurants, movie megaplexes, and of course, Kansas City International Airport. It's known, frankly, for being boring. But there is culinary life in the Northland—and how! The pint-size and utterly charming town of Parkville alone boasts several foodie-worthy destinations. One of K.C.'s most talked-about restaurants, the progressive **Justus Drugstore,** is up in the all-American hamlet of Smithville. Briarcliff Village's **Piropos** is as chic and elegant as anything at the Plaza, and it's got much more swoon-worthy views. And given the wide expanses of pasture and farm up in these parts, it's no surprise that the Northland is home to some of the Kansas City area's best local producers, including **Shatto Milk, Green Dirt Farm** (sheep's milk cheese and lamb), and **Campo Lindo Farms** (chicken and eggs).

That Missouri River crossing may pose a psychological barrier for those who live south of it, but hey, we're not talking Lewis-

and-Clark-style expeditions here. We have cars, and really, most of these Northland destinations aren't prohibitively distant. Parkville, especially, is much closer and easier to reach than you might think. Even if only for a Saturday afternoon, head up here and do some gourmet exploring.

Foodie Faves

Avalon Cafe, 608 Main St., Weston, MO; (816) 640-2835; www .avaloncafeweston.com. Tue through Sat 11 a.m. to 2 p.m. and 5 to 9 p.m., Sun 10 a.m. to 2 p.m.; $$–$$$. After Parkville, Weston (23 miles north) is the Northland's next most popular small town for an outing. It's got a cute little main street, antiques shops, and tastings at the Pirtle Winery (not reviewed here, www.pirtlewinery.com) as activities. The upscale-American Avalon Cafe is one of the best restaurants here, located in an adorable antebellum home that dates to 1847. Walk in past the lacy front porch and settle into comfy, classy American bistro fare that's become known for its game and unusual meats (though this hardly represents the majority of the offerings). It's just good food that pleases the palate, often utilizing delectable chutneys and compotes, or flavorful wine reductions, to complement the rich flavors of wild boar, lamb chops, or duckling. Return guests rave about the ostrich sirloin (with burgundy and wild berry compote, $24) and the pork tenderloin (pepper-crusted and stuffed with bell peppers and tomato, $20), but it's not all about heavy meat here. Avalon is also a place you can come and get a really satisfying soup-and-salad meal, or bistro comfort food like crab cakes ($11), baked brie ($12.50), pasta ($14.50 to $19), grilled sandwiches ($8 to $9), and steak burgers ($9.50). The wine list includes all the usual suspects from California, France, Italy, Argentina, and Australia, but Avalon also functions as a sort of extension of Pirtle Winery's tasting room, down the street; 7 Pirtle wines are poured by the glass ($4.50 to $5) and 13 are available by the bottle ($16 to $20). Most Pirtle wines are sweet, but try the dry and food-friendly white (Chardonel) and reds (Chambourcin and Norton).

Cafe Cedar, 2 E. 2nd St., Parkville, MO; (816) 505-2233; www.cafe cedar.com. $. Specializing in Mediterranean, Middle-Eastern, and good old American diner fare, Cafe Cedar (named for the national tree of Lebanon) is kind of a sleeper hit in historic Parkville. It's not romantic or picturesque in the way Piropos Grille or Cafe des Amis are, but the spacious and dark restaurant has its own quirky appeal, with murals of the Nile lining the booths and windows painted with Arabic village scenes. (You also walk in past museum-like rooms containing frontier-life and Native American memorabilia, and there's a red vintage car smack in the middle of the place—the ambience is definitely weird.) On the extensive, something-for-everyone-at-all-hours menu, choose from Greek and Middle-Eastern sandwiches like gyro ($7.75), falafel ($7.50), authentic entrees like mahshi (whole Cornish hen stuffed with rice, spices, sauteed beef, pine nuts, $15.95) and maltouf (sauteed beef, spiced rice and sea-sonings wrapped with cabbage leaves), as well as kofta and kebabs ($11.50 to $15.95). On Thursday nights, come for Chef Jehad's mystery appetizer—every week he creates a never-before-served app, which he tests on patrons free of charge in exchange for your honest opinion. However, for the less adventurous, Cedar also has its shorter "American Menu," with renditions of comfort food and kid-friendly fare—you've got to try the Southern American Southern Fried Chicken ($12.95 for four pieces plus sides), which has a light and exceptionally flavorful batter and tender, juicy meat. From Mon through Fri, lunch specials are only $6.25 (choose from one of four entrees plus a side).

Piropos Grille, 1 W. 1st St., Parkville, MO; (816) 741-9800; www .piroposgrille.com. Tues through Thurs 5 to 9 p.m., Fri through Sat 5 to 10 p.m.; $$$. On the hill directly overlooking historic downtown Parkville, Piropos Grille has the most charming restaurant setting in the Kansas City area. It's a romantic refuge, and this original loca-tion of **Piropos** restaurant (which moved to fancier digs at Briarcliff Village a few years ago), definitely has the adored feeling of the owners' "firstborn." Gary and Cristina Worden built the place practi-cally by hand, and there's a lot of love both in the architecture—a lofty split-level chalet with huge windows that take full advantage of the panoramic setting—and in what comes out of the kitchen. The food at Piropos Grille is a touch more casual (and slightly less expensive) than what is served at Piropos in Briarcliff, and instead of focusing strictly on Argentine fare, Piropos Grille's menu features specialties from all over South America, like Venezuelan *arepas* (corn cakes stuffed with black beans, queso fresco, and chicken or beef, $5), and the Caribbean-inspired *pescado caribe* (pan-seared grouper with rice, fried yuca, and mango–black bean salsa, $26). However, Piropos classics like empanadas ($3) and grilled meat entrees ($26 to $30) from the *carnes de parrilla* section of the menu are also available. Two of the best dishes, however, are the Trucha a la Cristina (Cristina's favorite—pan-seared trout with brown butter and almonds, rice, and grilled asparagus $24) and the *pollo al horno* (with mole and chimichurri, $20). Service is outstanding—the warm staff will make you feel like family. Come on Tuesday for the "gauchita" ribeye special, an 8- to 10-ounce steak with *papas fritas* and house-made chimichurri for $18; or on Wednesday, when wines by the bottle are half price. Perched here above Parkville, you can watch trains roll through town, or play a premeal round at the Wordens' minigolf course, directly adjacent. Gazing across to the opposite hill at the floodlit Gothic buildings of Park University, watching the comings and goings of Main Street Parkville below, you could almost be in Europe. I highly recommend Piropos Grille as a memorable date place for couples who can't quite get away for the weekend but want to feel like doing something out of the ordinary. The word *piropo* means a flirtatious compliment paid to a woman—and it kind of sums up Gary and Cristina's love story; the opening of Piropos a decade ago was the ultimate *piropo* that the K.C. businessman and amateur pilot could have given his worldly Argentine wife when she agreed to start a life with him in the Midwest after a seven-year long-distance romance. I can confidently say that any man who takes his lady to Piropos Grille for an evening will have paid her a lovely compliment.

A Picnic in Parkville

The banks of the Missouri River are fairly dismal throughout most of Kansas City, but a shining exception is where the Mighty Mo runs through Parkville. Here, just outside Parkville's charming downtown strip, is **English Landing Park,** a scenic riverside park with groves of big shade trees, recreation facilities, and 3 miles of walking paths. It's all very Midwest idyllic and—if you ignore the disc golf course—can feel like you're stepping back in time 150 years and hanging with Huck, Tom, Lewis, Clark, and the gang—too bad there are no keelboats or paddle wheelers to ride. Picnic tables and shelters aplenty make this park the perfect spot for a self-catered alfresco meal. Stock up on your provisions at **Red X,** the **Parkville Farmers' Market** (held in the park Wed and Sat in summer and fall), or pick up a pie to go from **Stone Canyon Pizza,** in downtown Parkville at 15 Main St.; (816) 746-8686.

Cafe des Amis, 112½ Main St., Parkville, MO; (816) 587-6767; www.cafedesamiskc.com. Tue through Sat 11:30 a.m. to 2:30 p.m. and 5:30 to 10 p.m., Sun noon to 3 p.m. and 5 to 8 p.m.; $$$. Authentic French cuisine in an atmosphere that transports you to Europe for a few hours—in the Northland? *Mais oui!* The sophisticated diners of K.C. have been onto the treasure that is Cafe des Amis for years. First of all, it's run and staffed by actual French people, whose cultural sensibility translates into an eating and drinking venue where a meal effortlessly adopts the pace of a Parisian bistro—where you're encouraged to stay for several hours, relax, and really enjoy the food and wine. The service is warm and knowledgeable, attentive but never rushed. Second, the location is utterly charming: The restaurant is in the heart of historic down-town Parkville, atop an antique shop in a building that dates to the 1840s; to access the restaurant you must climb a steepish exterior wooden staircase (potentially a problem for high heels and certainly for the mobility impaired). The interior dining rooms are cozy and intimate, like someone's apartment in a picturesque French village. It's all very romantic and homey without being cloying or dowdy in any way. The outdoor deck is enveloped in greenery and perched, like the rest of Cafe des Amis, one flight above street level; it's like a French treehouse, with red cafe umbrellas, sparkling white lights. (The al fresco atmosphere here is divine, but not when it's 90 and humid; so if outside seating is your thing, try to go in late spring or early fall, or during that odd string of 80 degree days in July.) Last

but certainly not least, the food: It's superbly executed, traditional French fare. If you're looking for progressive recipes, you might prefer **Le Fou Frog** (in downtown K.C., see p. 15), but for satisfying dishes that'll remind you of (or get you planning) your trip to France, Cafe des Amis is spot-on. Recommended hors d'oeuvre are the pâté maison (house-made pâté with black truffle, served with onion confit and cornichons, $8), and the *moules marinières facon Odile* (mussels steamed in sherry, shallots, herbs, and cream, $10.50). The warm goat-cheese salad ($11.50), with apricot, walnut, and baby greens, is also a favorite. Among the meat entrees, it's hard to go wrong with the duck confit ($28), the decadent quail ($29, stuffed with *foie gras* and black truffle, served with wild mushroom sauce), or the rack of lamb in herbes de Provence ($26). On the *poissons* side, the baked halibut filet ($24.50) in saffron and orange crème fraîche sauce is exquisite. This being a French restaurant, you'll want to save room for dessert—brûlées, souffles, flambés—they're all delicious. Be sure to start your meal with the fruit-garnished Champagne cocktail that your waiter will no doubt suggest, and then pair some lovely wine (most French, lots by the glass) with your meal. If you haven't already dined at Cafe des Amis, plan to do it right away. And then plan to linger.

Justus Drugstore, 106 W. Main St. (3 blocks east of US 169), Smithville, MO; (816) 532-2300; www.drugstorerestaurant.com. Tues through Sat 5:30 p.m. to 1:30 a.m., Sun 5:30 p.m. to midnight; $$$–$$$$. No self-respecting foodie can be in Kansas City for very long without making the trek 20 miles north of downtown to Smithville's very buzzed-about restaurant, Justus Drugstore. Executive Chef, owner, and Smithville native Jonathan Justus opened the restaurant in the building that used to be the family pharmacy. He is the mad professor of Kansas City chefs, the foodiest foodie I have ever met, and he goes to epic lengths to bring out the best in local ingredients in delightfully imaginative dishes. At 2 a.m., using his iPhone GPS for navigation, he and his staff forage for wild honeysuckle that will go into cocktail recipes the following day. Or for berries that will go into the sauce for an American Kobe beef entree. Justus and wife Camille Eklof, co-owner and head server, grow greens on their own land in Smithville, and they do all their butchering—of strictly local meats—in-house. I challenge anyone to find a more truly local locavore program anywhere in the country. But Justus Drugstore isn't just about sustainability—it's about really, really good food and savoring the experience of eating it. From the moment you sit down, servers will tell you that you will be here for a while, and until you've done it, it's hard to imagine that you can have an exciting night out in Smithville, Missouri—that Justus Drugstore can be a whole, big night in itself. But the fact that Justus Drugstore *is* in Smithville at all, and that it's thriving, is part of the excitement. Outside, Smithville is Small Town, USA, complete with a gazebo dedicated to veterans, but inside Justus Drugstore, the atmosphere is urban and fun. The room is not, as you might expect from a locavore joint in a rural town, languid and precious like a Martha Stewart shoot, sun streaming in through antique window panes over a tabletop of weathered wood. Instead, the room is modern and stylish, with clean lines and earth tones that give it an updated 1970s-Scandinavia feel. In the evening, tables are aglow with candlelight and lively conversation, and the restaurant hums with an infectious electricity. Justus Drugstore is also a theater where you watch the adrenaline-filled orchestra of Chef Justus and his staff in the open kitchen. With descriptors like "mulberry/red clover flower vinegar *gastrique*" and "house-brewed root beer braise," the menu can sometimes border on satire of the farm-to-table/forager movement, but most ingredient combinations work to stunning effect. Justus also plays around with the usual suspects of molecular gastronomy—unusual mousses (lemon basil in the Campo Lindo roast chicken entree), citrus gelées, savory ice creams (an arrestingly good blue cheese–black pepper in the Maytag blue cheese salad), foams, and such. But you never feel that substance and taste are sacrificed for fancy-pants showmanship; portions are generous for a restaurant of this caliber, and whatever stylish swagger a dish's presentation may have, there's always sophisticated, satisfying flavor to back it up. Justus, Eklof, and staff make the rounds of the dining room to talk about their approach to food—the nose-to-tail use of animals, the aggressive use of local produce, the rigorous (some might say insane) in-house production of everything from condiments to cured meats to vermouth, and most of all, the relaxed pace at which it is all delivered and enjoyed—with passion that's never preachy. Go to Justus Drugstore if only for the Newman Farms Berkshire Pork 2 Ways entree ($25, usually involves a grilled pork ribeye and a pork shoulder element; seasonal accompaniments vary but may be vermouth, berry, chestnut, barley, shallot, and chard in fall)—this has come to be a signature dish, and it's stupendous. The Farmer's Platter appetizer ($12 or $20) is another house favorite: It comes with wild persimmon seed–spiced rabbit terrine, house-made sausage, house-smoked Berkshire bacon, pickled and grilled vegetables, and bone marrow mousse. Even the salads are works of art; like the Maytag blue cheese with maple-port vinaigrette, pear, blue cheese–black pepper ice cream, arugula, and Missouri black walnut tuile. For each dish, there's a recommended wine pairing (by the half glass, $3.75 to $8; or glass, $7.25 to $15), and the list of wines by the bottle is modern and tight, with about 35 labels. Justus Drugstore has been profiled glowingly in the *New York Times, Food & Wine,* and *Travel & Leisure,* but some Show-Me-State critics haven't been quite as impressed with the reality behind the hype created by that national press. Granted, not every dish is perfect, and to charge these prices at this distance from the city, everything should be perfect. But overall, dining at Justus Drugstore is a fabulously memorable experience, a treat that jolts your taste buds as much as it does your attitude about the words "Kansas City" and "progressive" coexisting, all in a really warm and fun atmosphere.

A note about getting here: The drive to Smithville is straightforward and really not that long. It is exactly 20 minutes on US 169 north once you cross the Missouri River from downtown Kansas City. But for most of us, dining at Justus Drugstore means a drive home of 30 minutes to an hour—something to consider after a lengthy, wine-filled meal. Should you need it, there's a Super 8 motel just outside Smithville.

Piropos, 4141 N. Mulberry Dr. (in Briarcliff Village), Kansas City, MO; (816) 741-3600; www.piroposkc.com. Mon through Thurs 5 to 9 p.m., Fri through Sat 5 to 10 p.m., Sun 4 to 8 p.m.; $$$–$$$$. Piropos may have the distinction of being the only full-service Argentinean restaurant in Kansas City, but it's much more than an international niche filler. It's an elegant, decidedly grown-up destination with warm hospitality, refined food and drink, and some killer views. It's also a magnet for Northland movers and shakers (yes, they exist), who can regularly be seen crowding the bar or conversing over *provoleta asada* and Malbec along the restaurant's south windows. Those windows (and patio), you see, offer the best view of Kansas City's skyline of any restaurant in town. That you can drink the views in along with authentic empanadas (de rigueur for any social occasion back in owner Cristina's hometown of Buenos Aires, and they are phenomenal here) and Argentinean wine just makes the panorama even more special. Piropos is so chic that it makes you forget you're in Kansas City. Chalk it up to cosmopolitan owners Gary and Cristina Worden, who are two of my favorite restaurateurs in Kansas City, and who have managed to infuse their spirited personalities into the atmosphere of Piropos. The Wordens opened the original Piropos a decade ago on the hill in Parkville;

that location has now morphed into **Piropos Grille** (p. 213), which is more casual version of the Piropos concept. The new iteration of Piropos here at Briarcliff Village is bigger, showier, more polished, although Cristina's recipes didn't change much with the move. Argentinean food is about three-fourths European culinary traditions, one-fourth South American flourish. It's classic French, Italian, and Spanish fare, given saucy (but not too spicy) *sabor* by such accoutrements as chimichurri (garlicky green sauce with chopped parsley, cilantro, red pepper, cumin, olive oil, and vinegar) and *aji molido* (a sweet and smoky red pepper condiment). But really, it's not all that far removed from typical Midwestern steakhouse fare, with a lot of grilled meats (the *churrasco* is an Angus ribeye, $36), vegetable sides (garlic mashed potatoes, sautéed mushrooms, grilled asparagus), and seafood (the *parrilla de pescado* is a mix of fresh daily fish, shrimp, and scallops in Argentine lemon-butter sauce, $36). However, I recommend making a meal from the *aperitivos* (appetizers) list, which includes empanadas ($3 each), *calamarettis fritti* (breaded calamari with cilantro pesto aioli and lemon-tomato sauce, $12), *vieyras envueltas en panceta* (applewood-smoked-bacon-wrapped jumbo scallops with corn relish and chipotle aioli, $12), and a mixed gourmet cheese platter ($12 for 2, $16 for 3, $20 for 4). With the average entree price a bit north of $30, Piropos certainly isn't an everyday spot for a full meal, but with an enticing and extended happy hour ($6 for select appetizers, wines, and cocktails, Tues through Thurs 5 to 9 p.m., Fri through Sat 5 to 10 p.m., Sun 4 to 8 p.m. in the bar and on the patio) and vibrant bar scene—and oh those views!—it's a place to put on your regular rotation for small plates and drinks. And if ever you find yourself stuck for an empanada-and-Malbec buddy, give me a call.

The Vineyards, 505 Spring St., Weston, MO; (816) 640-5588; www .thevineyardsrestaurant.com. Wed through Fri 11 a.m. to 2 p.m. and 6 p.m. to 8:30 p.m., Sat 11 a.m. to 2 p.m. and 6 p.m. to 8:30 p.m., Sun 11 a.m. to 7 p.m.; $$$–$$$$. Set in an intimate cottage with white linen tablecloths, purposefully mismatched silver, and fresh cut wildflowers (and candlelight in the evenings), the Vineyards is a charming place with delicious and satisfying eclectic country fare. It's a popular lunch spot for day trippers to Weston (whose attractions are wineries and antique shops), and serves some wonderful sandwiches like the Spanish Pulled Pork (with apple and manchego, $8), and the balsamic marinated mushroom (caramelized red onions, red bell peppers, goat cheese, $9), but it's well worth making the trek up here for dinner, too. The seared duck breast (with balsamic and cherry reduction, $27) is fabulous, as is the braised lamb shank (locally raised at nearby Green Dirt Farm, served with gorgonzola cheese and bacon risotto, $29). Chef Rebecca's inventive seasonal risotto specials, like one with morels in spring, are worth the drive alone. Everything is made from scratch, so sit back and enjoy the wine (a smart and well-edited list includes inspired pairings for all the food they serve) while the kitchen hand-crafts each meal one by one. Due to its location up here in Weston (a good 45 minutes from central KC), the Vineyards may be hovering just off the average KC foodie's radar for now . . . but with Chef Rebecca's brilliant cooking and commitment to locavore practices, this place deserves a lot more attention.

Specialty Stores, Markets & Producers

Green Dirt Farm, 20363 Mount Bethel Rd., Weston, MO; (816) 386-2156; www.greendirtfarm.com. Tours by appointment May through Oct, Wed through Fri and Sun. One of the darlings of the Kansas City farmers' market circuit, Green Dirt Farm produces farmstead sheep's milk cheeses and 100 percent grass-fed lamb. The farmhouse, creamery, and grazing pastures are set in the bluffs that overlook the Missouri River Valley, 40 miles northwest of downtown Kansas City. Green Dirt's award-winning cheeses include Woolly Rind, a Camembert-style cheese; Dirt Lover, a firm and nutty ash-dusted French farmhouse cheese; and Bossa, a washed-rind cheese that you'll find on many a cheese plate in K.C.'s better restaurants. Green Dirt is owned and operated by women, and is certified Animal Welfare Approved for the spacious, open, natural, healthy habitat it provides for its free-roaming sheep. Farm tours are offered from May to Oct by appointment only and cost $8 per person. Tours last about 1 hour and are part nature walk, part food education—you'll stroll the pastures, learn about the farm's grazing regimen and how the animals' diet affect the flavor of the cheese and lamb from season to season, and have a look at the milking parlor and cheese kitchen. Oh, and for that $8 fee, you'd better believe you get to sample several cheeses. Event space in Green Dirt's lovely, Gothic-style barn can be booked for private dinners and cheese tastings. Can't make it up to Weston to visit in person? Green Dirt sells its cheese at several K.C.–area farmers' markets from spring through fall, but the Saturday outdoor markets in Brookside and Parkville are the only places where you can buy Green Dirt's lamb (unless you buy the whole 35-pound animal, from Green Dirt directly, for $250, which includes butchering into custom or standard cuts). Year-round retail locations where Green Dirt cheese is sold include **Cosentino's** Downtown and Brookside markets, the **Better Cheddar, Dean & Deluca,** and the **Cellar Rat.** You can also buy the cheeses online through www.localharvest.org.

Paradise Locker Meats, 405 W. Birch St., Trimble, MO; (816) 370-MEAT; www.paradisemeats.com. Mon through Fri 9 a.m. to 6 p.m., Sat 9 a.m. to 3 p.m. This high-end butcher shop really is paradise for meat lovers. The Fantasma family runs KC's premier processor and purveyor of meats from small, sustainable producers—you'll find Heritage pork breeds like Berkshire and Duroc from local farms; Wagyu beef (raised in Texas); Piedmontese beef (Italian breed, raised in Montana); domestic and New Zealand lamb; buffalo; and tons of gamemeat and exotics from elk to ostrich to wild boar to kangaroo, even alligator and turtle meat. Because of its out-of-the-way location, Paradise ships most of its meat to its customers (and counts several celebrity clients nationwide), but you can also make a trip to their facility and buy your steaks and chops directly from the store. Be sure to call ahead, however, to ensure availability of particular cuts. Paradise is also a wholesaler and provides meat for several of KC's top locavore restaurants, including **Justus Drugstore** in nearby Smithville. See Craig Adcock's recipe for **Wagyu Brisket,** made with meat from Paradise Locker, on p. 270.

Parkville Farmers' Market, English Landing Park, Historic Parkville, MO; (816) 699-9638. Apr through Oct, Sat 7 a.m. to noon; also Wed 2 to 5 p.m. (June through Oct only). The variety of locally produced goods ranges from elk meat to honey, baked goods, eggs and chicken, lamb (from **Green Dirt Farm**), fruit, flowers, and seasonal vegetables. The small-town atmosphere in Parkville is particularly appealing, and the location, within scenic riverside English Landing Park, makes it ideal for a family outing. The market is set up under the shade of a European-style pavilion, complete with picnic tables and hand-washing stations. Just make sure you get there early for the best selection.

Red X, 2401 W. Platte Rd., Riverside, MO; (816) 741-3377; www .riversideredx.com. Mon through Sat 7 a.m. to 10 p.m., Sun 9 a.m. to 9 p.m. On certain Friday nights, when the weird, wonderful, enormous store known as Red X is both doing a wine-tasting and serving fried frog legs (separate events), the parking lot is so packed that

CAMPO LINDO FARMS CHICKEN

The best chicken and eggs in Kansas City come from Campo Lindo Farms (not open to the public) in the rural community of Lathrop, 35 miles north of downtown. You'll see Campo Lindo chicken on the menu of K.C.'s best restaurants, including the American, bluestem, Michael Smith, Justus Drugstore, R Bar, and Room 39. Order a Campo Lindo chicken entree sometime (or buy some raw Campo Lindo meat at one of several area supermarkets—see list at **www.campolindo farms.com**); you'll pay a premium for these free-rangers, but you will absolutely taste the difference: The birds on this small farm have a higher quality of feed, a better quality of life, and a slower, cleaner process of butchering that involves more care and fewer chemicals than at conventional chicken operations.

you'd think the Rolling Stones were performing inside. What is Red X? It's kind of like an independent Wal-Mart, but a whole lot funkier (and usually cheaper)—the ultimate American roadside shopping experience. It's a supermarket, hardware store, liquor depot, toy store, dollar store, humidor, and an antiques museum all mashed into one low-slung emporium off SR 9. Since opening in 1950, it's been destroyed by two floods (1951 and 1993) and a fire (1957), but

Red X kept rebuilding and expanding, and thanks to the incorporation of Riverside as a separate city from Kansas City (which Red X founder E.H. Young lobbied for), Red X has never had to pay K.C.'s high taxes and has thus always been able to offer customers rock-bottom prices. When you walk in, you're almost knocked out by the state-fair-like smell of fried food, which is emanating from Red X's "deli," **Champs Chicken and Fish Too,** where you can get single pieces of fried chicken for about $1.50, or a 96-piece carton of it for $98.99 (call to pre-order the latter). Also on the menu are chicken livers and gizzards ($3.99/pound), battered fish fillets (served with hush puppies, $5.99), sides like breaded okra ($4.99/pound) and crab rangoon (4 for $2.59), and on Friday only, frog legs ($7.99/ pound or $6.99 for the "2 pair" dinner). But what makes Red X such a compelling destination for gourmets around the metro area is its surprisingly robust liquor department. They have a huge selection of wine, beer, and spirits at amazing prices, with lots of labels you will not find anywhere else in K.C. (If you need a bunch of booze for a wedding reception or other big party, definitely give Red X a call.) They can also special order just about anything that is legally available in the United States. In quintessential Red X fashion, the liquor section is mere feet from the plumbing aisles, so you can pick up a nice Napa Cab while also shopping for toilet tank parts.

Shatto Milk Company, 9406 N. Hwy. 33, Osborn, MO; (816) 930-3862; www.shattomilk.com. Tours offered Tues through Sat mornings, by appointment. The black-and-white Holstein cows of Shatto Milk Company are a pampered bunch of bovines. They graze in idyllic green pastures, they breathe the fresh air of the rural Missouri River Valley, they have never even heard of growth hormones, and their milk is processed with the utmost care and respect. The Shatto dairy farm is a small, family-run operation (owner Leroy Shatto delivers most of the milk himself) that believes in quality, freshness (Shatto bottles can be on store refrigerator shelves in as little as 12 hours after cows are milked), and limiting human interference as much as possible. The result is milk that is sweeter, purer, and just noticeably better than your regular supermarket milk. Shatto milk is sold strictly in glass bottles; this is an environmentally friendly practice as well as one that ensures better taste, as glass keeps milk colder than paper or plastic and imparts no foreign odors. Shatto, which is pronounced like "chateau" (not "shadow"), also does ice cream, cheese, and butter—the most spectacular butter on Earth—which have more limited distribution but can be found at higher-end food markets in town. You'll also see Shatto products show up in various foodie restaurants like **Blanc Burgers + Bottles** (the beer-battered cheese curds are a popular appetizer), **Starker's** (the curds are inside a burger also made with brown sugar-candied bacon), **Justus Drugstore** (the table butter is Shatto's), and others. The farm, which is about an hour's drive north from central Kansas City, welcomes visitors to tour the facility (by appointment Tues through Sat, $5, 1½ hours including tasting). While there, you can buy dairy products directly from the source, and simply hang out and enjoy the countryside that these 120 Holsteins (each producing

6 to 7 gallons a day) call home. During tours of this remarkably compact dairy operation, visitors get a very transparent look at every facet of the process, from seeing the bottling machinery and the bottle washer (it's no bigger than your family car and handles all the Shatto bottles in the entire K.C. area) in action, to learning how chocolate, strawberry, banana, orange, and root beer milks get their flavor, or how reduced-fat milk is skimmed, and watching cows being milked or even milking one yourself (if you get there early enough in the morning—milking is usually completed by 10 or 11 a.m.). There are always baby calves that kids can pet, too, and sometimes bottle feed. Tour participants also get to taste, in Dixie-cup portions, all of Shatto's flavored milks. In May 2011, Shatto held the grand opening of its newly expanded visitor areas, most exciting of which is a brand-new cheese-making facility. "Cheesemaker for a Day" courses may be offered to the public soon—check the website or call for more information.

Wines by Jennifer, 405 Main St. (between 4th and 5th Streets), Parkville, MO; (816) 505-9463; www.winesbyjennifer.com. Tues through Sat noon to 8 p.m. They tell me that nothing ever gets broken here, but I find that hard to believe. Wine glasses, bottles, ankles, all seem vulnerable in this cozy and tightly merchandised space in which copious amounts of wine flow. Wines by Jennifer is a converted 3-story cottage in which each room is dedicated to a different wine-growing country or region. While it's more than just a wine shop, it's not a full-fledged wine bar, either. Think of it as a wine-themed friend's house where acquaintances and strangers alike get together in little sitting areas to indulge in a bit o' the vine. In this environment, it doesn't take long for patrons to become bosom buddies. In warm weather, patrons spill out to the front porch and exterior patios—a delightful way to drink in a mild Missouri evening. The $12 "tasting," which includes samples of 3 whites and 3 reds, can be a tempting way to get to know the shop, but be aware that the pours are miniscule (less than "flight" size). If you really want to get your wine on, you're probably better off uncorking a bottle in one of the sitting areas. WBJ has interesting, high-quality wines, but because of the small spaces here, selection is limited. Most bottles are $15 and up—so perhaps don't shop here for your everyday vino needs (for that, there's Red X)—but when you visit Wines by Jennifer as a social venue, those bottle prices are actually quite a bargain. They also sell cheese, meats, and crackers to go with your imbibing session. Tip: The shop closes at 8 p.m., so it's fun to stop by Wines by Jennifer as an aperitivo destination before dinner at **Piropos Grille** or **Cafe des Amis.**

The Kansas Side: Johnson County

When people talk about "the Kansas Side" of metropolitan Kansas City, they're generally referring to the suburban sprawl of Johnson County, to the west and south of central K.C. This is the province of infinite beige subdivisions, upscale shopping centers, and cookie-cutter strip malls anchored by one giant mart or another. You might think such a place would translate to a bland food scene—which it is, to some extent: There are an awful lot of national-chain sports bars and grills here. But Johnson County, including the cities of Overland Park, Leawood, Prairie Village, and Lenexa, is also the most affluent part of greater Kansas City, with a ton of residents who are knowledgeable and curious about food, who care about high-quality ingredients, and who have proven to be an excellent customer base for some of K.C.'s most interesting markets and restaurants. Add to that a steady flow of business travelers and conventioneers passing through Overland Park's corporate district, and you've got plenty of

support for what is actually a surprisingly varied and sophis
gastronomic landscape.

Downtown foodies may hate to admit it, but the Kansas 'burbs
have even the Crossroads and Midtown beat when it comes to
gourmet markets and specialty stores—after all, the Midwest's
only **Dean & Deluca** is in Leawood, and K.C.'s only full-size **Whole
Foods** is in Overland Park. Also hidden among the vanilla housing
developments and big-box stores of Johnson County is the metro
area's highest concentration of international food markets, stocking
all kinds of exotic staples for the sizable Asian, Indian, and Middle
Eastern populations that have settled here. So, the next time you're
shopping at one of the myriad SuperTargets out here, visit an Indian
grocery or a Thai takeout while you're at it, and see for yourself the
delightful multicultural color behind all that beige.

Note that the few Kansas City, Kansas (Wyandotte County) food
businesses listed in this book are not in this chapter: Instead, they
appear within the chapter for the Kansas City, Missouri, neighborhood closest to them. For instance, Krizman's House of Sausage in
the Strawberry Hill district of K.C.K is listed in the West Bottoms
chapter (p. 54); and Oklahoma Joe's BBQ and Werner's Specialty
Foods are in the Plaza & Around chapter (pp. 146 and 156).

A logistical note: This chapter is by far the most spread out
"neighborhood" in this book, and you really will need to know
where to look to find the gems dispersed among the sprawling suburbs. Also, because Johnson County shopping centers can look so
identical (and be a pain to drive in and out of), double-check the
addresses and location details we've given (e.g., "southwest corner

icated

oodie Faves

Bangkok Pavilion, 7249 W. 97th St., Overland Park; (913) 341-3005. Mon through Thurs and Sun 11 a.m. to 9 p.m., Fri and Sat 11 a.m. to 10 p.m.; $–$$. During the week, it's a regular Thai restaurant, serving tasty but semi-Americanized dishes to the Asian-craving people of Johnson County. What many of those diners may not know, however, is that on the weekends (Sat and Sun from 11 a.m. to 2 p.m.), Bangkok Pavilion transforms into a buffet of truly authentic Thai dishes that draw the discerning palates of real southeast-Asian people from the entire Metro area. Standout items are the green papaya salad (done in both the Thai and Laotian styles), mushroom laab, beef ball noodle soup, sticky rice, and a plethora of seafood recipes like crispy fish with chili sauce.

El Porton Cafe, 4671 Indian Creek Pkwy. (106th St. and Roe), Overland Park; (913) 381-8060; www.elportoncafe.com. Tues through Sun 11 a.m. to 3 p.m., Wed through Sat also 5 p.m. to 9 p.m.; $$. If you like or are interested in learning more about South American food, seek this one out! El Porton is tucked away in the sleepy beige strip mall (the same one as Brobeck's) across from Suburban Lawn & Garden. Since opening here in 2010, Venezuelan-born KC restaurant veteran Jose Garcia has been refining his menu of South American and Caribbean food to focus on flavorful, authentic recipes that are hard to find elsewhere in the KC Metro Area. If you've never had one before, try one of the *arepas* (typical Venezuelan "hot pocket"-style sandwich made with white corn flour and stuffed with various combinations of meat, cheese, and vegetables). I am partial to the *de pabellon* (shredded beef, black beans, sweet plantains, aged cheese) and the *de guasacaca* (Venezuelan-style guacamole with queso fresco, but there are simpler *arepa* filling options like shredded chicken or beef. El Porton also has baguette sandwiches like the *pernil* (slow roasted pork in mojo with sofrito aioli) or the cubano, and entrees like *pollo adobado* (adobo-rubbed grilled chicken, pork hash, and *carne asada*, all served with rice, beans, and plantains. There is a lot of love coming out of this kitchen, so when possible, sit at the bar tables that face the cooking line, strike up a conversation with the people making the food, and go with whatever they recommend. But don't miss the yuca fries as an appetizer or side, and if you've got room for dessert, the tres leches cake is the best of the *postres* on offer. Note that El Porton does not serve alcohol, but you may BYO wine and beer, no corkage fee.

Mr. Gyros Greek Food & Pastry, 8234 Metcalf Ave., Overland Park; (913) 642-7500; www.mrgyroskc.com. Also at 8575 W. 135th St., Overland Park; (913) 851-7700. Mon through Sat 11 a.m. to 9 p.m.; $.

The proud neoclassical building, with columned facade resting atop a grassy knoll, could be that of a financial advisor's office. Look closely, however, and the Greek-key pattern running around the stucco exterior, along with the words "Mr. Gyros" etched into the stucco in an ancient-worlds font, let you know you're into something more interesting than mutual funds. Order your meal from the immaculate counter up front, where your tray will be ready seconds later, then find a table in the Greek-themed dining room and sink your teeth in. The gyros here are served deconstructed—with meat, pita, and tzatziki for you to assemble and dress as you wish. The meat is marvelously moist and tender but never greasy, delivering a flavorful bouquet of spices with a bit of kick. Portions are super generous—you won't run out of pita—and you can get out of here for less than what you'd pay for a fast-food combo meal. (Add an order of baklava for dessert, and you might go slightly over, however.) Even though this is a self-service joint, the dining room plays a role in the overall appeal of Mr. Gyros: With piped-in bouzouki music acting as soundtrack for the Greek-tourism video being looped on two flat screens, and replicas of ancient Greek vases, portrait busts of gods, and philosophers dotted throughout, the homage-to-Hellas touches are very endearing.

One Bite Japanese Grill, 8602 W. 133rd St., Overland Park; (913) 897-9388; www.onebitegrill.com. Tues through Sat 11 a.m. to 2:30 p.m. and 4:30 to 9:30 p.m.; Sun 11 a.m. to 2:30 p.m. and 4:30 to 8:30 p.m.; $$. If you spend a lot of time browsing the condiments and marinades section at the supermarket, chances are you've already come across One Bite, whose specialty sauces—with their sleek and eye-catching Japanese-pop labels—are sold in many area food stores. The dine-in One Bite experience is limited to this narrow, diner-style restaurant, which evokes the Peach Pit by way of . . . a Shinkansen train car, with just a handful of booths and bar stools. (Its location, deep within the newer developments of Johnson County, is in a secondary strip center off 135th and Antioch.) Most Kansas Citians equate "Japanese" either with sushi restaurants or teppanyaki communal griddle steakhouses (where you become a hapless sea lion that must catch flying shrimp in its mouth). Both types of eatery abound in KC, but One Bite is a different animal. There are no California rolls, no sashimi, no onion volcanoes. Think of One Bite as Japanese tapas, with a menu of mostly smaller plates meant to evoke something akin to Japanese street food, which, if not necessarily 100% authentic, at least seems more exotic. Most importantly, it's delicious. One Bite is especially distinctive for its *okonomi-yaki* ("grill what you like," from $8.95 including gyoza and house salad), a sort of Japanese pancake, born from the culinary traditions of Osaka and Hiroshima, whose batter is filled with your choice of meat or veggies and topped with a fried egg and either crispy noodles or fish flakes and drizzled with One Bite's fabulous sauces. *Okonomi-yaki* isn't a dainty dish: It's Japanese comfort food, and it'll fill your belly. Other dishes that get raves and return customers are *tonkatsu* (fried pork cutlet with plum sauce and cabbage, from $9.95), the best-selling Drunk'n Steak (skewered tender filet marinated in plum wine, with creamy corn salad, $13.99, dinner only), the Age Gorogoro appetizer (edamame and crispy tofu cubes with OB's Mogu Mogu and Motto dipping sauces, $7.50), and seaweed salad (with crispy noodles, $5.75). Wednesday is authentic Japanese Cuisine Night. With its sleek look and creative menu, One Bite definitely seems like the kind of place that should be downtown, or at least somewhere slightly hipper in the Metro Area rather than behind a Golf Galaxy deep in Johnson County. Late lunchers: Note that One Bite closes between 2:30 p.m. and 4:30 p.m.

Paradise India, 7119 W. 135th St. (southwest corner of 135th and Metcalf), Overland Park; (913) 814-0177; www.kcparadiseindia .com. Mon, Wed through Fri 11 a.m. to 2:30 p.m. and 5 to 9:30 p.m., Sat through Sun noon to 3 p.m. and 5 to 9:30 p.m. Closed Tues; $$. Everyone who walks into the K.C. area's most elegant Indian restaurant is greeted with a warm and reverent "Namaste" worthy of royalty. That respectful salutation sets the tone for any dining experience; Paradise takes great care to provide customers with a healthful meal by making everything from scratch, with only fresh ingredients, which means a slightly slower kitchen, but the delicious food is worth it. The samosas are plump perfection, the tandoor dishes expertly seasoned, and the curries velvety in texture and exploding with rich flavor. Given its anonymous location, in a spotless strip mall anchored by Staples, Paradise does its best with decor, making it a viable spot for a (somewhat) special occasion:

The softly lit dining room is divided into two levels, the upper dais area separated from the buffet by what could be, with some imagination, hitching posts for elephants. (Prefer alfresco? A few patio tables offer views of the T-Mobile store across 135th Street.) A very comprehensive menu of Mughlai (royal), Punjabi, Malabar, Madras, Hyderabadi, and southern Indian dishes makes 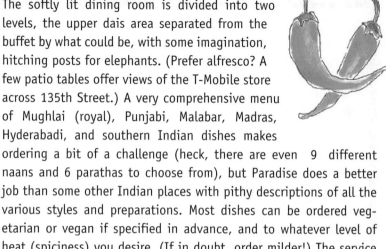 ordering a bit of a challenge (heck, there are even 9 different naans and 6 parathas to choose from), but Paradise does a better job than some other Indian places with pithy descriptions of all the various styles and preparations. Most dishes can be ordered vegetarian or vegan if specified in advance, and to whatever level of heat (spiciness) you desire. (If in doubt, order milder!) The service here cannot be beat, and chances are you'll hear the owner's earnest philosophy—fresh, healthy, we-are-here-for-our-customers—firsthand at some point during the meal.

SPIN! Neapolitan Pizza, 6541 W. 119th St., between Glenwood and Lamar, Overland Park; (913) 451-7746; www.spinpizza.com. Primary location reviewed in Plaza & Around chapter, p. 144.

Trezo Vino, 11570 Ash St. (Park Place, 115th and Nall), Leawood; (913) 327-8466; www.kctrezovino.com. Mon through Thurs 11:30 a.m. to 11 p.m., Fri through Sat 11:30 a.m. to midnight, Sun 3 to 9 p.m.; $$–$$$. Serving sharable contemporary American fare in a buzzy bistro setting, Trezo Vino is a bright light in Park Place, the

Go West: Expansion to the 'Burbs

A whole slew of Kansas City's most successful local food businesses, from independent pizzerias to BBQ places and confectioners, have satellite locations in suburban Johnson County. While I don't want to see any of these places turn into full-fledged chains, it's certainly convenient that they've brought their delicious offerings closer to the denizens of the 'burbs, many of whom are die-hard foodies but whose schedules make frequent treks to midtown or downtown K.C. unrealistic. The following is a short list of Kansas-side incarnations of restaurants and specialty shops that are reviewed elsewhere in this book in their "mothership" locations.

Andre's Confiserie Suisse, 4929 W. 119th St., at Metcalf Avenue, Overland Park; (913) 498-3440. Primary location reviewed in Plaza & Around chapter, p. 151.

Avenues Bistro, 10681 Mission Rd. (Mission Farms), Leawood; (913) 381-5678. Primary location reviewed in Brookside and Waldo chapter, p. 161.

Blanc Burgers + Bottles, 10583 Mission Rd., Leawood; (913) 381-4500; www.blancburgers.com. Primary location reviewed in Plaza & Around chapter, p. 131.

Bo Lings, 9055 Metcalf Ave., Overland Park; (913) 341-1718; also 7105 W. 135th St., Overland Park; (913) 239-8188; www.bolings .com. Primary location reviewed in Downtown chapter, p. 3.

Fiorella's Jack Stack BBQ, 9520 Metcalf Ave., Overland Park; (913) 385-7427; www.jackstackbbq.com. Primary locations reviewed in Crossroads chapter, p. 73, and South Kansas City chapter, p. 195.

Gates & Sons Bar-B-Q, 2001 W. 103rd Terrace, Leawood; (913) 383-1752; www.gatesbbq.com. Primary location reviewed in Downtown chapter, p. 11.

Glacé Artisan Ice Cream, opened summer 2011 at Leawood's One Nineteen shopping center (www.glaceicecream .com). No phone available at presstime. Primary location reviewed in Plaza & Around chapter, p. 154.

Oklahoma Joe's BBQ, 11950 S. Strang Line Rd., Olathe; (913) 782-6858; www .oklahomajoesbbq.com. Primary location reviewed in Plaza & Around chapter, p. 146.

Room 39, 10561 Mission Rd., Leawood; (913) 648-7639; www.rm39.com. Primary location reviewed in Midtown chapter, p. 100.

pseudo-urban eat-shop-live enclave that opened in 2009 opposite Town Center Mall. Certainly, with 45 wines available by the glass and 100 by the bottle, the vino part of the name is a strong suit, but this is way more than a wine bar. Foodies can also swoon over the robust menu of European-inflected and often decadent New American cuisine, as well as entree salads and wine bar standards like bruschetta and charcuterie. A lengthy list of "to share" plates (like tapas on steroids, most $12 to $18) comprises the bulk of the menu and includes a bit of everything from around the globe: crab and shrimp margarita ceviche ($12), gnocchi with fontina and truffle oil ($8), grilled lamb 2 ways ($26), even a bit of fusion flair in the ahi tuna tacos ($15). The airy bistro, with comfy and masculine, 1930s-meets-the-21st-century design inside and a congenial patio facing the W Hotel (yes, Leawood has arrived!) outside, has an upbeat energy to it, whether it's for midweek lunches or weekend nights out (the bar scene is big here and the kitchen stays open until midnight on Fri and Sat). This may be Johnson County's best spot for a classy, vibrant happy hour, a first date, or a girls' night out . . . in the suburbs.

Wai Wai, 8531 W. 135th St. (southeast corner of 135th and Antioch), Overland Park; (913) 402-THAI (8424); http://waiwai thaikc.com. Mon through Thurs 11 a.m. to 9 p.m., Fri through Sat

11 a.m. to 10 p.m.; $. If only it were closer to my house, I would get take-out dinners from this super-tasty Thai cafeteria in south Overland Park at least once a week. Started as an "express" version of the locally owned **Thai House** restaurant group (whose Westport location is reviewed on p. 191), stylish and immaculate Wai Wai offers huge portions of quick, made-to-order noodles, curries, and stir-fries. And in terms of both flavor and value, the student has surpassed the master. You won't find a better pad thai anywhere in town, and the entrees ($7.95 to $9.95 depending on your protein) are big enough to feed 2 hungry adults. However, you'll want to order your own dish so you can have leftovers the next day. Appetizers, filling salads (try the mint beef, $7.95) and hearty soups (like galanga chicken, with coconut milk, lemongrass, and Kaffir lime, $3.95) are also available. While a lot of their business is takeout for the Thai lovers of Overland Park, you can also sit down and eat in Wai Wai's casual dining room. There's no table service, but the sleek red-and-black decor is several cuts above your average fast food.

Old-Guard K.C.

Brobecks Barbeque, 4615 Indian Creek Pkwy. (106th St. and Roe), Overland Park; (913) 901-9700; www.brobecksbbq.com. Tues through Sat 11 a.m. to 9 p.m.; $$. Though it has only been open since 2007, Brobecks brings nearly thirty years of experience smoking meats and is Johnson County's best bet for down-home BBQ done right. Expect no frills or even any country atmosphere in the decor, but the dining room is comfy and the waitstaff couldn't be friendlier, and Brobecks delivers on superbly smoked, succulent meats that rank right up there with more famous K.C. barbecue institutions. The meat here is served dry (that is, without sauce—it has nothing to do with the juiciness or tenderness of the meat) because founder Doug Brobeck firmly believes that barbecued meat should be good enough to eat on its own, and should not have to be smothered in sauce to be palatable. (He does, however, dry rub his meats before cooking with a secret blend of herbs and spices.) But if you, like me, love to smother your meats in sauce anyway, you can do so with one of several different national and local brands (Gates, Arthur Bryant's, and K.C. Masterpiece) lined up in plastic pump containers at the front of the restaurant; Brobecks' 2 house sauces (a tomato-based K.C.–style and a sweet-mustard Carolina-style sauce, my personal fave) are also on every table. The pulled pork is a top seller here, while the combo platter ($11.95 for 3 ribs, sausage, and 1 sliced meat) is a great way to sample a bit of every-thing. And while all those smoked meat platters are well and good, it's Brobecks ham salad that really is to die for—the secret recipe includes ham, relish, mayo, and cinnamon . . . and that's about all we could wrestle out of him. Doug Brobeck could probably take everything off the menu *but* the ham salad and stay in business.

Cafe Provence, 3936 W. 69th Terrace (at Mission Rd.); (913) 384-5998; www.kcconcept.com/cafeprovence/. Mon through Sat 11 a.m to 10 p.m.; $$$. Hidden in the labyrinth of attractive but anonymous-looking merchants of the Prairie Village Shops is this French gem with gracious service, charming ambience, and classic French cuisine that's always reliable and often excellent. Cafe Provence was opened by the Quillec family a decade ago and maintains a warm atmosphere and high quality in its authentic bistro fare. At lunch, you can't go wrong with lighter options like *soupe à l'oignon* (French onion soup with bacon and gruyere, $8), *salade au poulpe* (warm octopus, arugula, fennel, and garlic chili vinaigrette, $15), *salade de poulet au curry* (curried chicken salad with grapes, shredded coconut, walnuts, and Bibb lettuce, $13), or the quiche of the day ($12). At dinner, try something a bit more substantial, like the *fletan Phillippe* (Alaskan halibut with truffle butter, potatoes, peas, and carrot jus, $32) or the seasonal *poulet aux Morilles* (Amish raised chicken breast with asparagus, potatoes, and Morel mushroom cream sauce, $27). While I tend to think of this as more of a special-treat lunch place, it's definitely a viable evening option (when the crowd definitely skews older) and is especially captivating on a warm night, when you can eat all this sumptuous fare on the sidewalk tables while sipping a nice Côtes du Rhône. The wine cellar, it should be mentioned, is surprisingly deep (mostly French, rounded out by California and Oregon) for a place this cozy and neighborhoody, and there are quite a few selections of whites, reds, rose,

and bubbly by the glass. On that note, feel free to drop by Provence just for drinks or dessert. The various crepes, gateaux, mousses, and tartes (all $7 to $8) alone are worth the trip.

Story, 3931 W. 69th Terrace (at Mission Rd.), Prairie Village; (913) 236-9955. Mon through Fri 11 a.m. to 10 p.m., Sat and Sun 10 a.m. to 10 p.m.; $$$. The latest addition to the fine dining scene in Kansas City is, believe it or not, in the Kansas-side burg of Prairie Village. Sleek and modern Story, which opened in May 2011, is the first proprietary restaurant for Chef Carl Thorne-Thomsen, who previously held chef-de-cuisine posts at Michael Smith, Extra Virgin, and 40 Sardines. His food is upscale New American, with a strong focus on really special, carefully sourced ingredients ("every ingredient has a story," says Thorne-Smith, hence the restaurant's name), exceptional seafood, and seasonal produce. All of the bread—batard, focaccia—is made in-house. Among the cold appetizers, the tuna tartare (American sturgeon caviar, fingerling chips, $14) and the ceviche (North Atlantic fluke, celery, pine nuts, cilantro, and Lucero Arbequina extra virgin olive oil, $12) are divine; hot apps include the smoked duck empanadas (with black beans, avocado puree, and jicama for crunch, $10) and the early-favorite fried soft shell crab, with tomatoes, cucumbers, and pancetta mayo, $12. The entree side of the menu features specialty seafood dishes like golden tilefish (crab fritter, english peas, and prosciutto broth, $27), as well as lamb, duck, and beef mains. At lunch, try the pork sandwich (confit, bacon, braised chard, ricotta, and BBQ sauce). From 2 to 5 p.m., a midday menu offers small plates like a cheese sampler with honey and fresh fruit ($12), or fried meatballs with roasted mole ($7). Every dish is as beautiful to look at as it is to taste: Story pays a lot of attention to visual aesthetics. The strikingly contemporary, crisp, and clean decor features gorgeous acrylic panels printed with photographs of birch trees by Ray K. Metzker (an acclaimed pho-tographer who has works on permanent col-lection at MOMA in New York, who recently had a show at the Nelson-Atkins Museum, and who happens to be chef Thorne-Thomsen's uncle) and faux-marble panels (also acrylic) forming a sort of dramatic drop ceiling. The vibe is completed by black tables and metallic accents, and waitstaff and hostesses rigorously clad in black, but Story man-ages to combine its stylish looks with warmth and conviviality: It's the kind of place where you share laughs with your server and end up asking nearby diners what that appetizer is or what wine they're drinking. Speaking of which, the wine list is beautifully restrained yet comprehensive, with selections from unique, small-production vineyards, and some wonderful choices by the glass ($7 to $14). Story is tucked into the quaint shopping center known as the Village (and with immediate neighbors like the Better Cheddar and Cafe Provence, this corner of the Village has become a foodie force). An ample patio, with its own miniature bar, is a boon in mild weather. (Before embarking on his second career in the food industry, Chef Thorne-Thomsen was a writer who spent more time cooking and thinking about food than writing. Hmm, sounds familiar.)

The Clocktower Bakery & Cafe, 7911 Santa Fe Dr., Overland Park; (913) 948-9559; www.clocktowerbakery.com. Mon through Sat 6:30 a.m. to 6 p.m. If you've ever wondered how a croissant, cinnamon roll, or challah bread is made, come on down to the Clocktower: All operations of this cherished downtown Overland Park bakery are in full view, and the jolly staff are more than happy to give you a play-by-play of what they're doing. On farmers' market mornings (Wed and Sat from May to Oct), the place does a brisk business selling pastries, scones, muffins (including the best-selling cinnamon sugar variety), breakfast pizzas, and coffee from K.C.'s own the **Roasterie,** but Johnson Country bread aficionados also know to stop in here for fresh handmade baguettes, dinner rolls, multigrain or wheat loaves, or their version of *fougasse* (an addictive and fun-to-pull-apart knot of flat baguette dough). If you're here around lunchtime, you must try the lamb and goat cheese pizza with lemon-rosemary crust. The Clocktower excels at cupcakes, with chocolate, red velvet, carrot, vanilla, and lemon dough and myriad frosting options, all laid on with pastry bag and tip in exquisite floral patterns. For dinner parties and holidays, you can special order anything in advance.

Culinary Center of Kansas City, 7920 Santa Fe Dr., Overland Park; (913) 341-4455; www.kcculinary.com. Part cooking school, part kitchen tools store, part restaurant, and part gourmet freezer case, the Culinary Center of K.C. is an ambitious enterprise staffed by a team of passionate foodies. The antique building that houses the center has 2 kitchen-classrooms where a kaleido- scopic range of courses—like "3-Day Cooking Basics," "Asian Party Fare," "Intensive on Autumn Vegetables," even Junior Chefs pro- grams for kids and less high-brow subjects like "Comfort Food for Weight Watchers" and "Secrets to Crockpot Cookery"—are taught daily (average fee $50 to $150 per ses- 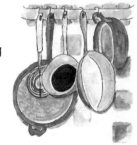 sion) by chefs and food experts from all over K.C. And, since this is the Midwest, the decidedly unsnobby Culinary Center also has a BBQ Institute ("The Art of Smokology") and beer-making curricula ("Home Brew Boot Camp"). On Tues from 11:30 a.m. to 1:30 p.m., anyone can show up for their weekly "Staff Lunch," when the menu is whatever the chefs feel like making that day; $12 includes drink and dessert. The front of the house is a boutique where you can browse nifty kitchen gadgets and pick up food from their "Dinners on Demand" program (the freezer is always stocked with a dozen or so different bake-and-serve entrees that they prepare in-house). The Culinary Center also organizes team-building cooking events and private cooking parties that can be tailored to any group size, experience level, and cuisine preference.

Dean & Deluca, 4700 W. 119th St. (at Roe, in southeast end of Town Center shopping area), Leawood; (913) 498-3131; www.dean deluca.com. Daily 10 a.m. to 8 p.m. As much as I love this store and its shelves full of epicurean ecstasy (and I do mean the hard stuff), Dean & Deluca takes the sport out of food shopping. It brings the most delectable cremas of Tuscany, the most prized teas of China, the best flavors from all over the globe, to one place—in the middle of Leawood. (And it makes a serious dent in your wallet while doing so; the tiniest packages of anything here seem to cost upward of $10.) Johnson County should be proud: Leawood's D&D is the best laid-out and merchandised store I've seen in this mini-chain that started in New York's Soho. Each steel rack is a tantalizing lineup of gourmet goodies in the prettiest packaging. Where else in this town can you find black truffle BBQ sauce, canned *ventresca* (tuna belly), an entire shelf devoted to demi-glace, or a $170 bottle of balsamic vinegar? As haute and exclusive as it all seems, not everything is imported; in fact, Dean & Deluca does a great job of sourcing its products locally whenever possible, and you'll find K.C.'s own chocolatier **Christopher Elbow,** cupcake mavens Three Women and an Oven, **Jude's Rum Cake,** and others represented here. A central deli case has all kinds of unusual charcuterie and olives, while another refrigerator case displays prepared cold dishes like chicken and grape salad with fried sage and toasted walnuts. D&D also has a grill serving upscale burgers and truffle fries, a gourmet salad and sandwich bar, a coffee bar, and bread bakery. As pricey as this place can get, it's always busy—proof positive that food lovers are alive and well in Kansas!

European Delights, 8841 W. 95th St. (southwest corner of Antioch and 95th Street), Overland Park; (913) 385-3876; www .europeandelightskc.com. Mon through Sat 10 a.m. to 8 p.m., Sun 10 a.m. to 6 p.m. Wrangle your closest Russian or Polish friend to help you make sense of the wares on offer at K.C.'s only north-central European market. Otherwise, the kindly owner, Oleg, will patiently answer any questions you have about halvah and the uses of various kinds of rusk. Personally, I skip all that, as well as the colorful and mind-boggling bins of bulk candy and head straight for the deli counter and Moscow salami (where I can also pick up caviar, cheese, and Russian dark chocolate). Being in this shop really is like going to the old country: You'll hear foreign languages both in the conversations between regular customers and staff and in the TV program playing in the background, usually a lurid "Russian Idol" type of reality show.

India Emporium, 10458 Metcalf Ave. (south side of the Furniture Deal$ strip mall), Overland Park; (913) 642-1161. They had me at the colorful window display of Bollywood movie posters, shiny cartons of curry mixes stacked 10 high, and a placard touting the "Easy Washing Personal Bidet." This is the best-stocked Indian market in the metropolitan area, selling all kinds of raw beans and flours, fresh produce, halal meats (drawing patrons from K.C.'s Islamic community), sauce mixes, spices, heat-and-serve packets of Indian standards like *palak paneer,* and in the freezer case, samosas,

Indian Ocean fish, even poppin' fresh Pillsbury naan (which comes to Kansas by way of General Mills' Mumbai office). An annex room sells household and personal care items, including hookahs and yes, bidets.

Jude's Rum Cake; (913) 526-6708; www.judesrumcake.com. Never had a rum cake before? Don't know what one is? I don't care. One taste of Jude's and you'll wonder how you ever lived without them. Loaded up with Mississippi pecans and drenched in a pirate-worthy amount of Barbancourt Haitian rum, Jude's Rum Cake is an insanely decadent treat. Owner, baker, and head dishwasher Craig Adcock used to work at Sprint, until massive layoffs gave him time to take stock of what he actually loved to do, which has always been food and drink. Named for Adcock's mother-in-law, Jude's Rum Cake is a secret recipe mastered following a family trip to Panama, and it's without a doubt one of the top 10 desserts I've ever had in my life. Rum cakes are common in the Caribbean, where they're a traditional holiday treat, but to have them coming out of a small-business kitchen in Kansas City is quite some good foodie fortune. Jude's has earned gushing reviews not only from local luminaries (like Jasper Mirabile of **Jasper's Restaurant,** and *KC Magazine*) but from national food glossy *Gourmet,* which has called the cakes "absolutely celestial." David Rosengarten has called them "the greatest rum cake I have ever tasted . . . the golden mean that gets everything right." Amen. For now, you can order the cakes online or by phone with Adcock directly, and they've recently been picked up by gourmet food boutique **Dean & Deluca,** which sells the cakes in its Leawood store (p. 250). Sizes range from two-bite "teaser" cakes ($12 for 5) to the large ring ($45 for about 16 large slices). Whenever possible, I recommend picking up the freshly baked cakes directly from Adcock's kitchen in old town Lenexa (call to make arrangements, as it's not normally open to the public). With any luck, Jude's Rum Cake will have its own retail venue sometime soon. Then you can come and shoot the breeze with Adcock, which is almost as much fun as devouring one of his cakes.

Louisburg Cider Mill, 14730 Hwy 68 (off MO 69), Louisburg, KS; (913) 837-2143; www.louisburgcidermill.com. Daily 9 a.m. to 4 p.m. Nothing says "fall in Kansas City" like the obligatory trek down to Louisburg (about 20 miles south of I-435 along MO) for homestyle apple cider, cider donuts, pumpkin patchin', corn mazin', and shopping at the country store. In business since 1977, the Louisburg Cider Mill is centered around a 120-year-old red hay barn (fully looking the part of old-fashioned, rural Kansas) where apples are pressed to make this operation's hallmark beverage—heavenly, 100% pure apple cider. The cider here is made using methods that date back 2,000 years: basically, apples (mostly from the Missouri River valley north of St. Joseph) are ground into a pulp, which is then pressed through mesh cloths to yield the juice that becomes Louisburg apple cider. After pressing, the cider is not filtered, which distinguishes it from apple juice and which gives it its cloudy composition and tangier taste than regular apple juice. (Louisburg's cider is pasteurized before bottling, however.) They also make their own root beer, called Lost Trail. The mill offers tours (Sept through Oct only, Mon through Fri 10 a.m. to 3 p.m., $3) which include observation of apples being unloaded and pressed and cider being bottled, as well as samples of cider and cider doughnuts. The doughnuts are made right in the cider mill's country store and let me tell you, there is nothing better on a chilly fall day. Also sold in the country store are some great home-style fruit butters, preserves, spreads, and jellies, as well as sauces and condiments made by local boutique producers. While you can find Louisburg Cider Mill drinks in area supermarkets, it's fun to come down to the source at least once a year, perhaps for Ciderfest (last weekend in Sept and first weekend in Oct) which features live music, all kinds of family activities (from hayrides to moonbounces), and of course product sampling.

Namaste India, 10563 Metcalf Ave. (southeast corner of 105th and Metcalf, in the Office Depot shopping center); (913) 901-8787; www.namasteindiakc.com. Daily 10 a.m. to 9 p.m. Among the several Indian specialty markets along this stretch of Metcalf, Namaste definitely seems to be the coolest. Case in point: In addition to being a grocery store, it also has a combination lottery, DVD rental (with strictly Indian films—Bollywood fans take note), and *chaat* (snack) counter where the young professional Indian population of Overland Park lines up for homemade snacks at midday. Another example? Prime merchandising space is given to prepared sauces (just add your protein and vegetables) that sell like hotcakes to those young professionals who don't have time to slave over a stove all day making butter chicken from scratch. If you do insist on doing it the old-fashioned way but are bewildered by all the exotic food-stuffs, the friendly staff can help you find what you need for your recipe, and even provide cooking tips.

Oriental Supermarket, 10336 Metcalf Ave. (north side of the Furniture Deal$ strip mall), Overland Park; (913) 341-3345. Twenty-four aisles, bright, wide, and clean, with no off-putting smell of dried fish flakes . . . this is an Asian market for the New World. Oriental sells mostly Korean and Japanese brands, although there are limited Chinese, Thai, and Filipino goods as well. Just about any noodle or rice variety from the Eastern Hemisphere is on these shelves, and there is a sizable fridge full of kimchee. I particularly love this market's reasonably priced packages of presliced meats (ribeye, pork, lamb) for Korean-style barbecue. Like any Asian market, this place has entire aisles devoted to things that will make no sense to most Westerners, like seaweed and pickled radishes, but there's also a lot of accessible stuff here, too, and at good prices: fresh shiitakes for $4.29/pound; 12-ounce bags of panko for $3; packages of frozen gyoza (dumplings) for $1.99. You'll also find tons of variations on soy sauce for stir-frying, marinating, or dipping. The point is, even an Asian cooking neophyte could come in here and walk out with the makings for an excellent pan-Asian party spread.

Not Your Average High School Cafeteria

Unbeknownst to many a Kansas City foodie, Overland Park has one of the nation's preeminent high-school-level culinary training programs. Broadmoor Technical center, part of Shawnee Mission School District, is home to the **Broadmoor Bistro,** a state of the art teaching kitchen where students hone their skills in preparing and serving food. From baking the bread to searing the *foie gras* to washing the dishes, the high school kids of Broadmoor (juniors and seniors) do it all, under the tutelage of two full-time chef/instructors. On Wednesday during the school year, the Broadmoor Bistro is open to the public for a four-course prix fixe menu ($30, reservations advised). You'll chuckle as you walk through corridors of lockers and other nostalgic reminders of your youth to get to the Bistro, but once you're there, it's serious stuff. The dining room is contemporary, and the plates that these 17- and 18-year-olds are putting out are as ambitious and technical as at $30 entree restaurants elsewhere in town. Even the city's star chefs, many of whom are frequent visitors and guest instructors at Broadmoor, are ga-ga for the fancy equipment (e.g., a sous-vide machine) these students have access to and green with envy at their kitchen square footage—at nearly 5,000 square feet, Broadmoor's display kitchen is like something out of a Las Vegas hotel restaurant. This being a high school, no alcohol is served or allowed in the Bistro, but you may enjoy bottomless glasses of ice water, and they make a mean cappuccino.

The Broadmoor Bistro is located inside Broadmoor Technical Center, 6701 W. 83rd St. (at Glenwood), Overland Park; www.broadmoorbistro.org. Open for dinner on Wednesday only during the academic year (mid-September to mid-May). Make reservations online.

Overland Park Farmers' Market, between Santa Fe Dr. and Marty Dr., and between 79th and 80th Streets, Overland Park; no phone; www.downtownop.org. Mid-April through May open Sat 6:30 a.m. to sellout, from June to Sept Wed 7:30 a.m. and Sat 6:30 a.m. to sellout; Oct open Sat only 6:30 a.m. to sellout. Under a vaulted and patinated pavilion that evokes a European city marketplace, the biggest and best farmers' market in Johnson County has more than 60 vendors selling homegrown tomatoes, peaches, zucchini, apples, eggplant, potatoes, herbs, flowers and plants, bread and pasta, even wine, all from carefully selected local producers. Though Saturday mornings can get very busy after 10 a.m.,

it's still a much more relaxed scene than downtown Kansas City's larger City Market. This market has been a major contributor to the revitalization and community development of historic downtown Overland Park, and the businesses on Santa Fe Drive, just above the pavilion (including the **Tasteful Olive, Penzey's Spices,** and **Clocktower Bakery & Cafe**) are packed on market days.

Penzey's Spices, 7937 Santa Fe Dr., Overland Park; (913) 341-1775; www.penzeys.com. Mon through Fri 9:30 a.m. to 5:30 p.m., Sat 9:30 a.m. to 5 p.m., Sun 11 a.m. to 5 p.m. Appropriately located on the historic Santa Fe Trail, the new foodie strip where a century ago horse-drawn wagons delivered goods from all over to bustling downtown Overland Park, Penzey's is an encyclopedic emporium of spices and dried herbs from around the globe—as if the caravans of the ancient spice road somehow detoured from the Middle East and found themselves in the Midwest. Not only does Penzey's stock dozens of hand-selected varieties of chile peppers and powders, cinnamons, and curry powders, they've also developed a wide array of signature seasoning blends and dry rubs—Bangkok Blend, Barbecue Seasoning of the Americas, bouquet garni, just to name a few—that will simplify and enhance your own at-home preparations of everything from poultry and pork to sandwiches and salads to steak and lamb kebabs. Everything Penzey's sells can be sniffed from glass jars atop each spice display—just watch out for those pequín chiles. You could spend a lot of time in here just gawking at all the "essential" spices you've never heard of (annatto seed, for Central American and Caribbean cuisine, or zaatar for Middle Eastern dishes); it can make your pantry feel a little inadequate, actually. Penzey's has stores nationwide but is family owned and operated out of Wisconsin. Prices are $2 to $3 for a ¼-cup jar.

The Tasteful Olive, 7945 Santa Fe Dr., Overland Park; (913) 649-7900; www.thetastefulolive.com. Mon through Fri 10 a.m. to 6 p.m., Sat 8 a.m. to 5:30 p.m. Also open 6 to 9 p.m. on the third Fri of the month. No gourmet kitchen is complete without really good olive oil, and this spacious shop on downtown O.P.'s burgeoning foodie strip delivers it—extra-virgin olive oil from the best olive oil regions around the world made the old-fashioned way: The olives are stone-milled, crushed within four hours of hand-selection, and pressed through woven wooden mats. In all, there are 20 oils from both hemispheres available as well as 18 aged balsamic vinegars from Modena, Italy. Many of the oils and vinegars are "fusions," or flavored with natural fruits and herbs at the time of production. The best thing about the store is that you can sample everything: The oils and vinegars are merchandised below stainless steel *fusti* (spigoted drums), from which you can dispense some of the liquid into little paper cups and try out different flavored pairings, like Tuscan herb olive oil with lemon balsamic vinegar. The knowledgeable staff can recommend innovative uses, from salad dressings to cooking glazes to dessert toppings, for all their products and provide recipe cards. Prices—about $15 to $17 for 375 milliliters; $29 to $33 for 750 milliliters—are on par with what you'd pay for high-quality oil or vinegar anywhere, and no other retailer in the K.C. area offers the Tasteful Olive's selection or sampling setup. They also stock a broad range of sea salts, spice blends, tapenades, and other gourmet items—including *fusti*, for the ultimate home kitchen showpiece. See the Tasteful Olive's recipe for **Blood Orange Olive Oil Brownies** on p. 278.

Whole Foods Market, 7401 W. 91st St. (west side of Metcalf Ave.), Overland Park; (913) 652-9633; www.wholefoodsmarket.com. Mon through Thurs 7:30 a.m. to 9 p.m., Fri and Sat 7:30 a.m. to 10 p.m. Overland Park's outpost of the natural and organics-focused supermarket is your best bet in the Metro area for hard-to-find produce, bulk grains, gourmet deli items, and baked goods all under one roof. The seafood and butcher counters are both excellent (and expensive), but this store is not as strong on dry-goods aisles as other Whole Foods branches around the country, and is not as large and comprehensive overall. But, as with all Whole Foods stores, this one is equipped with a tantalizing prepared foods bar—fancy salads, exotic rice dishes, specialty olives, etc.—where it's quite easy to spend your Whole Paycheck. There is another Whole Foods in Overland Park, at 119th St. and Metcalf, but that location has much more scaled-back offerings.

Recipes

In this section, I've collected recipes from some of the most acclaimed chefs, restaurants, and specialty shops in Kansas City. Covering (almost) all of the culinary spectrum, from soup to salad to BBQ to brownies, and all courses from breakfast through dessert, these recipes are customer and chef favorites from all over town. The ingredient lists are enough to make your mouth water, but it's

the details of preparation that give you a privileged glimpse at each chef's unique sensibilities. While some of the recipes may be more ingredient- and labor-intensive than others, they are all meant to be accessible—something that the dedicated home chef could conceivably recreate reasonably well, and where applicable, the chef-authors of these recipes have given tips for shortcuts and substitutions that you may find handy.

Chorizo & Fig Stuffed Chicken Thighs

The menu at the Crossroads small-plates hotspot Extra Virgin changes a bit each season, but one item Chef Michael Smith can't take off the menu, for fear of a popular uprising, are these sweet and savory chicken thighs.

Yield: 8–10 pieces

Chorizo Chicken Braising Sauce

3 or 4 tablespoons canola oil

1 yellow onion, thinly sliced

1 teaspoon chopped fresh garlic

⅓ cup sugar

⅓ cup sherry vinegar

1 tablespoon Peruvian Roccoto or Panca chile paste

3 teaspoons tomato paste

1 sprig fresh oregano

2 cups meat stock

Reserved chicken thigh bones (if available)

Chicken Thigh Filling

3 or 4 tablespoons canola oil

1 yellow onion, finely diced

1 teaspoon minced garlic

1 cup rough-medium chopped Spanish chorizo

6 dried figs, chopped

1 sprig fresh thyme, leaves picked

1 sprig fresh oregano, leaves picked and chopped

1 tablespoon chopped fresh parsley

Salt and pepper to taste

Chicken

8 to 10 pieces large skin-on chicken thighs, center bones removed (reserve for sauce) but skin intact

To make the braising sauce, heat a large soup pot with canola oil over high heat. Add onions and garlic and brown them well. Add sugar and let it caramelize to a medium golden brown. Add sherry vinegar. Add chile paste, tomato paste, and oregano Bring to a boil and cook for 5 minutes. Add meat stock and reserved thigh bones and bring to a boil. Reduce heat and simmer for 15 minutes. Strain sauce and set aside.

To make the filling, heat a large braising pan with canola oil over high heat. Sauté onions and garlic until softened and lightly colored. Add remaining ingredients and cook for 10 minutes.

Combine all ingredients in food processor and chop until relatively smooth. Season with salt and pepper if desired. Cool and set aside.

Lay chicken thighs on a flat surface and season them with salt and pepper. Place a medium spoonful of filling in the center of the thigh. Roll the thigh closed and tie with kitchen twine in two spots to keep them closed during cooking.

Place a heavy skillet with canola oil over medium heat. When oil is hot, sear thighs until golden brown. Pour excess oil out of pan and add braising liquid just to cover the thighs by about three-quarters. Place in a 400 degree oven and bake for about 30 to 40 minutes.

Serve without delay.

Courtesy of Chef Michael Smith of Extra Virgin (p. 61).

Room 39 Oven Eggs

Chef-Owner Ted Habiger's favorite breakfast dish was an accidental invention, when he found some odd-shaped pans lying around his kitchen and decided that they needed a vocation. You don't have to have the half-moon cut-out pans that Habiger uses to make these oven eggs—a large-format muffin pan is fine—but be sure to use great-quality farm eggs, such as those from Campo Lindo Farms. For an extra luxurious touch, drizzle these with truffle oil when they are finished baking.

Yield: 1 serving

1 brioche bun
3–4 thin slices Genoa salami
1 slice gruyère cheese
2 farm egg yolks

Extra-virgin olive oil
Sea salt
Fresh-cracked black pepper

Preheat oven to 375 degrees.

Cut the top, then the sides of the bun with a large round cutter or a serrated knife. Dig out a round center, making the bun into a sort of bowl. Lay the salami around the outside rim of the bun. Place the gruyère on top of the bun and put in the oven just long enough to slightly melt the cheese.

Place two egg yolks in the center, drizzle with high-quality olive oil, season lightly with sea salt and fresh-cracked black pepper.

Bake in the oven for 5 to 7 minutes or until the yolk is warm but still runny.

Serve with a side of fruit and another drizzle of olive oil.

Recipe courtesy of Chef-Owner Ted Habiger of Room 39 (p. 100).

Carrot Thai Curry Soup

Chef Celina Tio came up with this tangy, fragrant, and gorgeously sunshine-colored soup while cameras were rolling when she was a contestant on season 3 of The Next Iron Chef. Don't let the few semi-exotic ingredients fool you: Tio calls this soup "embarrassingly easy" to make. You can add a few tablespoons of coconut milk, and use shallots instead of onions, for a little added richness.

Yield: 4 servings

1 tablespoon grapeseed oil
1¾ ounces diced onion, weighed after dicing
10½ ounces sliced carrots, weighed after peeling and dicing
3¾ cups vegetable stock

Thai red curry paste (Mae Ploy brand recommended)
½ ounce kosher salt
⅓ ounce fresh galangal (may substitute ginger)
1 small lime, juiced
1 tablespoon honey

In a saucepan over medium-high heat, add the grapeseed oil and sweat the onion and carrots for about 2 minutes. Add the vegetable stock, Thai curry paste to taste (one teaspoon at a time), salt, and galangal (or ginger). Bring almost to a boil then lower the heat to medium and cook until the carrots are tender. Add the lime juice and honey and puree in a blender on high until smooth. Strain through a fine-meshed strainer, if necessary.

Recipe courtesy of Chef-Owner Celina Tio of Julian (p. 168).

Osso Buco Milanese

Osso buco *literally means "bone hole" and is a hearty cornerstone of authentic Italian cooking as well as one of the top-selling meat dishes at Jasper's. Slow roasting is essential to release the marrow from inside the* osso buco *and results in exceptionally luxurious flavor.*

4 servings

- 4 tablespoons (½ stick) butter
- 4 pounds veal shanks, cut into 3½-inch lengths
- ¼ cup brandy
- 2 teaspoons salt
- 2 medium onions, chopped
- 8–10 baby carrots, chopped
- 2 stalks celery, coarsely chopped
- 1 750-milliliter bottle Chianti
- 1 28-ounce can San Marzano tomatoes, crushed by hand
- ½ teaspoon hot red pepper flakes
- 2 sprigs rosemary
- 4 medium potatoes, cut into ¾-inch cubes

Preheat the oven to 375 degrees.

Melt the butter in a large skillet over high heat. Sear the veal shank pieces, 2 to 3 minutes on each side. Add the brandy and season with the salt.

Toss the onions, carrots, and celery in a large roasting pan. Add the veal shanks, wine, crushed tomatoes, red pepper flakes, and rosemary and stir. Roast for 2 hours and 15 minutes. Add the potatoes and cook for another 45 minutes. Serve at once.

Courtesy of Chef-Owner Jasper J. Mirabile Jr. of Jasper's Restaurant (p. 196).

The Rieger Pork Soup

Chef-Owner Howard Hanna created the base for this soup for a pork-centric competition called Cochon 555, which travels the country giving whole pigs to local chefs and turning them loose with them. The current form of the Rieger Pork Soup was born when it occurred to Hanna to mimic French onion soup, but with pork substitutions (my kinda guy): shredded pork confit in place of onions, and crispy pork skin floating on top, in lieu of a crouton, to hold up the oozy, melted gruyère. While the soup is extremely rich and hearty, the bitters and the vinegar balance it out and cut the fat, and the gruyère smoothes it all out. The soup was a smash hit the first winter the Rieger was open, and has become such a signature dish that it stays on the menu year-round.

8 servings

- 2 quarts rich pork stock*
- 1 cup roasted garlic (about 15 whole heads), smashed with a fork
- 1 cup braised pork shoulder, shredded**
- ½ cup sherry vinegar
- ½ tablespoon Angostura bitters
- kosher salt, to taste
- freshly ground black pepper, to taste
- 8 each chicharrones***
- 8 ounces gruyère, grated
- 2 tablespoons parsley, chopped

Preheat oven to 400 degrees.

Bring the pork stock to a boil in a medium-size, heavy bottomed stockpot over high heat. Reduce heat to medium and add the roasted garlic. Whisk thoroughly to incorporate, then season to taste with salt and pepper. Add braised pork, the vinegar and the bitters, and whisk again to break up and mix in the pork. Let simmer for 10 minutes to allow the flavors to mingle, then taste again and adjust seasoning as needed.

To finish, pour soup into 8 soup bowls, on a sheet pan or baking sheet. Break up one chicharron into each bowl, top with the gruyère, and place the sheet pan into the oven. Cook for 5 minutes or so until the cheese is bubbly and starting to brown. Remove from oven, top with parsley, and serve.

Notes:

*At the Rieger, we use pork bones and pork trim from other preparations along with carrots, onions, celery, and herbs to make a nice stock for the base of this soup. We also add in some pigs' feet, or trotters, which give a rich, gelatinous mouthfeel and a great body to the stock. If this isn't possible at home, just use chicken stock to braise the pork shoulder and then use that stock for the soup and you will still have a great result.

**On our menu, we call the meat in this soup "pork confit," and it is actually pork shoulder that we cook sous vide with aromatics and a good dollop of lard sealed in a vacuum pouch. We poach it in a water bath at 85 degrees celsius for 12 hours and it becomes incredibly juicy and tender. At home, you can simply use braised pork shoulder that has been cooked until it is fall off the bone tender, and shred that up for the soup. Leftover carnitas will also work well.

***Since we try to use whole animals at the restaurant, we like to make our own chicharrones with the skins. To do this we boil pork skin in salted water for an hour and a half, cool it completely, carefully scrape every bit of fat from it, then dry it in a dehydrator overnight. At that point it is brittle and glassy and can be stored for weeks. Before service, we break off a few pieces of the dried skin and fry them in the fryer, where they puff up magically, turn a beautiful clean white color, and become light, airy, and amazingly crispy. If this sounds like too much work for you, you can buy chicharrones at your local Mexican market or at a lot of convenience stations or supermarkets. Just look for the ones with the least artificial ingredients because we just want them for the texture, not for a lot of chile/lime or other flavors.

Courtesy of Chef-Owner Howard Hanna of the Rieger Hotel Grill & Exchange (p. 80).

Wagyu Brisket

After many years smoking Wagyu brisket from Paradise Locker Meats, Craig Adcock has hit upon the perfect formula for making this decadent BBQ meat: Pull the brisket from the smoker when it's reached an internal temperature of 150 to 160 degrees (that is, cook it less than you would a normal beef brisket) to achieve the elegant, prime-rib-like taste that is the hallmark of Wagyu.

At first glance, the finished brisket looks very, very fatty, but that's just the marbling that makes Wagyu so rich and silky. Slice by hand into ⅛-inch thick slices. (Adcock does not use sauce for this recipe, but if you prefer to, brush your sauce on the top of the brisket only when it's reached the 155-degree mark or after slicing.)

All Wagyu briskets sold from Paradise Locker come with Adcock's instructions; he may indeed be the foremost expert on Wagyu brisket smoking in the nation.

Adcock also has some advice for anyone thinking about getting into smoking meat at home: Resist the temptation to splurge on one of those locomotive-sized black behemoths that you've no doubt seen displayed at home improvement stores (alongside that ride-on lawnmower you also probably don't need). For beginners, bigger isn't better, and Adcock recommends starting out with the small-footprint, relatively small-investment Weber Smokey Mountain Cooker. Entry-level or not, this is a great smoker that can accommodate all the meat your family and friends can eat on a given weekend. The Weber cooker can be bought for about $300 at your local hardware store, and owning one will give you a good sense—before you get into more expensive, space-hogging equipment—of how much you actually end up smoking meat at home.

Serves: A lot of people (makes 5 to 10 pounds of meat)

Wagyu Brisket (8 to 14 pounds, untrimmed)

1 cup Belly Up BBQ Beef Seasoning (available at Pryde's of Old Westport, Cellar Rat Wine Merchants, or Paradise Locker Meats)

Peach orchard wood (small log—8 to 12 inches long x 3 inches in diameter—or equivalent amount of wood chunks) or similar, such as wild cherry, pecan, oak, etc.

Lump Charcoal

Prepare your fire.* Remove brisket from cryovac bag and slightly trim fatcap if desired (I leave the cap intact). Lightly sprinkle all sides of the brisket with beef seasoning. I add about half of the amount of seasonings that I would for a traditional brisket—this allows the smoke, spice, and characteristic of the meat to complement each other in harmony. Place the brisket in the smoker fat-side up and allow the smoker to come to 220 degrees. I use fruit wood because the smoke seems to penetrate the meat throughout; granted, I sacrifice a smoke ring (the trademark layer of crimson-pink discoloration just under the meat crust, sought after in the world of competition BBQ and obtained by exposing the meat to heavy smoke), but I'm not looking for rings—I'm looking for the best possible end result.

Check the brisket periodically—an 11-pound brisket will need to cook for anywhere between 6 to 9 hours based on outside temperature, the elements, etc. When an internal temperature of 160 is reached in the largest part of the brisket, remove it, rest it, and slice/serve as desired. Anticipate a 25 to 30 percent reduction in brisket size while cooking.

Note:

I use a layered system when preparing my fire: I place my log of peach wood at the bottom, cover that with a chimney of unlit lump charcoal so a bit of the wood is exposed, then I add a chimney of lit coal. This allows for a slow release burn (heat rises, so if one places unlit wood or charcoal on top of lit coal, the heat will rise more quickly and the charcoal or wood will be exhausted more quickly). The smoker internal temperature takes about 1 hour and 20 minutes to reach 220 degrees and smoke will be present from the start as the smoker temperature rises.

Courtesy of Craig Adcock, Chef-Owner of
Belly Up BBQ & Seasonings and Jude's Rum Cake (p. 252).

Cafe Sebastienne Crab Cakes

No other chef in town has the same winning combination of bright flavor and simple cooking style as Chef Jennifer Maloney. These crab cakes are a classic menu item at Cafe Sebastienne that may appear on their own or as part of Maloney's take on eggs Benedict, the Cafe Benny, at brunch on Sunday. If you're feeling extra fancy, you can add some lobster meat to the mix.

Maloney suggests serving these crab cakes with shrimp remoulade (recipe in the Cafe Sebastienne cookbook), sliced tomatoes, cabbage slaw, and a buttery Chardonnay.

Makes 10 crab cakes

2 pounds lump crab meat
½ medium red onion, diced
1 red pepper, seeded and diced
½ cup diced celery
4 eggs

¼ cup Dijon mustard
¾ cup mayonnaise
1 pinch Old Bay seasonings
1 cup bread crumbs
1 tablespoon olive oil

Mix together all ingredients except bread crumbs and oil. Form crab mixture into 4-ounce cakes (about 2½ inches in diameter and 1½ inches thick). Coat cakes with bread crumbs.

Preheat oven to 400 degrees. In a medium sauté pan, heat olive oil. Add crab cakes. Cook until golden brown on one side. Transfer pan to oven for 5 minutes. Serve immediately.

Courtesy of Chef Jennifer Maloney of Cafe Sebastienne (p. 133).

Ensalada de Ayocote Morado
(purple runner bean salad)

One taste of an heirloom bean, and you'll never go back to the canned and bagged stuff. Chef-Owner Patrick Ryan makes beautiful use of heirloom beans (from California's Rancho Gordo) in this Mexican salad, served at his converted Airstream food truck, Port Fonda. Simple, bursting with flavor, and with just the right amount of queso fresco to give body to all the fresh veggies and herbs, this is a fantastic warm weather dish.

Serves 4

2 cups Rancho Gordo ayocote morado heirloom beans (or another heirloom bean)

salt for the beans

8 radishes (6 quartered, 2 sliced into thin sticks)

6 turnips, quartered

2 shallots, sliced thin

olive oil

salt and pepper to taste

4 basil leaves, torn

12 cilantro leaves, torn

4 large mint leaves, torn

4 tablespoons queso fresco

1 teaspoon ancho chile powder

Heirloom Bean Vinaigrette (recipe follows)

Cooking directions: *Cook beans over medium heat in unsalted water until tender and no longer al dente. Let beans cool in their liquid and salt the beans and bean liquid generously. Cool and reserve.*

Toss quartered radishes, quartered turnips, and sliced shallots with some olive oil, salt, and pepper. Grill over a medium-high heat until slightly browned and smoky tasting. Cool and reserve.

Assembly directions: *Drain the beans and reserve a small amount of the bean liquid for bean vinaigrette (see recipe below). In an appropriate-size bowl, add the beans, grilled radishes/turnips/shallots, torn basil/cilantro/mint, a few tablespoons of the bean vinaigrette, and toss gently to incorporate. Divide bean mixture into 4 appropriate-size bowls and garnish with queso fresco, ancho chile powder, and the thinly sliced radishes.*

Heirloom Bean Vinaigrette

⅛ cup bean cooking liquid   ¼ cup vinegar of your choice
¼ cup good extra virgin olive oil

Combine all vinaigrette ingredients well.

Courtesy of Patrick Ryan, Chef-Owner of Port Fonda food truck (p. 70).

Chocolate Truffle Cookies

Owner and pastry chef Megan Garrelts is the "sweet" half of the husband and wife team in the kitchen at acclaimed and James-Beard-Award recognized bluestem. Nothing against Colby, who's a really nice guy, but Megan's desserts are to die for. Unfortunately, you will probably gobble these cookies down in less time than it takes to make them.

Makes about 50 truffle cookies

2 ounces unsweetened chocolate, chopped

3 tablespoons unsalted butter

½ cup all-purpose flour

½ cup granulated sugar

1 tablespoon unsweetened cocoa powder (preferably Dutch-processed)

⅛ teaspoon baking powder

¼ teaspoon kosher salt

2 large eggs

1 teaspoon vanilla extract

5 ounces miniature bittersweet or semisweet chocolate chips

⅛ cup confectioners' sugar

1 lime, for zesting

In a double boiler (or a bowl set over a saucepan containing 1 inch of simmering water), melt the unsweetened chocolate and butter together over medium-low heat. Stir the chocolate and butter in the double boiler until it is melted and smooth. Remove the mixture from heat and set aside to cool slightly.

Combine the flour, granulated sugar, cocoa powder, baking powder, and salt in a medium bowl.

In the bowl of a stand mixer fitted with a paddle attachment, beat together the eggs and vanilla on medium speed until combined, about 2 minutes. Add the dry ingredients and resume mixing on medium speed until incorporated, scraping the bowl as needed, about 2 minutes. At this point, it should resemble cake batter.

Add the melted chocolate mixture to the batter and continue to mix, scraping the bowl as needed, until the batter thickens. Using a rubber spatula, fold in the chocolate chips by hand.

Cover the batter with plastic wrap and refrigerate for 1 hour.

Preheat the oven to 350 degrees. Line a baking sheet with parchment paper or a nonstick baking liner. You can bake 2 sheets at a time, rotating halfway through baking.

Using a small melon baller or a sturdy rounded spoon, scoop the chilled batter into balls and arrange them on the prepared baking sheet, leaving at least 1 inch between them. For a softer, truffle-like cookie, bake for 6 minutes. For a harder, cookie-like texture, bake them for 7 minutes.

Transfer the baking sheet to a wire rack and let the cookies cool slightly. Cooled cookies can be stored in an airtight container for up to 3 days. When ready to serve, dust them with confectioners' sugar. Using a Microplane zester, grate fresh lime zest over the top. Serve immediately.

Courtesy of Chef-Owner Megan Garrelts of bluestem (p. 119).

Note: Recipe excerpted from *bluestem, the cookbook* by Colby and Megan Garrelts.

Blood Orange Olive Oil Brownies

Once, when I lived in Italy, I gave a friend a recipe for chocolate chip cookies. Not having Crisco in the cucina, *she substituted olive oil for shortening, and, needless to say, it was a disaster. With that experience in mind, I never could have imagined olive oil having any part in brownies—that is, until I tasted the blood orange olive oil at the Tasteful Olive. The citrus component in the oil is deep and assertive, a magnificent complement to the chocolate, but there's still plenty of butter to maintain the proper texture in baking.*

Yield: 12 servings

4 ounces unsweetened chocolate	½ cup (1 stick) butter
1 ounce bittersweet chocolate	½ cup Tasteful Olive Blood Orange Olive Oil
1 cup all-purpose flour	4 eggs
2 cups white sugar	1 tablespoon vanilla flavoring
1 teaspoon baking powder	1 cup coarsely crushed walnuts
¾ teaspoon salt	

Preheat oven to 350 degrees. Butter a 9 x 12-inch baking pan.

On low heat, melt both chocolates in pan, stirring continually. Set aside to cool.

In separate bowl, sift flour, sugar, baking powder, and salt.

In a saucepan, melt butter and add the olive oil. Mix in 1 egg at a time. Add vanilla and then chocolate. Fold into dry ingredients (include walnuts) but don't overmix. Pour into pan and smooth off the top.

Bake 25 to 30 minutes or until brownies pull away from side of pan.

Courtesy of Laura McGill of the Tasteful Olive (p. 258).

Appendix A: Eateries by Cuisine

American (Classic, New, Progressive)
American, The, 97
Avalon Cafe, 211
Avenues Bistro, 161, 240
Blue Bird Bistro, 29
bluestem, 119
Cafe Sebastienne, 133
Cafe Trio, 135
Farmhouse, The, 4
Genessee Royale Bistro, 33
Grand Street Cafe, 138
JJ's, 139
Justus Drugstore, 217
Michael Smith, 78
Pot Pie, 111
Rieger Hotel Grill & Exchange, The, 80
Room 39, 110, 241
Starker's, 148
Story, 246
Trezo Vino, 239
Vineyards, The, 223
Westside Local, The, 39
You Say Tomato, 95

Argentinean
Piropos, 213, 221

Asian/Pan-Asian
Bo Lings, 3, 133, 240
Lulu's Thai Noodle Shop, 66
Nara, 68
Po's Dumpling Bar, 93
Sung Son, 113

Austrian
Grünauer, 63

Westport Cafe & Bar, 115
Westside Local, The, 39

Coffee
Bella Napoli Alimentari, 177
Broadway Cafe & Roastery,
    The, 121
Chez Elle, 31
Coffee Girls, 179
Filling Station, The, 105
Roasterie Cafe, The, 185

Deli
Bella Napoli Alimentari, 177
Cupini's, 110
Dean & Deluca, 250
European Delights, 251
Marco Polo's, 206
Werner's Specialty Foods, 155
Whole Foods Market, 260

Eastern European
European Delights, 251

Eclectic
Avenues Bistro, 161, 240
Blue Grotto, 163

Extra Virgin, 61
Justus Drugstore, 217
R Bar, 38

Farm-to-Table/Locavore
bluestem, 119
Blue Bird Bistro, 29
Farmhouse, The, 4
Julian, 168
Justus Drugstore, 217
R Bar, 38
Room 39, 100, 241
Westside Local, The, 39

Food Trucks
Fresher than Fresh Snow
    Cones, 52
Port Fonda, 70

French
Aixois, 159
Cafe des Amis, 216
Cafe Provence, 245
Chez Elle, 31
Le Fou Frog, 15
Westport Cafe & Bar, 115

Mediterranean
Aladdin Cafe, 90
Avenues Bistro, 161, 240
Cafe Cedar, 212
Extra Virgin, 61

Mexican
Bonito Michoacan, 41
El Camino Real, 41
El Patron, 41
El Pueblito, 41
Los Alamos Market y Cocina, 36
Los Amigos, 41
Los Tules, 65
Taqueria Mexico No. 1, 41
Tortilleria San Antonio, 41

Middle Eastern
Aladdin Cafe, 90
Cafe Cedar, 212
Habashi House, 23
Jerusalem Bakery, 122
Olive Cafe, 189
Papu's Cafe, 175

Pizza
Blue Grotto, 163

Minsky's Pizza, 145
Pizza Bella, 69
SPIN! Neapolitan Pizza, 144, 239
Waldo Pizza, 176

Polish
Pieroguys, 25

Sandwiches
Bella Napoli Alimentari, 177
Coffee Girls, 179
Filling Station, The, 105
Happy Gillis Cafe & Hangout, 6
Marco Polo's, 206

Seafood
Bristol Seafood Grill, 13
Story, 246

Small Plates
Avenues Bistro, 161, 240
Extra Virgin, 61, 262
La Bodega, 34
One Bite Japanese Grill, 236
Tannin Wine Bar & Kitchen, 72
Trezo Vino, 239

Appendix B: Specialty Stores & Producers by Category

Other Specialty Stores

Wine & Liquor Stores

Appendix C: Restaurants by Special Feature & Atmosphere

Index